THE FOUNDATIONS OF NIGERIA'S FINANCIAL INFRASTRUCTURE

THE FOUNDATIONS OF NIGERIA'S FINANCIAL INFRASTRUCTURE

Edited by J.K. Onoh

CROOM HELM LONDON

© 1980 J.K. Onoh
Croom Helm Ltd, 2-10 St. John's Road, London SW11

British Library Cataloguing in Publication Data

The foundations of Nigeria's financial infrastructure.
1. Finance — Nigeria
I. Onoh, J K
332'.09669   HJ1609.N5

ISBN 0-7099-0448-7
ISBN 0-7099-0449-5 Pbk

Printed in Great Britain by
Biddles Ltd, Guildford, Surrey

CONTENTS

FOREWORD

Opinions differ on the type of modality of financial system that is best suited for rapid economic development, particularly of developing countries. Some argue that the system should be dynamic, able and willing to lead and finance as well as service the economy. Others believe it should be cautious and avoid stimulating instability and inflation. All are agreed that the system should act as a catalyst in development and that this requires a good infrastructure. This is what *The Foundations of Nigeria's Infrastructure* has set out to do.

In five parts and twenty-one chapters the authors have achieved three important objectives. First, they have assembled into one piece many different aspects of Nigeria's financial infrastructure. Secondly, in so doing, they have challenged future scholars, practitioners and policy-makers to provide the 'superstructure'. Thirdly and finally, they have presented the 'dynamic' and 'cautious' views and agree on the 'catalytic' role of the financial system in economic development.

One may not totally agree with all the views and conclusions expressed in the book, but there should be no disagreement over the fact that it is an important contribution to the scanty literature on the Nigerian financial system.

Professor G.O. Nwankwo
Executive Director
Banking Operations
Central Bank of Nigeria
Lagos

PREFACE

28 January 1892 will remain a landmark in the financial history of Nigeria. It was on that date that the Crown Agents concluded the agreement by which the African Banking Corporation was permitted to import new UK silver coins from the Royal Mint into Lagos Colony. The African Banking Corporation began operations in Lagos in 1891 as the London Board minutes of a meeting of 4 June 1891 reveal.[1] The African Banking Corporation became the first bank to be actively engaged in the monetisation of the Nigerian barter economy.

Another landmark in the monetisation of the economy was reached in 1912 with the establishment of the West African Currency Board, which was empowered to replace the United Kingdom coins with the West African Currency Board coins and notes.

Between 1912 and 1979 a number of banks and financial institutions have been established which continue to play a great role in the economic development of Nigeria. The Central Bank of Nigeria was established by the Central Bank of Nigeria Act of 15 May 1958 but it began actual operation on 1 July 1959. More than 18 commercial banks with over 500 branches have been established. A number of financial institutions other than banks have taken their rightful places in the Nigerian economy. Unfortunately no serious efforts have been made to bring together the various aspects of Nigeria's financial developments and experiences into an integrated framework. The importance of financial aggregates and their analysis for economic and related policy decisions in a rapidly developing economy requires no emphasis. This fact is recognised by both Nigerian financial practitioners and academic financial specialists but as one practitioner puts it 'bringing together Nigeria's financial experiences into one arena is like fitting a complex jig-saw puzzle'. The statement has some elements of truth in it. Common facts and figures relating to Nigeria's financial aggregates are scattered in various official and semi-official documents or tucked away in 'SECRET' files beyond the reach of researchers.

This book in my view has broken the barrier. It has attempted to fit the jig-saw puzzle by bringing together the most important of Nigeria's financial happenings, and any measure of success attributable to it is owed to the devoted financial scholars, practitioners, and with all modesty, the humble editor, who have monitored Nigeria's financial dispositions over the years, picked up the pieces of information and facts and built up formidable essays on the structure of the Nigerian financial system and how the system should or should not operate. A majority of the contributors are academic dons. Some of them have been privileged to act as advisers to the Government on financial matters. Others have conducted various researches in the areas of finance and economics and have participated in local and international conferences on financial themes; all have taught financial subjects for many years. They have not come up with any curious financial theory but a perfect blend of theory and practice.

As the editor, I have taken great pains to edit the various contributions. I have in some cases rearranged the works of the contributors and in other cases I have expanded their thoughts, without of course altering the trends, arguments or conclusions. In doing this the benefit of readers has been at the back of my mind. If in the attempt to please I have in any way misrepresented a contributor's views then the blame squarely rests on me.

I sincerely hope that this book will be of value to reference libraries the world over, to policy makers and administrators in the developed and developing countries who may wish to learn in greater depth the Nigerian financial experiences and above all to the students of economics, finance, accounting and business studies. Politicians and businessmen will also find the book useful. While maintaining a high level of analysis and abstraction the use of financial jargon has been reduced to the minimum so that financial laymen will also comprehend the issues with the minimum of effort.

J.K. Onoh

Note
1. Richard Fry, *Bankers in West Africa, The Story of the Bank of British West Africa Limited*, (Hutchinson Benham, London, 1976), p. 19.

Part One

A GENERAL SURVEY OF NIGERIA'S FINANCIAL SYSTEM

1 NIGERIA'S TRADITIONAL FINANCIAL SYSTEM*

J.K. Onoh

1. Introduction

Like the modern financial institutions which include the Central Bank, commercial banks, savings banks, building societies, hire purchase finance companies, insurance companies, pension funds, investment trusts and development banks, the traditional financial institutions engage to a large extent as financial intermediaries by channelling funds from surplus economic subjects to deficit economic subjects.

In the place of commodity 'currencies' modern Nigerian currency is now used. In the pre-banking era traditional financial institutions served Nigerian communities relatively well and performed some of the functions of modern banks though in an unrefined and limited manner. They still outnumber the modern financial institutions in terms of units but not necessarily in the volume of business. There are no records which show their numbers but as many as five or more can be found in a village of less than 500 people and as many as 20 or more in a Nigerian rural 'town'. A rural 'town' is normally an amalgam of villages and in many Nigerian 'towns' there are no banks or savings institutions. The traditional financial system has perpetuated itself in such 'towns'. The cities are no exceptions. In spite of their array of banks and networks of other financial intermediaries, traditional financial institutions continue to exist side by side with the modern financial system in the cities.

This chapter will examine the different types of traditional financial institutions, their objectives, how they are organised, managed and how they function as well as the causes for their unabated proliferation. A study in traditional financial intermediation is in itself a study in rural sociology – the behaviour patterns, customs and norms of the rural people. The chapter, however, will limit itself to the operational mechanics of the system as a large-scale study of strictly sociological overtones is beyond the scope of this book.

* N = naira throughout

11

2. Types and Objectives of Traditional Financial Institutions

In the modern financial system there are various shades of financial institutions with slightly varying modes of operations. Their short- or long-term objectives determine their organisational, managerial and operational structures. The only common denominator to the modern financial institutions is the principle of financial prudence.

In the traditional system there are also variants of financial institutions. Their mosaic nature arises from the obvious fact that they are not nationally standardised as there are no statutory provisions regulating their organisational forms and mechanics of operations. With more and more proliferation of the traditional financial units it becomes all the more difficult to group them into main and sub-units.

(a) *Types of Traditional Financial Institutions*

The earliest but the most primitive means of traditional financial intermediation were slavery, forced human labour and child marriages. The first two have been forced out of existence by laws because of their disregard for human values although it has not been possible to stamp out child marriages which are now contracted under various guises such as 'housemaid' and 'apprentice'. Because of the crushing poverty to which many families were subjected and the tempting offers by unscrupulous middlemen, some families took recourse to seizing a member who was considered a trouble-maker, a weakling or a sluggard and selling him into slavery. Through such deals financially hard-pressed families generated money for satisfying immediate needs. With the assault on the Long Juju in Arochukwu, Imo State, in 1901, the slave trade was dealt a very severe blow and with it the slave institution as a means of raising funds. The Long Juju constituted the nerve centre of the slave traffic.

In the Yoruba land a primitive form of traditional finance also has been stamped out of existence because of its debasement of human dignity. The system was called *iwofa*. By that system a borrower sent either his son or daughter, or in the absence of any child, his wife, to the lender to work for him for an agreed number of days a week. The service rendered was regarded as the interest for the borrowed money because the principal sum was still to be repaid. If a boy was sent he lived with the lender and was expected to make at least 200 earth heaps for the planting of yams during the planting season. If a girl was sent she was expected to work with the wives of the lender. Such a girl was not allowed to return to her father's house without being relieved of her duty as an *iwofa* and she could only be relieved of her services to the lender's family if the amount borrowed were fully repaid to the lender. A married woman was allowed to serve the lender from her husband's house until the amount borrowed was fully repaid. The *iwofa* system operated in a manner akin to pawning; it was a person-to-person arrangement. The practice also existed in some parts of Ibo land. Daughters were pledged to raise money for the training of the first son. If the father defaulted the son repaid the amount. If the money was not repaid the girl was customarily married and absorbed into the family of the creditor. Like *iwofa* the practice has been phased out in Ibo land.

The most popular and most widespread of traditional financial institutions are those engaged in savings, loan and mutual-aid schemes. These schemes are integrated in a system referred to in local parlance as *isusu* in Ibo land and *susu* in the Isoko areas of Bendel State. Traditional financial units which operate loan, savings and mutual aid schemes are popularly known by the above names in most areas, especially in the southern parts of Nigeria. There are variants of *isusu*, also referred to as *esusu* or *osusu* in some places. For example the variation *ogba* is found in the Nsukka area and *oha* (mitiri)[1] in the Ideator and Mbaise areas of the Ibo land. In a place like Ututu in the Arochukwu/Ohafia Local Government Area the savings/loan schemes are simply called *isusu*. In the Yoruba land there are variations such as the *ajo* and the *egbe*. Both differ slightly from *esusu* but the *egbe* system is a modern development of the *ajo* system.

Traditional financial intermediaries or units may be classified into the following groups. Each group has its variations, and the number of variations vary from locality to locality. The main systems are:

(a) finance through slavery, human labour and child marriages;
(b) *isusu* (*esusu, osusu, susu*) group;
(c) age grade associations;
(d) village administration contributions;
(e) village rural development schemes;
(f) men's revolving loan associations;
(g) married women's associations;
(h) family fund pools;
(i) extended family co-operative fund;
(j) town unions;
(k) local money lenders;
(l) social clubs.

(b) *Objectives of Traditional Financial Institutions*

The names of the different types of financial associations suggest strongly their objectives and natures. While the *isusu* scheme is concerned with loan, savings and mutual aid matters, the *age grade associations* are in most cases assigned certain village projects for the benefit of the entire community. They also organise schemes for the benefit of age-grade members. When a young man is of age he is expected, especially in Ibo land, to join an age grade. The community is full of expectation about the roles and achievements of the mature young man in the society. He is expected to perform certain functions if he is to be respected in his community. For example, he will be expected to marry, build a home and own other assets such as a bicycle, a motor cycle or a car, large farms, livestock or any other meaningful business if he is to establish his social position. In order to respond to the financial challenges facing him, it is imperative for the young man to join an age grade if he is to raise the fund he needs for fulfilling the expected duties.

Village administration contributions aim at providing the necessary funds for certain village services such as the cost of operations of a health centre, fuel costs of a village generator or entertainment costs of a village potentate. All the village's recurrent expenditures are taken care of by the administration contributions of the entire village. Unlike the *isusu* the contribution is not voluntary but mandatory. While the objective of an *isusu* scheme is the satisfaction of the immediate financial needs of members only, the village administration contribution is for the maintenance of village services which are of general interest. Funds for inter-village land litigation are also provided by the administration contributions of villagers.

Unlike the administration contributions *village rural development schemes* are capital-project oriented. Rural-scheme contributions are also mandatory on all villagers living at home and 'abroad' — that is, outside the village confines. Village projects such as a hall, connecting roads and culverts are the main objectives of rural-development-scheme contributions. Unlike *isusu*, where the contributions are revolvable and recoverable, village and town-union contributions are not refundable.

Men's revolving loan associations are formed by a small group of men in the village or in the urban areas, who are, in most cases, friends. Members contribute monthly. The monthly contributions are passed to members whose financial capacity may be inadequate for the projects they may have at hand. The revolving scheme continues until each member has benefited from the scheme. The programme also serves as an avenue for socialisation and merriment. At the monthly meetings members are entertained with drinks and food. The cost of the entertainment is borne by all the members — a part of the monthly collection is used for offsetting the cost of entertainment as well as other charges on the association. This is normally met from the general fund subtracted from the monthly contributions. The balance constitutes the *rotating fund* which is lent to members.

Married women's associations, like the men's counterpart, have the objective of catering for the welfare of the married women members. Contributions revolve among the members. After childbirth and during the nursing period a married woman is rendered unproductive in terms of economic activities. To supplement family income she contributes funds which will later revolve to her in many folds, especially during the pregnancy and nursing periods. A woman may also want to join the association because of anticipated future commitments such as the marriage of a daughter or a son or a close relation in which she may be expected to discharge certain traditional duties, which can only be performed with adequate funds.

The objective of *family fund pools* is to promote the well-being of the members of the family. In Nigeria, especially among the Ibos, the family is an 'insurance corporation'. The father educates a son or daughter who in turn educates brothers and sisters. As the family grows larger and more people are educated a family fund pool is created. Every month each of the income-earning members of the family contributes his or her own quota into the general family pool. From such a pool other children within the immediate family circle are educated. Other projects such as the building of a larger family house are also met from such funds. In some places the family fund pool is the strongest binder of the members of the family. Married women who were educated from the funds are known to have continued their contributions for a long time after they have been married and thereafter occasionally made token contributions to show their continued solidarity. In some cases family funds are invested in economic projects such as transport, garri-grating machines etc.

The *extended family co-operative fund* is an extension of the family fund pools system. It is wider in scope than the simple family fund and commands a larger fund. The objectives of the two are basically the same, except that in the case of the family fund pools the benefit derived by a member may not be repaid, but the beneficiary is obliged to make contributions to the fund as long as he or she lives. In the final analysis his total contribution may be many times greater than the benfit received. The difference is, of course, never regarded as a loss as nothing contributed for the benefit of the family is ever regarded as a loss in the African sense. In the case of the extended family co-operative fund, which also has the objective of assisting members of the extended family in financial needs, the financial help rendered to a member for a particular project must be repaid. An extended family co-operative fund has aided progressive members of the extended family to promote viable projects and to contain emergency situations.

The *town union* is a post-First World War phenomenon. With the development of urban towns by colonial authorities, people began to move from their villages to urban centres in search of better paying jobs and for trading purposes. People who were originally from the same towns but were now living in remote urban centres far from home met at least once a month to exchange news about home. The postal system was not as developed as it is today and communication with home was difficult. Town union meetings offered a forum for the exchange of news which reached individual members in trickles. In the course of time members found it worth while to contribute funds for their general good. Businessmen are financed from such funds. There are also provisions for emergency funding for members who have suffered reverses in business, and for the conveyance of dead members back to their native homes. In an urban town there are as many town unions as there are representatives from various places. Many of the unions now form the vanguards of rural developments. Besides the assistance to members, unions launch annual development-fund programmes in their respective towns for the purpose of starting certain high-cost projects such as schools, colleges, pipe-borne water, rural electrification, town halls, health centres, hospitals and scholarship awards for the benefit of the native town. Ironically in most cases town unions do not have a strong home branch, the real beneficiary of all the projects. All the ideas and funds originate mainly from the town 'boys' and women living 'abroad'. The developments of many communities today are attributed to the activities of town unions.

 Local money-lenders are well established in Nigeria. They provide the quickest but the costliest and often the most embarrassing means of securing urgent funds. The main sources of money-lenders' funds are their personal savings or funds set up by a union of money-lenders.

Social clubs are the latest addition to the traditional financial system. In the seventies they have experienced astronomic proliferation. Essentially they are a form of mutal insurance association. They provide a condolence purse to the dependants of a deceased member and take over from the dependants burial expenses such as the purchase of suitable coffin and entertainment costs of mourners, besides the conveyance of the corpse to the place of burial. By providing a condolence fund to dependants, social clubs alleviate the hardship which dependants frequently experience after the death of the bread-winner. Most people prefer joining social clubs to taking out a life assurance policy because of the past experiences of dependants. Obtaining letters of administration or probate is fraught with difficulties in Nigeria, where the deceased died intestate, i.e. without leaving a Will. Many dependants have suffered hardships because of the delay in issuing letters of administration which in some cases may not be released for many years because of counterclaims by immediate or distant relations of the deceased. The constitutions of the social clubs on the other hand are quite clear about the recipients of the condolence purse — the wife and the children of the deceased.

3. Organisation and Management of Traditional Financial Institutions

Apart from the social clubs whose members number up to 500 or more, the traditional financial units are normally not large and therefore require no sophisticated organisational and managerial competence. Although the organisation and management are simple, varying from locality to locality, the pattern of administration is a crude version of the modern financial administration.

(a) *Organisation*. Organisation suggests a division of job functions. In the traditional financial system there may or may not be a permanent leader, a treasurer or a secretary. In many of the organisations the meeting-place rotates. The monthly or fortnightly meeting is normally held in the houses of members and any member who hosts a meeting becomes automatically the chairman of the day.

Although there may be no permanent chairman, inner leaders of the association are acknowledged by members. In the case of *isusu* the inner leaders are those who recommend new members. The extent of the influence of the leaders is determined by the number of acceptable new members each of them recommended.

In the olden days it was difficult to find any literate person for miles around. Members relied on their retentive memories for keeping account of those who had or had not paid their dues, as well as those who had received the revolving funds and those who had not. Retentive memory was backed up by chalk markings on the wall. Now there is no village without some literate people. Some of the members of modern *isusu* organisations can read and write and may act as a permanent or occasional 'secretary' as the case may be. It is however, customary to employ an independent 'secretary'. Here the services of village primary school pupils are very handy, for a small token fee they cover the monthly or fortnightly proceedings of the organisations.

In some organisations the treasury rotates. The chairman of the day collects the contributions; in most cases the meeting of the organisation is held in the house of the member whose turn it is to receive the monthly contribution.

There are no written laws, rules or regulations to guide the operation of the older financial units. The conventions are, however, known by members who keep to them and respect them like any written laws. The frequency of meeting, the day, time and place as well as the amount to be paid by each member is determined either by the inner leaders or by general consensus.

Social clubs, which are recent developments have a guiding constitution, a complete set of principal officers and they are organised on modern lines; unlike the early traditional financial units they keep bank accounts.

(b) *Management*. The funds raised by the traditional financial units are usually small with the exception of the social clubs which control larger funds. But there is no clear information about how the social clubs invest their idle funds, which may remain after the presentation of the condolence purse to the dependants of the deceased and after meeting burial expenses.

In the case of *isusu*, which is a credit organisation, little financial management is involved. A member collects his turn on the very day that the fortnightly or monthly meeting is held. No interest is paid on the credit so the problem of interest management therefore does not arise. *Isusu* is the most popular of the traditional financial institutions; all that is required of members is the regular payment of contributions. Payments can also be made in advance, for example, in the *oha* variant of *isusu*. Double payments by members are frequent during the harvest seasons, particularly during the palmfruit harvesting season. When double payments are made, two or more members receive their dues at the same time.

Any member of *oha* who defaults in payment of his dues without a very good and acceptable reason is immediately expelled. Such a defaulter is held in contempt by the community, so defaulters are rare because of the fear of censure. Potential defaulters are eliminated in the process of screening. Any member who fails to contribute his dues after taking his turn is stigmatised. He loses the respect and trust of fellow members and is unlikely to be admitted into another association in his community.

There is a type of *oha* which does not permit the revolving of contributions. The weekly, fortnightly or monthly payments are stored in a common cash-box called *igbe oha*. The cash-box is given to a trusted member and the key to another member. The fund so raised is used to finance a common project like the award of a scholarship to a bright village boy, whose parents are not financially able to sponsor his education. Members who have personal financial problems may borrow from the common fund and some token interest is charged on the money so borrowed. The interest realised is added to the common fund.

In the *ajo* variant of the *isusu* the individual who promotes the association automatically becomes the manager. Promoters of *ajo* (*baba ajo*) are normally men of integrity, who can engineer the confidence of the people. The promoter is sometimes a full-time manager but he may also choose to operate on a part-time basis. He visits the houses of members in turn collecting their daily savings, which are usually quite small; each member contributes the same amount each day. They may not necessary contribute equal amounts but the voluntarily agreed contribution by a member for each month must remain constant for easy accounting purposes. At the end of each month every member forgoes a day's contribution. The sum of money collected from such forgone daily contributions serves as the salary of the promoter. The promoter manages the daily contributions of members, he can even invest them in a business with a very rapid turnover to his advantage; but he must pay out the members' contributions to them at the end of the month. Such bulk payments can then be better utilised by them.

The management of the funds of the village administration contributions and the village rural development scheme is normally vested in a village committee made up of a chairman and a few selected members of the village. The chairman is normally chosen by virtue of his age and not necessarily on account of his wisdom or financial prudence. Very often village funds are mismanaged because of incompetence in financial management. People are normally nominated to the committee to represent the different compounds that make up the village. Quite often trouble-makers are selected since they manipulate themselves into being chosen. A village financial committee may exist for the lifetime of a given project, or it may be a permanent committee which can be dissolved only if obvious mismanagement is observed.

The contributions of the married women's association are kept in a common cash-box and deposited with a trusted member of the association. The money so collected is held for the benefit of members. At the end of the year or half year as the association may decide, the money is distributed to the members according to their relative contributions. No proper records are kept about the amount of contributions made by each member. The association relies on the memory of members and the periodic entries of the schoolboy secretary.

The contributions generated from family fund pools and the extended family co-operative fund for specific family projects are kept in the custody of the oldest member of the family. The decision on how to spend or invest the fund is, however, a matter for the entire family. The various families engaged in the contributions have to sit over any proposal and approve it before the family fund is disbursed. In educated families which still respect the age-old tradition of family financing, any money collected is invested in a family trust and managed by trustees, who report to the entire family at the yearly family gatherings — a type of annual general meeting.

The town union and the social club are more sophisticated than the older traditional financial institutions already discussed. Their members include both the élites and the illiterates. The funds of both associations are normally banked in savings or current accounts. A member of a town union may borrow from the union's fund if he is in financial need, such a loan may require the guarantee of some members, although the loan may also be given on the basis of trust to the borrowing member depending on his integrity and general standing in the union in terms of financial commitments. Project-oriented contributions of a town union are normally transferred to the headquarters of the union or banked and cashed only for the purpose of presentation during the annual launching of the town's development fund. Members are in most cases not allowed to borrow from such specific funds. They may only borrow from the normal monthly or fortnightly contributions of members. Social clubs have larger amounts of funds which are neither invested in financial nor real assets. The fund of a club must be readily available for meeting its obligations in respect of deceased members, as the main provisions of the constitutions concern the clubs' obligation towards their members. Social clubs also consider themselves philanthropic organisations which help the disabled, the motherless babies in Cheshire Homes and other less fortunate ones in society but the extent of their commitment in philanthropic activities is very dubious. Only a very insignificant proportion of their funds are devoted to works of charity.

4. Functions of the Traditional Financial Institutions

Traditional financial institutions perform functions similar to those of modern financial institutions. However because of the lack of legislation guiding and standardising their operations those functions are still performed in a crude manner. They include savings, credit, discounting and development finance functions.

(a) *Savings Function*

The *isusu* organisation is a good example of a traditional financial institution which engaged mainly in savings and credit businesses. Like the modern financial institutions saving is voluntary; members are admitted into the *isusu* organisation on a voluntary basis.

In some of the *isusu* organisations the amount to be saved monthly or fortnightly is determined by the members of the association in order to make recording easy. In the *ajo* organisation which is a variant of the *isusu* association and the married women's associations, members contribute according to their ability. The amount collected constitutes savings for the members, which will be returned to them after the expiration of an agreed period, following the subtraction of certain service costs. The basic difference between the two associations is that the married women's associations share their funds among members at the end of the year while the contributions of the *isusu* association revolve to members in turn. Unlike the modern savings and loans departments of commercial banks no interest is paid on the money saved as the savings are traditionally never invested.

While modern savings institutions allow members to deposit any amount at any time, whenever the saver wants, the traditional system makes it mandatory to deposit the agreed amount at the agreed time.

(b) *Credit Function*

A good number of the traditional financial institutions perform credit functions, providing credit to their members, on which interest is charged by some associations, while others provide interest-free credit. Some demand some form of collateral security while others rely on the integrity of members.

In the *isusu* association the fund that revolves to a member each time is usually many times greater than the contributions made by the member originally. Only the last recipient receives an amount equal to the total of his contributions, assuming no administration costs are incurred. In most organisations members receive an amount less than their total contributions, as expenses for the purchase of minute-books and for the payment of the hired schoolboy clerk are normally incurred. The recipient of the revolving fund receives a form of credit which is repaid at a future date on the basis of contributions; no interest is charged by the association. Married women's associations provide credit to members who may be in dire need of funds to finance personal programmes. The amount so lent out must, however, be repaid before or on the date fixed by the association for sharing the fund among the member. Token interest may be charged in the case of borrowing members but non-members who are judged fit to borrow from the association pay higher interest charges. Town unions provide members with interest-free loans but the men's revolving loan associations and the money-lenders charge interest for any credit they provide. The interest charges of money-lenders are normally very high and many people join one or more associations to ensure that they are not forced by circumstances to borrow from money-lenders. Family pools funds do not provide credit directly, but the fact that members of the family who benefited from the fund later contribute to the fund qualifies the financial assistances as credit. Extended family co-operative funds provide interest-free credit to extended family members.

Like modern financial institutions credit may be granted if men of substance guarantee the borrower or if the borrower is prepared to provide some collateral security. The traditional collateral security normally demanded is farmland or a palm plantation. In the case of farmland the lender uses the land for farming purposes until the borrower repays the money borrowed. In the event of default the lender continues to utilise the land until a member of the borrower's family repays the money. Where a palm plantation is used as collateral the lender harvests the palm fruits until the loan is repaid. Movable property may also be pledged and in the case of default, the pledged properties are carried away by force.

(c) *Discounting Function*

In the modern financial system commercial banks and acceptances discount bills. A bill is discounted when funds are urgently needed. Bills discounted normally attract a penalty in the form of discount rate. The discount rate is regulated or fixed by the monetary authorities. In the traditional system a man or woman urgently in need of funds may want to buy the right of a member whose turn it is to receive the revolving fund. The purchaser of the right can resell the right further.[2] The first seller is, however, responsible in the event of default. Any member who purchases a member's turn discounts his own turn to receive the revolving fund in the future. The 'discount rate', that is, the amount the purchaser pays to buy another person's turn from him is not fixed. It is negotiated and rises according to the number of people wishing to purchase the right.

(d) *Developmental Function*

Because of the absence of banks and financial houses in most rural areas the traditional institutions play the role of financiers. They conceive projects, plan them, organise their implementation and raise the necessary funds. The age grade association is very much involved in development finance. Each age grade chooses or is assigned a particular project which it must execute for the benefit of the community. Town unions, social clubs and village rural development schemes also undertake certain projects. In some cases all the project-oriented associations combine to carry out a major project which requires a very large financial base. Unlike the modern financial institutions the amount invested in community projects is not refundable.

5. A Critical Appraisal of the Associations

There is no doubt that the traditional financial associations have contributed enormously to encouraging thrift, communal development and the promotion of general business and industry. Those areas where they are most evident manifest a higher level of development. In the absence of commercial banks and other financial institutions they have constituted the only sources for the harnessing of funds of the relatively surplus economic units and transferring them to the very deficient economic units of the rural and urban areas.

In spite of their positive contributions they have a number of shortcomings which become more and more obvious in the increasingly sophisticated economic environment in which they operate. The absence of rules and legislation relating to their operations has made it difficult to harmonise them. The fear is real, however, that if any attempt is made to regulate them their operations may be stifled as a good number of the associations may not be able to conform with the minimum conditions which such rules or legislation may impose.

Because of the absence of regulations relating to their operations there is no definite process for bringing defaulters to book. Traditional financial associations often resort to unfair practices. Properties of defaulters which have a value over and above the amount borrowed are normally pledged as they have no scientific means of determining the real value of such properties. The seizure of such properties in the event of default has very often led to feuding which may spread over generations.

Money-lenders are the biggest culprits in the arena of traditional finance. Their interest-rate charges are in some cases over 100 per cent of the actual value of the credit provided; they often seek security in the form of a piece of land with cash crops and harvest the crops until repayment is completed. If both lender and borrower should die the relevant documents may not be found and the family of the lender regard the mortgaged piece of land as their patrimonial bequest. Many years later, elders in the village may resurrect the issue in order to create a situation of arbitration — through such an arbitration exercise opportunities for drinking and dining are created at the expense of the disputants, to the pleasure of the elders. Where settlement is impossible the elders may force one of the disputants to swear before a local 'juju'. If the claim is false he would be expected to die within a year. In order to sustain his claim the counter-claimant may resort to plotting to precipitate the death of the other through poisoning; where he succeeds, a family vendetta is generated.

The traditional financial institutions, especially the much older ones, have no accounting system, no good records and no auditing process. The security of the savings of members depends on the honesty and personal integrity of the promoter. There is no legal cushion against fraud. In some associations those who keep the associations' funds swear an oath promising not to appropriate them. It is generally believed by members that any misappropriation will lead to the death of the custodian. Some associations do not rely on the power of 'juju' for auditing the account, rather they keep a watchful eye on the custodian of the association's funds. If his style of living is considered excessive in terms of his normal income an emergency meeting is immediately summoned. A quick accounting is made of the money lent out and the balance is cross-checked. If the cash balance with the custodian is incomplete, punitive actions are taken against him in the traditional ways allowed by the customs of the area. He could be brought in disgrace before the village elders to explain himself or his house may be looted and properties seized.

Of all the traditional financial associations the town union and the social club have come under the fire of criticisms in recent times. The 'big two' in the arena of traditional finance have been criticised as platforms for demonstrations of affluence and for taunting and tempting the 'have nots' in our communities into illegitimate actions in the pursuit of wealth. At the end of each year town unions launch development-fund programmes. Rich businessmen now use the occasion to demonstrate the extent of their wealth by the amount of money they donate. Before the civil war which began in 1967, town unions diligently executed town projects in the spirit of brotherhood and oneness and in the absence of rivalry. The post-civil-war town unions are now full of an outcrop of young and rich businessmen who see the launching of a development programme as an occasion for challenging a rival townsman. The financial battle of the giants has created such disunity in most towns that it has been impossible to carry out important projects because the financial heavyweights disagree on how best to implement the project. Each would like the project to be carried out along the lines he suggested if the amount he pledged is to be released. Sometimes a battle line is drawn between the supporters of one financier and the other. The humble villager who is full of good intentions is discouraged from contributing the usual widow's mite as it appears shamefully low in comparison with the pledges and donations of businessmen. He is psychologically converted into a dummy without any say on a project which affects him more than the city businessmen. Money power substitutes village wisdom. Not all the town unions have faulted in their objectives, there are still some which are genuinely and strongly committed to communal developments without bitterness.

Social clubs have been under severe criticism because of their objectives. As stated before, they are aimed primarily at giving a dead member a fitting burial and secondly, providing a handsome purse to the deceased member's family. Obiechina has elegantly referred to them as the 'Mortuary Clubs'.[3] Ostentatious living, pomp and pageantry characterise the organisation. He observed that the professed objectives of providing succour to the needy and services to the communities are a cover-up of their main intention because about 'two-thirds of the provisions of these "constitutions" are devoted to mortuary obligations'.[4] The following observations of Obiechina aptly summarise the ironic realities of the social clubs vis-à-vis their publicly avowed humanitarian objectives.

In other words the interest in the poor and materially deprived of our society is a mere ruse, a pretence and a front of respectability behind which the most disgusting self-indulgence is promoted. There is no sight as offensive to the sense of propriety as the scene in which already over-weight men and women sit greedily concentrated and businesslike, one person to a huge whole chicken and a hillock of jollof rice and twenty-four bottles of lager beer forming a thick wall behind these and a large bottle of whisky winking in the corner to complete the full picture of an orgiastic Bacchanalian setting.[5]

The epicurean style of living of the socialites does not permit them to think of the society in terms of the future, as their attention is primarily focused on the present and short-term needs. The social clubs consider themselves a kind of mutual insurance which provides benefits to members without tears because unlike life insurance companies, no letters of administration are required by the deceased's relations.

Their mode of operation is likened to the funeral societies of medieval Europe, and can in no way be compared with the benefits of modern life assurances. Modern life assurances have a number of advantages.

1. The assured is free to borrow the surrender value of his life policy which he may invest in activities beneficial to him and his dependants while he is still alive, without jeopardising the benefits to his dependants after his death.

2. Life policies provide for different ages, various premiums and maturities.

3. An assured may decide to break the scheme at any time and still recover a large portion of the amount already paid.

The 'mutual assurance' provided by the social clubs lack the above advantages. Ogwo[6] aptly observed that as the 'mutual assurance' of the social clubs has no age provision, the younger members of the club are compelled to pay the same annual dues as the very old members. In the final analysis the family of a member who joined the club as a young person may receive a condolence purse much smaller than his total contributions over the years.

Should there be a change in the outlook of future generations, the membership strength of the social clubs may drop. Such a situation will increase the burden of contribution on the few members still living who must pay the same amount as condolence purse to the dependants of bereaved members as stipulated in the 'constitution' of the club. The cost of operating the scheme may become so prohibitive that the social clubs may disband without some dependants of members reaping the ultimate benefits.

The danger of fund mismanagement is there and the benefits of members may suffer. Above all members stand the chance of losing their benefits if the government should consider the activities of social clubs incompatible with the spirit of justice or countervailing to social norms and proscribe them as was the case of the *Oka Society* in 1966.[7]

6. Reasons for Their Continued Proliferation

Many factors quantifiable and unquantifiable account for the continued proliferation of the traditional financial institutions. These factors can be grouped under two broad categories — ignorance and banking rigidities.

(i) *Ignorance*. The majority of the Nigerian people are still illiterate. They do not understand what banking business is all about and do not appreciate the facilities offered by modern financial institutions. Many of them still regard banks as a creation of the rich where no moderate- or low-income people are expected to show their faces.

It took the older generation of rural people decades to accept and appreciate modern money and then the acceptance was restricted to metallic coins. It took more decades before currency notes gained general acceptance. The approach to modern monetary institutions by the rural people has always been a cautious one.

When banking institutions were established the older generations did not trust them and would not part with their monies to the banks for safe-keeping. The younger generations of the rural people adopted the financial habits of their fathers and also preferred hoarding their monies. This lack of trust for the banks was reinforced by tales of the crash of mushroom banks in the fifties which led to financial ruin for many depositors. The Nigerian civil war (1966-70) brought about other bitter banking experiences for the depositors in the war zones which further confirmed the fear of the rural people about the safety of a depositor's money with the banks.

Little attempt has been made to inculcate banking habits in the rural people. Rudiments of financial habits are not taught in schools. In an advanced country like West Germany a bank may open a free savings account for a newborn baby. As the child grows more deposits are made for him or her by the parents. When the child is older he or she goes personally to the savings bank and makes the deposit, and so gets acquainted with banking procedures, develops banking habits and later behaves rationally with respect to money. No encouragement has been given to potential savers in Nigeria. Consequently many people are estranged from banks and what they stand for. Given the option to choose, the rural people will, under the circumstances, prefer the traditional financial system they know, to the system that they hardly know about.

(ii) Banking Rigidities. In order to maintain a higher standard of banking practice, legislation is passed to regulate the operations of financial institutions that carry out the functions of modern banks. The question often asked is whether banking developments are not paralysed in the effort to set a very high standard. The Nigerian Banking Decree (Decree No. 1, 1969) as amended is one such law which has raised eybrows. By that decree a bank can only be licensed to operate if the capital requirement of N1.5 million for foreign-sponsored banks or N0.6 million for indigenous banks is met. In a country with an estimated population potential of about 80 million there are less than 20 commercial banking institutions and barely 500 branches. Consequently in some areas of the country banking facilities are not available for 100 km. Because of this absence the rural people are left with the available 'financial system'. The existing banks concentrate in the urban areas where in their view banking business is available. Although the Central Bank has directed that a new bank branch in an urban area can only be permitted if such a bank can open a rural branch simultaneously, the directive has not led to any significant growth of rural banks.

Where bank facilities are available a number of problems are encountered by potential depositors. First of all a depositor intending to operate a chequeable account has to be recommended by two depositors who hold accounts with the bank in question; then a high level of initial deposit is expected. In the actual operation of the account a number of problems are encountered before a cheque can be cashed as they take a long time to process. In some cases it may take a whole day to cash a cheque issued by a bank customer. Intercity cheques may take weeks, and in some cases months, before they are cleared. The clearing systems for cheques are still to be mechanised.

The attitude of bank officials are at times outright hostile. The cardinal principle that the customer is king is still to be accepted as a business maxim by many Nigerian business houses including banking institutions. Discrimination against customers abounds. Some 'big' customers are given preferential treatment with all the courtesy denied the ordinary customers.

Unlike the traditional financial associations which make credit easily available on the basis of mortgaged properties or farmland or cash-crop plantations, the modern financial institutions demand the guarantees of men of substance or collateral securities acceptable to them before any loan is granted. The condition for loans may be difficult to comply with by a small saver intending to borrow from a bank.

When small savers consider the inconveniences, the embarrassment and the delays of modern banks as well as the sometimes long distance to the banking houses, they tend to prefer the near, friendly and easily accessible local financial associations and money lenders. In short, ignorance, the rigidities of the modern financial institutions and the government's apparent indifference in encouraging rural banking have tended to enhance the proliferations of the traditional financial intermediaries.

7. Conclusion

Traditional financial institutions have definitely contributed to the development of the Nigerian economy in spite of their imperfections. Their modes of operation can be improved to the greater advantage of the economy if the Nigerian monetary authorities create an atmosphere more conducive for their proper development. The newly created local governments can play a great role in this respect if a department responsible for Rural Thrift, which will take over the responsibility of advising financial associations, is established in each local government area. The Rural Thrift department will conduct village seminars from time to time, encourage local financial associations and educate them on the benefits of investing their funds instead of hoarding them. Mobile savings banks should be put at the disposal of the local governments to enable villages and towns to be visited on market days so that associations and individuals may deposit their savings.

Notes

1. 'Mitiri' is a corrupted word from 'meeting'.
2. See E. Iwu, *Die Bedeutung ursprunglicher sozio-oekonomischer Organisa-tions Formen in Afrika fuer die Industrialisierung* (Eukerdruck K.G. Marburg, 1973), p. 44.
3. E. Obiechina, 'Ring In The New Year – A New Year Essay', *Daily Star* (Enugu), 1 January 1979, pp. 5-6.
4. Ibid., p. 6.
5. Ibid.
6. S.A. Ogwo, 'Life Assurance and Social Clubs' in *The Bond* (The Universal Insurance Company, Enugu October/November/December 1978), vol. I, no. 2, p. 2.
7. Ibid.

2 A SURVEY OF NIGERIA'S MODERN FINANCIAL SYSTEM

W. Okefie Uzoaga

1. Introduction

A financial system comprises the entire congeries of institutions and institutional arrangements established to serve the needs of modern economies. This service is rendered through provision of financial resources to meet the borrowing needs of individuals, business enterprises and governments; of facilities to collect and to invest savings funds and of a sound payments mechanism.

It must be noted that financial institutions could not develop until the barter economy gave way to the money economy and until the latter was superseded by the credit economy. The invention of double-entry bookkeeping, the evolution of the concept of negotiability, and of negotiable instruments, the development of the law of contract, of real property, of partnerships and corporations, the evolution of the instruments of finance, of capital markets and stock exchanges, the growth of trade and commerce; all these constitute the basic infra-structure that encouraged the rise of financial institutions. Their growth accentuated the accumulation of large aggregates of savings funds necessary for the establishment of various enterprises that produce great quantities of goods and services.

Financial institutions may be publicly, privately or jointly owned. They may be general or specialised in character. They might have evolved in response to developing needs or they might have been deliberately created and superimposed on the economy to meet specific credit needs.

In economies where private ownership is nonexistent, financial institutions are state owned and controlled and besides form an important part of the control machinery of the state. The organisational structure is relatively simple and normally comprises one huge bank which performs both commercial and central-banking functions such as the Gosbank in Russia, a network of savings banks serving the needs of individuals and a group of specialised credit institutions. The role of financial institutions in such economies is purely that of financing and implementing the production plan. They do not initiate the establishment of enterprises. They do not exercise any discretionary authority in credit allocation. Once the production plan is set in motion the currency and credit are mobilised towards the fulfilment of the plan. In other words a bank manager in such an economy cannot select the establishments to which the funds are loaned. He merely disburses funds according to plan and ensures that loans are repaid on schedule. In this way he acts as one of the control organisations of the state with responsibility for the achievement of the plan.

This stands in contrast with competitive capitalistic society where financial institutions are usually privately owned and managed. The financial structure is much more complicated and the role of financial institutions is more difficult and much more aggressive and involved. Goods and services are produced not according to a predetermined all-embracing plan but primarily in response to price changes which reflect varying intensity of demand on the part of consumers, business enterprises and the government. Market competition is thus the major factor determining the allocation of the factors of production; and financial institutions stand ready to finance those enterprises which on the basis of market demand, are considered the most eligible risk. Before financing these enterprises, financial institutions attempt to *evaluate* the credit standing of the prospective risk, to *appraise* its management capability and to *forecast* the demand for goods and services produced. They are thus active participants in the market plan.

The funds for disbursement by these institutions comprise savings funds and credit created in the process of lending. In the exercise of disbursing and collecting savings funds, the rate of interest plays an important role by serving to ration the loan demand, to cover the credit risk and to reward the thrifty. But in noncapitalistic economies the rate of interest has no economic significance since it serves rather as a service charge to offset the bookkeeping costs of the lending institution.

The general trend has been strongly towards state ownership of financial institutions even in rugged capitalistic societies. In the United States of America, state intervention in the ownership and control of financial institutions has been significant as evidenced by a host of federal credit institutions and state guarantee of loans particularly in such areas as rural credits, urban mortgage credits, small business loans and export credit. Even in those few areas where private ownership persists, including the federal reserve banks, activities of financial institutions are strongly state oriented.

The Commonwealth of Australia established the Commonwealth Bank to perform central banking and commercial-banking functions and to compete actively with private commercial banks. The state bank of India, the successor of the presidency banks, was nationalised in order to facilitate the transmission of banking facilities to the rural areas of that country.

The wave of socialisation which spread over post-war Europe culminated in the nationalisation of the Bank of England but barely missed the British joint-stock banks. In France an extensive programme of socialisation during the early post-war period netted the four large commercial banks which are permitted to maintain their individuality and compete as usual but within the new framework of socialised institutions.

2. Survey of Colonial Financial Arrangement

Since independence from British colonial rule the trend in Nigeria has been strongly in the direction of public ownership of financial institutions. The colonial experience in Nigeria was one in which private transnational commercial banks dominated the banking arrangement. Multinational trading firms similarly controlled sources of trade credit, which they extended only to their *bona fide* customers who were largely foreigners. The private indigenous financial institutions, mainly commercial banks, in time sprang up to provide credit to the bulk of indigenous enterprises who for various reasons could not secure adequate financial assistance from expatriate banks and the trading firms. The supra-territorial enterprises were primarily interested in financing export – import transactions of expatriate trading firms and in providing the short-term financial needs of the colonial administration and seasonal loans for collection of primary export products.

Such public financial institutions as existed during the colonial period comprised the West African Currency Board, which issued and redeemed the currency and invested its resources in sterling securities. The Nigeria Development Loans Board (1945), later decentralised along regional lines and known as Regional Development Boards (1949), was established to provide medium-term loan capital to Nigerian entrepreneurs and public bodies for public works, land development and utilisation and development of village crafts. In practice virtually all the boards' loans were made to public enterprises.

There were also co-operative 'banks' established in the various regions at the apex of co-operative organisations in each region. They functioned as the co-operatives' central financial institutions – as depositories of the funds of a region's thrift and credit societies as well as a source of credit to the co-operative organisation. Initially they did not accept deposits from the public since they were not banking institutions within the meaning of the Nigerian Banking Ordinance (1952). They obtained the bulk of their funds from regional governments, shares and deposits of member co-operative societies. Their loans and advances were made to member societies to finance marketing of export crops. The emphasis was on the marketing aspect of their activities rather than on long-term production credit. The credit operations were thus of short-term character and in small amounts. Moreover, the thrift and loan societies organised by salaried workers were concentrated in urban centres while the thrift and credit societies were essentially rural. Both groups were pestered with problems of mismanagement, accounting confusion and defalcation of funds.

The Post Office Savings Bank (now the Federal Savings Bank) which mobilised small savings through its network of branches and whose liabilities were guaranteed by the government was required by law to ensure that 'not more than one-third' of its funds should at any time be or remain invested in securities of the government of the colony. In other words not less than two-thirds of its money should be remitted to London for investment by the Secretary of State. In practice, much less than one-third of the bank's resources was invested in Nigeria. For instance in 1956 only 0.4 per cent of the bank's total investments of £4.2 million was placed in Nigeria. In 1959 the bank's sterling asset holdings of £2.9 million constituted 80 per cent of the bank's deposit liabilities of £3.6 million in that year. Thus the bank was designed to facilitate export of capital and not to mobilise savings for domestic economic development even though its funds were the most suitable for medium- and long-term capital. And so the demand for this type of capital remained unsatisfied.

Under normal circumstances the insurance industry could have contributed significantly to meeting the need for long-term capital in Nigeria during the colonial period. A number of British insurance companies were represented, in four cases directly and in others through agencies. As in commercial banking and commerce, indigenous insurance companies were still in their rudimentary stages of development. The close connection with London firms meant that the premiums collected by these companies and agencies in Nigeria were repatriated to London for investment. Once again a possible source of medium- and long-term capital for local development could not be harnessed because of institutional dependence on British firms and the British capital market. To the extent that this type of fund was induced either by law or association or both to leave the country, the development of organised capital and securities markets was constricted.

With this sketch of Nigerian financial arrangements and their inadequacies during the colonial period it can be seen that there was no financial 'system' as such during this period. The country was merely an appendage of the British economy and the financial arrangements were purely an integral part of the British financial system. There could not have been a financial system without a national pivotal financial institution, to regulate the issue and redemption of a national currency, and to moderate in the interest of the local economy the flow of funds in and out of the country. But it must be said that the arrangement was efficient in ensuring that institutional and individual savings even in the remotest village if deposited in one of these institutions readily contributed to the sustenance of the metropolitan country's economy.

3. Nigerian Federal Government Intervention Since Independence

The humiliation experienced during the operation of the colonial financial arrangement and subsequent abuses and indifference to local economic conditions largely explain the systematic state intervention in the financial system since political independence. As in other countries state intervention in the financial system in Nigeria has occurred for various reasons — economic, political and social.

Central banks are usually public-owned institutions and the purpose is to ensure co-operation in implementation of monetary policy towards a nation's economic goals. The British colonial monetary policy ensured that the financial institutions in the colonies geared their efforts and resources towards achievement of Britain's national economic objectives. It was only fair that Nigeria, in common with other former colonial territories, would found her own central bank.

Unlike the Bank of England which evolved from the banking system, the Central Bank of Nigeria, like the federal reserve system of the United States, was deliberately organised and superimposed on the existing financial institutions. But unlike the US federal reserve system the Central Bank of Nigeria is wholly owned by the Federal Government of Nigeria. Like other central banks therefore it was established to *exact co-operation* and give direction towards the achievement of national economic objectives. To this end, the West African Currency

Board was abolished and some of its functions were taken over and refined by the Central Bank of Nigeria. The anachronistic regulations that governed the operations of the Postal Savings Bank and investments of funds of similar public bodies were amended and redirected. The custodianship of the nation's foreign-exchange reserves and the composition of these reserves were centralised and decentralised respectively. The movement of funds in and out of the country was regulated through the Exchange Control Act, 1962. The development of local capital and securities markets was encouraged.

For once indigenous commercial banks were offered the opportunity of operating under a well-defined body of regulations geared towards their safety and that of the depositors. These banks, since the establishment of the Central Bank, have had the opportunity of ease of accommodation and of sound banking supervision and bank examination instead of the ridicule to which British officials subjected them during the colonial period. Expatriate banks on the other hand are constantly being required to adapt their operations to local needs and to seek out and use local investment outlets for their excess reserves. To ensure compliance some 60 per cent of their ownership is mutualised.

Other reasons for intervention include the desire to promote competition, to provide banking accommodation to a wider sector of the population, to provide banking facilities to the rural areas and to check the dominance of transnational banks, which if unchecked, would have conferred a virtual monopoly of the banking system on foreign interests. Thus the Nigerian Federal and State governments by outright establishment of new banks and subsidisation of existing indigenous banks as well as direct participation in ownership of equity interests in foreign banks have attempted, through intervention, to sustain competition in the banking system.

At the local level State governments have sponsored the establishment of commercial banks, co-operative banks and other credit institutions, to fill the gap created over the years by inadequate banking and credit facilities. The indigenous commercial banks which started in the thirties as private institutions have in the course of their difficulties become virtually state owned or mutualised institutions through substantial financial assistance which they were forced to seek and obtain from the State and Federal governments as their private resources became clearly inadequate. Through the Central Bank's guidelines to commercial banks, effort is being made to increase the proportion of total advances available to indigenous businesses.

Other than the few facilities largely provided by the Federal Savings

Bank (formerly the Post Office Savings Bank) and co-operative banks, the rural communities are still badly in need of banking facilities. The plea of various rural communities for banking facilities has continued to fall on deaf ears as the existing banks prefer to concentrate their activities on centres of trade and government rather than branch out to the outlying but rapidly developing communities. The trend to concentrate activities in the urban centres is now under check. The Central Bank has now made it mandatory for any bank wishing to open up a new branch in an urban area to simultaneously create an outpost in a rural area if the new urban branch is to receive approval. Specialised credit institutions in agriculture, industry, and housing have been established to facilitate lending in these sectors. But, due to physical and financial constraints, these facilities are yet to expand into the rural communities.

Indeed Nigeria has not embarked on an extreme programme of nationalisation of the financial system, but has combined the factors of outright ownership and participation in various segments of the financial system to achieve a dominant presence in the system. But in appraising this trend towards increased state intervention, it is important to bear in mind that socialisation *per se* would not guarantee efficiency as the performance of public enterprises in this country has since proved. If the financial system is completely nationalised, the principal advantage would be the dampening of the rigorous competitive profit-and-loss economy. But the temptation to extend credits to state-owned enterprises on better terms rather than to private enterprise, as was rife during the era of the Regional Loan Boards, may prevail. It would also be necessary to consider the fate of individuals, professionals and firms whose views and legitimate operations fall short of the expectations of a political party in power. Would these still have the opportunity to be appraised on the basis of their credit worthiness when they seek bank accommodation? Finally, there is the danger of the chronic inefficiency that has been the lot of public enterprises generally.

In sum the ownership in the financial system though mixed in character is strongly in favour of state ownership achieved largely by deliberate action in founding new institutions, and in mutualisation of existing ones sometimes at the request of the affected institutions.

Whether privately or publicly owned, financial institutions would still be required to provide facilities which are adequate to the growing needs and the changing requirements of an economy. Traditionally, commercial banks in Nigeria, and indeed in other countries, lend out money only on a short-term basis and mainly to activities of a commercial nature. They do not provide long-term financial accommodations.

It therefore became necessary for the government to establish specialised credit institutions to provide long-term capital.

4. Specialised Credit Institutions

It was the inability of the commercial banking system in Nigeria, as
indeed in other countries, to meet long-term credit needs of various sectors of the economy that made it necessary for the Federal Government
to undertake to establish specialised credit institutions such as the
Nigeria Industrial Development Bank (1964, after reconstruction of the
Investment Company of Nigeria), the Nigerian Agricultural Bank
(1973) and the Nigeria Bank for Industry and Commerce (1973). In
addition the Federal Military Government acquired the Building
Society with plans to develop it into a full-fledged Federal Mortgage
Bank. Similarly the Federal Savings Bank, formerly Postal Savings
Bank, is being strengthened.

Through the agency of the National Insurance Corporation of
Nigeria the Federal Government set out through ownership of equity
shares to mutualise non-bank financial institutions such as foreign
insurance companies in Nigeria. So far eleven private foreign insurance
companies have been affected. Various State governments have also
established insurance companies. Taken together the rapid expansion of
the financial system in the last few years has occurred largely from
direct government intervention aimed at restructuring and controlling
the financial system in the public interest. With such presence it is
hoped that the government would be better placed to correct the
abuses and disabilities that have over the years combined to restrain the
availability of medium- and long-term credit and its equitable distribution among the various sub-sectors of the national economy.

But in this exercise to domesticate the financial system and direct
its resources towards achievement of national objectives, the Federal
Government has not lost sight of the desirability of institutional specialisation in lending functions. The fundamental characteristic of a sound
financial system is its ability to finance credit needs which contribute
to economic growth without injury to stability. In other words the goal
of a sound credit policy is economic growth within the framework of a
relatively stable price level.

A financial system can finance economic growth in various ways.
This can be done through:

(a) the medium of commercial banks and their credit-creating powers or

(b) the agency of financial intermediaries and their utilisation of financial savings or

(c) the services of the capital markets in selling securities to financial intermediaries and other members of the investing public. Business enterprises can also finance their need for funds through retention of earnings. Whichever means of financing is preferred, it would still be necessary to underscore the need to contribute to economic growth without stimulating inflationary pressures.

A financial system in which institutions specialise in lending functions would appear to be best suited to finance credit needs of growth without causing inflation because of a number of reasons: first, specialisation is necessary to ensure that the maturity of assets of financial institutions is related to the maturity of their liabilities. The character of liabilities of commercial banks demands that short-term funds should not be employed to finance long-term requirements. The use of short-term funds to finance long-term requirements would aggravate the liquidity problems of commercial banks and ultimately lead to failure and economic instability. Several commercial banks in Nigeria had attempted to defy this basic principle of commercial banking and the result was a high failure rate such as occurred in the fifties. And those private indigenous commercial banks that survived after engaging in this practice paid for their survival by losing their position as private institutions once they accepted large infusions of public funds. The result is that today all indigenous banks which started as private institutions are for all intents and purposes mutualised institutions.

Experiences of other countries are no less relevant. Lacking long-term funds in the twenties, German commercial banks used short-term funds to finance the long-term requirements of German industry. But no sooner had the Great Depression of the thirties set in than these banks found that their assets had been frozen and therefore not available to meet depositors' demands. Indeed such assets could be shifted to the Central Bank — the lender of last resort and the losses thereby socialised. But if the assets so transferred are large in amount, as was the case in Austria, the currency itself may be ruined or at best devalued. We should therefore reject the assumption that the Central Bank has a magic well-spring of funds. There is a limit to what a central bank can absorb without injury to economic stability. True it has a monopoly of note issue but the conversion of all types of assets into paper money would be disastrous. Inflation as we have since experienced in this country is a very unjust and inequitable levy on the populace whose welfare policy definitions tend to underscore.

Secondly, institutional specialisation in lending is important, to restrict monetisation by commercial banks of those types of debt which induce cyclical swings in business activity such as urban and rural mortgage debt, government debt and long-term corporate debt. The financing of debts of this character should be related to *savings* and so should largely be provided by financial intermediaries. Thirdly, specialised institutions acquire expertise in various fields of lending such as consumer credit, mortgage credit and agricultural credit. In this regard they are better able to exercise independent judgement in evaluating credit risks. Such expertise and objectivity in risk appraisal are not normally available in an institution such as a commercial bank burdened with varied functions including production of means-of-payment. We should therefore resist the temptation, in this period of great liquidity flood which many think will never subside, to force commercial banks to enter vigorously into fields of lending which neither the character of their liabilities nor their managerial capability would sustain.

The Federal Government must have recognised the dangers inherent in such action when years ago it repeatedly proscribed certain activities of licenced commercial banks in all banking legislation since 1952 and more recently under Section 13 (1) of the Banking Decree 1969 (Amended 1970) and proceeded to establish specialised credit institutions for various sectors of the national economy. To mitigate the difficulties of marginal and sub-marginal credit risks in securing bank accommodation the Federal Government has gone further to provide in its 1976/77 budget for a guarantee scheme, the scope of which is yet to be known but which one assumes is intended to sweeten the financial position of prospective risks — those who otherwise would not qualify for bank loans on the basis of their own assets including their credit history or who are incapable of convincing even their relations or friends with bankable assets to guarantee repayment of principal and interest on the amount they wish to borrow from banks. Perhaps, the guarantee scheme would have provisions also to subsidise the initial cost incurred by financial institutions that expand into outlying districts and thus accelerate the reduction of low banking density that tends to constrict economic activities in developing rural areas.

5. Commercial or Department-Store Banking

The question then arises as to what credit needs should be financed by commercial banks and what by other financial intermediaries? Some of the activities which are proscribed by the Banking Decree for commercial banks in Nigeria may be summarised to enable us to appreciate the framework of the regulation of bank credit within which commercial banks are required to operate:

A licensed bank is prohibited from granting to any person any advance, loan or credit facility or financial guarantee in excess of 33.33 per cent of the sum of the paid-up capital and statutory reserves of the bank. It should also not grant *unsecured* advances or loans of an aggregate amount in excess of N1,000 to any of its directors or to any firm, partnership or private company in which any of its directors is interested as a director, partner, manager or agent or to any public company in which any of its directors has direct or indirect interest. Unsecured credit to any of a bank's officials or employees is limited to the amount of the annual salary of such officials or employees.

Commercial banks are also proscribed from acquiring or holding any part of the share capital of any financial, commercial, agricultural, industrial or other undertaking. Exceptions are:

(i) shareholding as a licensed bank may, with the prior approval of the Central Bank, be acquired in the course of satisfaction of debt due to it or

(ii) any shareholding approved by the Central Bank in any *statutory corporation* established for the purpose of promoting the development of money and capital markets;

(iii) all shareholdings approved by the Central Bank in *other undertakings*, the aggregate value of which does not at any time exceed 25 per cent of the sum of the paid-up capital and reserves of the commercial bank. Prohibited also is the purchase, acquisition or lease of *real estate* except for the purpose of the business of the commercial bank or the housing of its staff. But a commercial bank may secure a debt on any real estate and in default of repayment may acquire such property and dispose of it at the earliest possible moment.

At first sight these prohibitions may appear quite stringent and restrictive for a banking system operating in a developing economy suffering from all manner of shortages in housing, food supply, consumer and durable goods. The justification may be found in the history of the commercial-banking development in this country, the credit behaviour of our professionals and businessmen, the high failure rate among indigenous banks and the resultant need to protect bank capital and reserves (stockholders) as well as to provide adequate protection for their depositors. But to moderate the effect of the stringent regulation of the commercial-banking system on bank credit, additional sources of bank credit have been created through the establishment of specialised financial institutions. This would appear to support the preference of commercial banks as sources for short-term credit, even though the people have always looked up to this group of banks as a source of all types of funds — short, medium and long term. The problem therefore is no longer so much of a dearth of institutional facilities for medium- and long-term credit as ignorance of the new and expanding specialised sources of bank credit available to various sub-sectors of the economy; the physical and institutional constraints under which these new institutions operate; the wondrous credit behaviour of Nigerians; and the dearth of trained, responsible and experienced manpower necessary to cope with the rapid expansion and scope of credit operations.

6. Credit Needs

Evaluation of desirability or undesirability of certain types of loans underlies all legislation intended to regulate, in the public interest, the assets which commercial banks and financial intermediaries may or may not hold. They also form the basis of the classification of loans into those of an essential or of non-essential character. Credit needs with respect to their relevance to economic growth and stability may be *roughly* classified as follows:

    (i) credit demand which contributes little or nothing to economic growth but causes economic instability and inflation;

    (ii) credit demand which contributes to economic growth and at the same time causes economic instability and inflation; and

    (iii) credit demand which contributes to growth without inducing economic instability and inflation.

Commercial bank financing of loans for security trading and speculation such as occurred under the Enterprises Promotion Decree 1972 falls under the first category. This type of loan made little or no contribution to economic growth and yet induced economic instability and inflationary pressures. True, a small amount of stock-market credit is required for efficient functioning of the securities market. But it is an invitation to harm to permit commercial banks to provide a very large proportion of such credit. In the interest of stability such credit should be subject to a high margin requirement.

The second category of loans, whether it stimulates growth or not, induces instability and inflation. This includes working-capital loans, consumer credits, urban mortgage loans and plant and equipment loans. Working-capital loans or overdrafts constitute a large proportion of business loans made by commercial banks. They are difficult to control because their heterogeneous nature does not lend itself to qualitative credit control. They are not self-liquidating since they are abetted by frequent renewals of promissory notes or by the practice of revolving credits. Thus their effect on the economy could be unstabilising. Their control rests with the individual commercial banker in his own interest, through review of the financial position of the borrowing firm. The other possible source of control is the bank examiner who should ensure that banks with a large volume of such loans have an adequate cushion of capital funds and sufficient earning power to absorb possible losses. In view of the unreliable sources of effective control it is doubtful whether commercial banks in a sound financial system should be encouraged to grant such credits unless their long-term liabilities in the form of capital and reserve funds, and savings accounts, are clearly adequate to offset sudden losses. Without such long-term liabilities, working-capital loans would best be financed from the equity funds of business enterprises, from the capital market or from loans obtainable from specialised credit institutions.

Most of the various types of consumer credit facilitates the purchase of status symbols. A small amount of instalment credit contributes to growth, for instance loans extended to an employee to purchase a vehicle which he needs for his work or loans extended to a student for his education. It would be better for the consumers and for the economy if they were to save their funds to purchase goods of the kind that do contribute to economic growth. Commercial banks should extend such loans only if they possess the offsetting savings funds.

An efficient financial system would ensure that mortgage credit demand is met in such a way that inflation and instability are not encouraged. By its very nature and viewed from the intricacies of land-tenure problems, of appraisal and of maturity terms, urban mortgage loan is one which should be handled by specialised savings institutions. Structurally mortgage institutions should be co-ordinated by a central mortgage institution which can extend loans to member institutions in case of need and which can grant member institutions access to the capital market. Some important features of a well-functioning mortgage market are a reliable land policy and availability of funds of savings institutions linked together by a central mortgage bank. Residential construction exhibits wide cyclical swings. These swings are intensified if mortgage credits are the result of credit creation rather than savings.

Another type of credit which in stimulating growth may cause economic instability is that to finance plant and equipment expenditures. These loans should be obtained from financial intermediaries or from the capital markets. Except in those cases where their capital funds and other offsetting long-term liabilities were large, the experience of commercial banks in financing such expenditures has rarely been a happy one.

The American commercial-banking practice of granting term loans subject to amortisation of up to ten years' maturity has often been cited by advocates of commercial banks' involvement in long-term capital outlay for plant and equipment. Even the Radcliffe Report recommended it to British bankers. In spite of its popularity it is still difficult to accept that in a well-functioning financial system directed toward the objectives of economic stability and growth such loans should be made by commercial banks unless they possess a sizeable buffer of capital resources. Otherwise funds for capital expansion should be obtained from the internal earnings of business enterprise, from the sale of securities and from financial intermediaries. Thus development banks and specialised credit institutions are admirably fitted to make capital loans to industry and can play an important role in financing the equity needs of new and small businesses.

Finally the third group of loans contributes to growth without inducing economic instability. This refers to loans extended to finance seasonal expansion in production and marketing of goods. It is appropriate for commercial banks to finance this category of credit needs because the maturity of the liabilities of a commercial bank should govern the maturity of its assets. Borrowing short and lending long have caused the failure of many commercial banks in this country and elsewhere. In other words commercial banks should play a cautious role in economic development since they are primarily sources of short-term credit. Long-term involvement on their part would necessarily be limited by the magnitude of their long-term liabilities which in any case are normally meagre in relation to long-term needs of industry. This situation therefore leaves the development banks and specialised credit institutions and other financial intermediaries with the primary responsibility of playing the dynamic role in stimulating economic growth.

Indeed the post-war inflation and oil boom have induced sharp increases in the capital resources and savings accounts at the commercial banks. These resources, as has been mentioned, are suitable for long-term commitment but it should not be understood that this transient development qualifies commercial banks for all time as other than a sustaining force in economic development.

Conversion of commercial banks into department-store banking of American fame will aggravate inflationary pressures on the economy. American commercial banks have monetised all types of debt since the end of the Second World War but this has also meant persistent inflationary pressures, and a humiliating loss of the reserve currency status of the dollar. Italy has since set up several credit institutions to help to bail out its commercial banks which without success had attempted to combine commercial and investment-banking practices. France, prior to the Second World War and since, had a specialised set of credit institutions. There are the commercial banks operating in the financing of short-term credit needs, and the investment banks operating in the long-term field. The investment bankers are able to accumulate the savings funds of France through the sale of debentures and shares throughout the French economy. The commercial banks finance mainly short-term credit needs. There has always been a separation of functions and the economy has opportunity for orderly and rapid growth.

In Germany the large banks operate in both the long-term and the short-term sectors of the economy. But in operating these two sectors, they operate as two institutions using their very large volume of capital resources to finance the long-term credit needs of industry. In turn, proceeds from the sale of their own stock are used to finance long-term credit needs so that essentially they operate as investment trusts. It is noteworthy that in both France and Germany the money and capital markets, although close, are not mixed up as is sometimes assumed by advocates of mixed banking. Incautious integration of credit functions could be dangerous as the banking experience in several countries has since demonstrated. It could prove more dangerous in a banking system where the recipients of credit more often than not prefer investment in status symbols.

7. Mobilisation and Collection of Savings

A developing economy needs a large volume of savings if the expanding capital needs are to be met without stimulating inflationary pressures. In communist economies savings are forced in the form of taxes levied on the consumer and incorporated in the price of goods which he buys. In capitalistic economies savings used to finance social capital needs are forced but those used to finance gross private domestic investment are largely induced.

A sound financial system should play an important role in the mobilisation and collection of individual savings through:

(a) establishment of an adequate number of savings institutions conveniently located and efficiently operated; and

(b) provision of savings plans and programmes with widespread appeal.

Specialised institutions interested in promoting thrift should be encouraged. Such institutions include the postal savings bank, co-operative credit unions, investment companies, savings and loans associations, insurance companies and mutual savings banks. These institutions if encouraged can play a more active role than time and savings departments in commercial banks. But the definitions of 'banking business' under the Nigerian Banking Decree 1969, the restrictive capital requirement that has to be met in organising some of these institutions are clearly restraining factors. The postal savings bank in spite of its change of name has continued to fail to win public patronage. To this may be added the matter of yield rates, service and convenience offered by the existing institutions. Savings institutions are normally directed to the saver, and commercial banks and specialised credit institutions toward the borrower.

8. Central Banking

In addition to its customary functions of issue and redemption of national currency, regulation of bank credit, protection of the domestic and external value of the national currency and conservation and administration of the nation's foreign-exchange reserves, a central bank in a developing economy has the responsibilities to subject its traditional functions to constant review in the light of defined national objectives. Secondly it should exercise a great deal of alertness and leadership to produce the various options required by a national government to accommodate or resist the results of economic and political developments stemming from efforts of other national governments to protect their economic position by impediments to trade and capital movements, tariffs, quotas and exchange control. Thirdly a great deal of co-operation between a central bank and fiscal authorities in a developing country is required if ridiculous and contradictory monetary and fiscal policies are to be avoided. Fourthly a central bank operating in an economy dominated by foreign financial institutions should recognise the ineffectiveness of moral suasion as an instrument of monetary policy and in its place incorporate a measure that would yield overt co-operation in the effort to achieve desirable national objectives.

The beauty of the currency and banking arrangement during the colonial period was its capability to mobilise financial resources from the smallest public institution in the remotest village for the achievement of imperial objectives. But today many Nigerians and foreigners have appointed themselves custodians of foreign-exchange resources. In the circumstances they have all but usurped the strategic position to dictate the direction of trade and movement of capital. To this may be added individual and institutional indiscipline in the financial system which the Central Bank has seemed unable to contain. A good financial system must be able to transfer funds cheaply and expeditiously. In Nigeria internal and external transfers of funds have been so costly, and riddled with nauseating bureaucracy and corrupt practices that people have been driven to resort to all sorts of means to facilitate payments – and speculators and unauthorised dealers have not spared efforts to take advantage of the situation.

In recent years Nigeria has enjoyed sharp increases in foreign-exchange earnings primarily due to crude-oil exports. In turn this has swollen the capacity of the banking system to create money. Although the Central Bank has attempted to exonerate the system and exaggerate public spending as the root cause of domestic inflation one cannot but observe that regardless of the cause of inflation the Central Bank has the primary responsibility to protect the value of the national currency. For this purpose a basketful of measures has been provided but rarely used. Some of them like treasury bills and treasury certificates issues

were being stagnated or being phased out in a manner that did not consider their stabilisation and regulatory functions. What was considered
was the rising revenue of the Government and therefore the needless-
ness of Government borrowing, but certainly not their uses as instruments of credit control and as means to regulate the quality of commercial banks' assets. One would have thought that rates paid by the
Federal Government to holders of these instruments were pretty cheap
as costs for stabilisation and safety. Indeed the Bankers Unit Fund and
Certificate of Deposit have been introduced — after a time-lag — during
which outlets for commercial banks' investments were constricted.

Other instruments of control such as stabilisation securities, special
deposits, cash reserves ratio and liquidity ratio were held almost constant as the problems they were intended to solve loomed large. For
instance, if the cash reserve ratio designed for various classes of banks
were to be applied, it would be found that some of those classes of
banks holding the assumed deposits no longer exist in the banking
system. In a period of sharp growth in bank deposits, there was no
noticeable effort on the part of monetary authorities to moderate the
growth by applying the provision of the Banking Decree on special
deposits. Similarly, the provision for stabilisation securities was applied
quite reluctantly for a long period as inflation raged. Finally the
liquidity ratio is virtually blanket and constant for the banking system
in an era of raging inflation.

The Central Bank on its part is required to maintain at all times a
reserve of external assets, the value of which shall not be less than 25
per cent of aggregate demand liabilities of the Bank. In practice the
Central Bank has maintained a multiple of the reserve requirement.
But this practice should be strengthened by law and raised significantly
to support the Central Bank's experience that the minimum external
reserves requirement is anachronistic. It was reduced to that level to
facilitate the achievement of a national objective several years ago.
While the Central Bank's recent effort in the recomposition of the
nation's external reserves is commendable, a great deal of effort in the
direction of *timely* and *systematic* application of the various instruments of monetary and credit control remains to be made. Rigidity
in the use of these instruments, dearth of systematic supervision and
examination of the banking system and leniency with defaulting
institutions and individuals create immense problems.

There is also the problem of inadequacy of trained manpower to
manage efficiently the several institutions being established or mutualised by the Federal Government. The increasing specialisation in credit

functions makes training and retraining of bank personnel of primary importance if an efficient financial system is to be realised. As an adviser to the Federal Government and as a leader in the development of the financial system the Central Bank is better placed to guide and stimulate training programmes directly or through the aegis of public financial institutions for the benefit of bank personnel.

There is need also to increase the Federal Government's scholarship awards to students of banking and finance and to support research and teaching in the few faculties in national universities that emphasise degree courses in monetary and banking studies. Ultimately the effectiveness of the financial system will depend on the quality of the men who manage it.

9. Banking Density

The enlargement of banking personnel generally through education and training would also help to alleviate the problem of banking density. Traditionally commercial banks have raked up all manner of excuses, some financial, others psychological to delay extension of their services to the rural areas. Even co-operative banks prefer to operate in urban areas until 'facilities' are available in the rural areas lest they suffer the loss of their staff who prefer to live and work in urban areas. Since these institutions are virtually owned by governments and since rural development is high in the programme of national development the financial cost of bank expansion into developing rural communities should be assured by the present Government. In the circumstances there is no reason why co-operative banks and commercial banks should not be induced to extend their services to rural communities and thus help to provide some of the services they wish to extend. Only by the existence of such financial intermediaries in the rural communities would the full benefit of services provided by specialised credit institutions such as the Nigerian Agricultural Bank and the Nigerian Industrial Development Bank be realised. Similarly monetary policy would stand a better chance of effectiveness if the financial system is rooted physically and psychologically in all facets of the economy in both urban and rural communities. It would be self-defeating if co-operative and commercial banks are allowed to continue the practice of expanding into the suburbs of an urban community as an answer to public demand for banking facilities in rural areas. This merely intensifies the existing concentration of banking facilities in urban centres to the disadvantage of rural communities, the members of which have still to travel some 80km to reach a banking office.

10. Conclusion

The acid test of a sound financial system is the capability to promote and sustain growth and promptness to stifle actions calculated to stimulate instability or inflation. This would be contingent in part on the extent of co-operation between the monetary and fiscal authorities.

The capacity of the Central Bank to socialise losses is not unlimited. Therefore those financial institutions endowed with the power to create money should exercise care and caution in the exercise of this power in the interest of stability and enduring growth. The power to create money does not exempt them from guarding against stretching their resources into activities most unsuitable to the character of their liabilities. It is fairness in the distribution of available bank credit, riddance of corrupt practices in employment, risk selection and efficient administration of the payments system that appear to be a major contribution that commercial banks in Nigeria should make. Mere pressure to enlarge their loan assets which ignores the mode of distribution of available bank credit would serve only to multiply the frustrations levied on the excluded borrowers who must also share the burden of inflationary pressures as the value of money bottoms out.

With the increased mutualisation of commercial banks the Federal Military Government was in a singular position to provide for a fairer distribution of bank credit among the various sectors of the national economy. But in this exercise it would be necessary to ensure that commercial banks are not goaded into borrowing short and lending long — a practice, as already stated, that has caused the breakdown of many commercial banks in this country and elsewhere. Changes in commercial bank portfolios demand constant supervision and intervention by the Central Bank. In sum, commercial banks, because of the character of their liabilities should play a cautious role in economic development while the specialised credit institutions should play the dynamic role in stimulating economic growth.

Specialised credit institutions have since been established in Nigeria to undertake the financing of long-term credit needs — an area in which commercial banks' involvement is fraught with difficulties. By fostering the establishment of these institutions the Federal Government underscores the desirability of institutional specialisation in lending functions. These institutions which are now available in the areas of housing, agriculture and industry would appear to be best suited to finance credit needs of growth without stimulating inflationary pressures.

Institutions in the financial system are faced with various constraints principally in the area of trained and experienced personnel and organisation and management of prospective borrowing enterprises. Planned programmes of training and development involving personnel of financial institutions is required to update the operations of these institutions. Educational institutions running long-term programmes in banking and finance should also be encouraged with funds and facilities for increased research in monetary and banking studies.

Commercial and co-operative banks, now virtually mutualised institutions, should be induced to extend their services to the outlying rural communities. Concentration of their services around and within centres of trade and government frustrates the development of emerging and active rural areas. The absence of these financial intermediaries limits to a great extent the impact of specialised credit institutions on the rural economy.

The defects of the Nigerian financial system demanded a positive action by the Federal Military Government. It also required an aggressive central-banking policy — one which would be concerned with the control of the sensitive points in the financial system as well as the determination of appropriate techniques to deal with the problems peculiar to the Nigerian monetary and banking system.

Moreover, effective programmes of an educational and promotional nature would be required to reform the attitude of Nigerians towards credit from public financial institutions, and to encourage the habit of savings and capital formation.

While the achievement of any real degree of sustained economic growth requires an increase in the magnitude, range and variety of institutional credit facilities available to different forms of economic enterprise, credit *alone* would be patently inadequate to solve the immense and complex problems of Nigeria's economic development. Thus direct government intervention would be necessary to ensure the removal of restraints that constrict the volume and availability of bank credit.

Part Two

THE BANKING SYSTEM AND THE FINANCIAL MARKETS

3 DEVELOPMENTS IN THE CENTRAL BANK OF NIGERIA ACT

C.S. Inyang and C.A. Okeke

1. Introduction

The motion to create a Central Bank for Nigeria was first tabled in the House of Representatives in Lagos on 21 March 1952. The motion was formally debated on 9 April 1952 with the following amendments by the Financial Secretary to the Nigerian Government:

that as a practical means of marshalling the financial resources of this country for the purpose of aiding commercial development in all its phases, the government should examine the possibility of establishing a Central Bank, and report to the House as soon as possible.[1]

The amended motion was accepted, and the government invited Mr J.L. Fisher, an adviser to the Bank of England, to examine the 'desirability and practicability' of establishing a central bank in Nigeria for promoting the economic development of the country.

Fisher's Report of 1953 held the following reservations about the feasibility of a central bank in Nigeria:

(i) the financial environment hardly existed for a central bank to function in Nigeria except semi-automatically as a bank of issue;

(ii) that it was doubtful if a central bank could be adequately staffed in Nigeria;

(iii) that the operation of a central bank would be costly for the country at that time.

He therefore recommended that the currency board system should be continued instead of a fully fledged central bank.

2. International Bank Mission

The International Bank Mission which visited Nigeria in the latter part of 1953 supported the creation of a State Bank of Nigeria, in view of the constitutional progress towards self-government. The encouragement by the International Bank Mission revived Nigeria's interest in the scheme.

In 1957, the Federal Government invited Mr J.B. Loynes to advise the government on a wide range of anticipated banking problems which might arise from the establishment of a central bank in Nigeria and in the light of the recommendations made by the International Bank Mission. Loynes's Report favoured the proposal. Accordingly the Central Bank of Nigeria Ordinance was passed in 1958.

3. The Central Bank of Nigeria Ordinance, 1958

The Central Bank of Nigeria was established by the Central Bank of Nigeria Act, 1958 with the following provisions:

Constitution. It stipulated that:

(i) the bank be called the Central Bank of Nigeria, and
(ii) it shall be a body corporate and shall have perpetual succession and a common seal, and may sue and be sued in its own name, and subject to the limitations contained in this Ordinance. It may acquire, hold, and dispose of movable and immovable property for the purpose of its functions.

Objects. The principal objects of the Bank shall be the following:

(i) to issue legal tender currency in Nigeria,
(ii) to maintain external reserves in order to safeguard the international value of that currency,
(iii) to promote monetary stability and a sound financial structure in Nigeria, and
(iv) to act as banker and financial adviser to the Federal Government.

Chief Office and Bankers. In accordance with the decisions of the board, the Bank shall have its chief office in Lagos and may open branches in Nigeria and appoint agents and correspondents.

Capital and Reserve.

(i) The authorised capital of the Bank shall be £1.5 million. The capital was to be paid up by such amount as should be resolved by the bank and confirmed by the minister. This amount was to be subscribed and paid up by the Federal Government upon the establishment of the Bank.

(ii) The paid-up portion of the authorised capital may be increased by such amount as the board may, from time to time, resolve with the agreement of the minister, and the Federal Government shall subscribe and pay up at par the amount of such increase.

(iii) All paid-up capital shall be subscribed and held only by the Federal Government.

General Reserve Fund. The Bank was to establish a general reserve fund to which the following shall be allocated at the end of each financial year of the Bank:

(i) 1/8 of the net profits if the total reserve fund is less than the paid-up capital of the Bank;

(ii) 1/16 of the net profits of the Bank if the total reserve fund is not less than the paid-up capital of the Bank;

(iii) half of the remainder of the profits shall be used for retirement of any outstanding obligations of the Federal Government to the Bank arising from the financing of the cost of printing, minting and shipment of the initial stock of the bank's notes and coins;

(iv) the remainder of the net profit shall be paid to the Federal Government;

(v) the net profit is to be determined after meeting current expenditure including provisions for bad debts, depreciation in assets, contributions to staff and superannuation funds, and all other contingencies.[2]

Administration. There shall be a board of directors of the Bank which shall be responsible for the policy and the general administration of the affairs and business of the Bank.

The Board was to be composed of the following:

1. a governor,
2. a deputy governor, and
3. five other Directors.

(i) Appointment and Functions of Governor and Deputy Governor

(a) The governor or, in his absence, the deputy governor shall be in charge of the day-to-day management of the Bank and shall be answerable to the board for their acts and decisions.

(b) The governor and the deputy governor were to be persons of recognised financial experience and should be appointed by the Governor-General by instrument under the public seal on such terms and conditions as may be set out in their respective letters of appointment.

(c) The governor and deputy governor shall devote the whole of their professional experience to the service of the Bank and shall not hold any other office other than the one in the Bank.

(ii) Appointment of Directors

(a) The five other directors shall be appointed by the Prime Minister of the Federation;

(b) A director shall be a person of recognised standing and experience in affairs and shall not act as a delegate on the board from any federal or regional authority or from any commercial, financial, agricultural, industrial or other interests with which he may be or may have been connected;

(c) A director shall hold office for three years and be eligible for reappointment;

(d) A director shall be entitled to fees and in accordance with such rules as the board, subject to confirmation by the minister, may lay down; and

(e) No person shall be qualified as a governor, deputy governor or other director of the Bank who is a member of the Federal Legislative House, a Regional Legislative House, a director or salaried official or shareholder of any licensed bank under the provisions of the Banking Ordinance or is an officer in the public service of the Federal or a Regional Government.

(iii) Resignation of Office

(a) The governor or deputy governor may resign his office on giving at least three months' notice in writing to the Governor-General of his intention;

(b) Any director may resign on giving at least one month's notice in writing to the Governor-General of his intention;

(c) The governor, deputy governor or any other director shall cease to hold office in the Bank if he becomes of unsound mind, bankrupt, is convicted of a felony or of any offence involving dishonesty, is guilty of serious misconduct in relation to his duties or he is disqualified or suspended from practising his profession in any part of Her Majesty's dominions; and

(d) If any, that is, the governor, deputy governor, or director of the Bank dies, resigns or vacates his office before the expiration of the term, another person shall be appointed in his place.

Meeting of Board. The meeting of the board shall take place as often as may be required but not less frequently than once in each of any ten months in every financial year of the Bank. The governor or his deputy shall be chairman of the board and in the absence of both from the meeting, the other directors appoint a chairman from among them. Four members of the board shall form a quorum at any meeting and decisions shall be adopted by a simple majority of the votes of members present. In the case of an equal vote, the chairman shall have a casting vote.

All appointments of officials and other employees shall be only to positions created by decision of the board and on such terms and conditions as shall be laid down by the board.

Advisory Committee. There shall be an advisory committee of the Bank which shall consist of:

(a) the minister or his alternative,
(b) the minister charged with responsibility for finance in respect of each region or his alternative, and
(c) the governor or deputy governor.

This committee shall meet not less than twice a year to consider matters of common interest. The meeting of the committee shall take place in Lagos or in such other places as may be agreed from time to time.

Currency Matters. The unit of currency in Nigeria was the Nigerian pound which was divided into (20s) twenty shillings, each shilling being divided into twelve pence (12d). The parity of the Nigerian pound was to be one Nigerian pound to one pound sterling.

The bank held the sole right of issuing notes and coins throughout Nigeria and neither the Federal Government nor any Regional Government nor any other person was allowed to issue currency notes, bank notes, coins or any documents or tokens payable to bearer on demand being documents or tokens which are likely to pass as legal tender. It was further provided that:

(a) the Bank shall arrange for the printing of notes and minting of coins;

(b) the issue, reissue and exchange of notes and coins at the Bank's offices and at such agencies as the Bank may, from time to time, establish or appoint;

(c) the safe custody of unissued stocks of currency and the preparation, safe custody and destruction of plates and paper for the printing of notes and of dies for the minting of coins, and

(d) the notes and coins issued by the Bank shall be in such denominations of the pound or fractions thereof as shall be approved by the minister on the recommendation of the Bank, and should be of such forms and designs and bear such devices as shall be approved by the minister on the recommendation of the Bank.

The standard weight and composition of the coins issued by the Bank and the amount of remedy and variation shall be determined by the minister on the recommendation of the Bank.

Notes issued by the Bank shall be legal tender in Nigeria at their face value for the payment of any amount. Coins issued by the Bank shall, if such coins have not been tampered with, be legal tender in Nigeria at their face value up to an amount not exceeding £10 in the case of coins of denomination of not less than 6d and up to an amount of not exceeding 1s in the case of coins of a lower denomination.

The Bank shall not be liable to the payment of any stamp duty under the Stamp Duties Ordinance in respect of its notes issued as currency.

External Reserve. The external reserve maintained by the Bank shall consist of the following:

(a) gold coin or bullion,

(b) sterling notes, coins, bank balances and money at call with banks in the United Kingdom,

(c) treasury bills of the Government of the United Kingdom maturing within a period not exceeding 93 days,

(d) bills of exchange,

(e) sterling securities guaranteed by the government of the United

Kingdom and maturing within five years,
    (f) coins of West African Currency Board.

The value of the reserve shall not be less than the aggregate of the amount representing 60 per cent of the Bank's notes and coins in circulation together with an amount representing 35 per cent of the Bank's other demand liabilities.

After five years, the reserve will be reduced to 40 per cent of the aggregate of the Bank's notes and coins in circulation and other demand liabilities.

The Bank shall on demand sell sterling for immediate delivery in London at a rate of not less than £99 5s sterling for £N100. It was also required to buy sterling for immediate delivery in London at a rate not more than £100 15s sterling for £N100, provided the Bank was not required to buy or sell sterling for an amount less than £10,000 in respect of any one transaction.

General Powers of the Bank. The Bank may:

    (a) issue drafts and effect other kinds of remittances payable at its own offices or at the offices of agencies or correspondents;
    (b) purchase and sell gold coins or bullions;
    (c) open accounts for and accept deposits from the Federal Government, the Regional Governments, Government institutions and Corporations etc.;
    (d) purchase, sell, discount and rediscount inland bills of exchange and promissory notes bearing two or more good signatures, drawn mainly to finance seasonal agricultural operations or marketing of crops etc.;
    (e) purchase, sell, discount and rediscount inland bills of exchange and promissory notes arising out of *bona fide* commercial transactions bearing two or more good signatures;
    (f) purchase, sell, discount and rediscount treasury bills of the Federal Government of Nigeria;
    (g) purchase and sell Federal Government securities;
    (h) invest in Federal Government securities;
    (i) subscribe and hold shares of approved corporations;
    (j) grant advances for fixed periods not exceeding three months against publicly issued treasury bills of the Federal Government maturing within 93 days;
    (k) grant advances for periods not exceeding three months at a mini-

mum rate of interest of at least 1 per cent above the Bank's minimum rediscount rate;

(l) purchase and sell external currencies, purchase, sell, discount and rediscount bills of exchange and treasury bills drawn on places abroad maturing within 90 days;

(m) maintain account with central banks and other banks abroad;

(n) purchase and sell sterling securities of, or guaranteed by, the government of the United Kingdom;

(o) act as correspondent banker or agent for any central bank or other monetary authority and for any international bank or international monetary authority established under governmental auspices;

(p) undertake the public issue and management of loans in Nigeria on behalf of the Federal or Regional Government or by the Federal or regional public bodies;

(q) accept from customers for custody, securities and other articles of value;

(r) promote the establishment of clearing systems and give facilities for the conduct of clearing business in premises belonging to the Bank.

The Bank is prohibited from:

(a) engaging in trade or developing direct interest in a specific institution;

(b) the purchase of shares of any institutions;

(c) granting loans on securities or any shares;

(d) granting unsecured loans or advances;

(e) purchasing or acquiring or leasing real property except in accordance with the provision to (d) above;

(f) drawing or accepting bills payable otherwise than on demand;

(g) paying interest on deposits;

(h) accepting for discount, or as security for an advance made by the Bank, bills or notes signed by members of the board of the Central Bank or by the Bank's officials or other employees;

(i) opening accounts for and accepting deposits from persons other than as provided by the Act.

Relations with the Federal Government. The Bank shall be responsible for the banking and foreign exchange transactions of the Federal Government internally and externally. It shall receive and disburse Federal Government monies and keep accounts thereof without remuneration for such services. Where the Bank has no branch, it may appoint another bank to act as its agent for the collection and payment of Federal Government monies.

The Bank may grant temporary advances to the Federal Government in respect of temporary deficiencies of the budget revenue at such rates of interest as the Bank may determine. Such advances shall not exceed 12.5 per cent of the preceding year's government budget. The percentage of temporary advances which the Federal Government may receive is subject to review from time to time. All advances shall be repaid as soon as possible, and shall in any event be repayable in the financial year in which they are granted.

The Bank shall be entrusted with the issue and management of Federal Government loans publicly issued in Nigeria. It may act as a banker to any fund, institution or corporation of the Federal Government or of a Regional Government (*vide*, (c), (f), (g), (h), (j) and (p) of the *General Powers of the Bank*).

Relations With Other Banks. The Bank may act as a banker to other banks in Nigeria and abroad. The Bank shall seek the co-operation of, and co-operate with, other banks in Nigeria:

(a) to promote and maintain adequate and reasonable banking services for the public;

(b) to ensure a high standard of conduct and management throughout the banking system; and

(c) to further such policies not inconsistent with the Ordinance as shall be in the national interest.

The Bank may prescribe from time to time by publications the amount of specified liquid assets which each bank operating in Nigeria under the Banking Ordinance is required to hold as a minimum in Nigerian pounds or in sterling. This required ratio shall be expressed as a percentage of the gross demand liabilities of each such bank due in Nigerian pounds.

The Bank may require any bank to furnish such information in such form as the Bank may deem necessary to satisfy itself that the bank concerned is holding not less than the prescribed minimum amount of specified liquid assets.

The Bank may appoint one or more banks in Nigeria to act as its agents for issue, reissue, exchange and withdrawal of notes and coins or for other purposes.

It shall be the duty of the Bank to facilitate the clearing of cheques and other credit instruments for banks carrying on business in Nigeria. For this purpose, the Bank shall, in conjunction with other banks, organise a clearing-house in Lagos and in such other place or places as may be desirable in the premises provided by the Bank.

The financial year of the Bank shall begin on 1 April and end on 31 March or shall be such other period as shall be prescribed by the minister. The account shall be audited by an auditor appointed by the Bank and approved by the minister.

The minister may from time to time request the Director of Federal Audit to make an examination and submit the report on the accounts relating to issue, reissue, exchange and withdrawal of notes and coins by the Bank. Annual accounts and reports of the Bank shall be published regularly.

4. Central Bank of Nigeria (Amendment) Act, 1962, No. 17

After two years of operation of the Central Bank, it became necessary to amend the Ordinance. On 23 June 1962, an Amendment Act was passed with the following provisions:

(i) the parity of the Nigerian pound was fixed at 2.48828 grams of fine gold per pound. The parity of the pound could be changed from time to time by the Central Bank with the approval of the Council of Ministers, and

(ii) external reserves may be maintained with any of the following or a combination of them:

(a) balances at any bank outside Nigeria where the currency is sterling or is freely convertible into sterling, for example, coins, bills of exchange;

(b) treasury bills having a maturity not exceeding 184 days issued by any government outside Nigeria whose currency is in sterling or is freely convertible into gold or sterling; and

(c) securities guaranteed by a government of any country outside Nigeria whose currency is sterling or is freely convertible into gold or sterling.

The value of the reserve of external assets shall not be less than 40 per cent of the total demand liabilities of the Bank. The Central Bank has the obligation to issue and redeem Nigerian currency against gold or other currencies eligible to be included in the external reserves.

Amendment Act, 1962, No. 19

A further amendment was made under the Amendment Act, 1962, no. 19 as follows:

(i) Rates of interest charged on advances or other credit facilities by licensed banks were to be linked with the minimum rediscount rate of the Central Bank subject to a stated minimum rate of interest;

(ii) The interest rate structure of every licensed bank should be subject to the approval of the Central Bank as shall be uniform for all licensed banks;

(iii) All licensed banks were to hold specific liquid assets as prescribed by the Central Bank. These specific liquid assets include: notes and coins, balances at the Central Bank, net balances at other banks in Nigeria, treasury bills, inland bills of exchange, promissory notes rediscounted at central banks, net balances at banks, money at call.[3]

5. Central Bank of Nigeria Act (Amendment) Decree 1968, No. 17

In 1968, the following amendments of the Central Bank Act were made retroactive from 29 November 1967:

(i) the Central Bank of Nigeria may in any return prepared by the Bank disclose the gold tranche position of Nigeria in the International Monetary Fund, and

(ii) the gold tranche position in the International Monetary Fund shall form part of the external reserve of assets of the Bank.

The decree gave the Bank the power to recommend different cash-reserve ratios for the three different classes of commercial banks. The cash reserves of the commercial banks were to be determined within such period as the Central Bank may from time to time specify, on the basis of the period balances of the institution's deposit liabilities.

The Central Bank was authorised from time to time to require each institution to prepare and deliver to the bank a true correct statement showing the positions of the deposit liabilities of the institution.

The Bank was also given power to demand information and statistics from commercial banks for purposes of satisfying itself that the institution concerned was in compliance with the provision of that subsection.

The Bank was given power:

(a) to vary the composition of specified liquid assets of the commercial banks;

(b) to vary the proportion of each category of specified liquid assets; and

(c) to require that all applications to each institution for loans exceeding such amounts as the Bank may specify shall be submitted to the Central Bank for approval.

6. Central Bank of Nigeria Act (Amendment) (No. 2) Decree 1968, No. 28

On 8 May 1968, a second amendment Decree was promulgated. This decree authorised the Federal Commissioner for Finance in consultation with the Central Bank of Nigeria to make available to the marketing board, on application, by way of advance:

(a) an amount not exceeding 90 per cent of the total value of the crops to be purchased in any given year in the state concerned, as estimated before the opening of the relevant crop season by the marketing board; and

(b) an amount which the Federal Government may guarantee where the value of the crops is unknown or cannot be estimated.

Therefore, marketing boards were given guarantee of funds for purchase and marketing of crops, or for any particular purposes accidental to crops generally and acceptable to the Federal Military Government.

7. Central Bank Currency Conversion (Amendment) Decree 1968, No. 48

Under this decree it became an offence for any person 'to have in his possession in Nigeria or under his apparent control any note issue, which immediately before the conversion date, was in circulation in Nigeria as legitimate currency in Nigeria, after the time or extended time . . . fixed for its conversion in the area where the offender at the time is, has elapsed'.[4] It has to be placed on record that the Central Bank of Nigeria currency notes had witnessed the following conversions, in 1959, 1968 and lastly in 1973 by which Nigerian currency was decimalised.

8. The Central Bank of Nigeria Act (Amendment) (No. 3) Decree 1968, No. 50

On 19 September 1968, another amendment, Decree No. 50, was made, empowering the Central Bank as follows:

(i) to finance the purchasing and marketing operation of marketing boards;

(ii) to regulate advances to indigenous persons and in consultation with the Commissioner for Finance to prescribe a minimum ratio of total loans, advances and discounts, granted to indigenous persons, to be maintained by each bank licenced under the Banking Act;

(iii) to issue directions from time to time requiring each licensed bank to adhere to the following:

(a) to maintain at all times in the form of cost reserves with the Bank at its Head Office, a sum equal to a ratio of the institution's deposit liabilities. Banks were classified in A, B and C institutions;

(b) to hold a minimum amount of specified liquid assets which shall be expressed as a ratio of deposit liabilities of the institution;

(c) to maintain special deposits with the Bank as may be prescribed from time to time;

(d) to fix ceiling on the volume of loans, advances and discounts outstanding at each institution (different ceilings may be fixed for different categories of such loans, advances etc.); and

(e) to fix a ceiling on the aggregate amount of loans, advances and discounts granted by any institution and outstanding at any time.

For the purpose of maintaining monetary stability, the Bank may issue, place, sell, repurchase, amortise or redeem securities to be known as stabilisation securities and the securities shall be issued at such rate of interest and under such conditions of maturity, amortisation, negotiability and redemption as the Bank may deem appropriate.

The Bank was further empowered to sell or place by allocation to each institution any stabilisation securities issued by the Bank, and to repurchase, amortise or redeem, in such manner as the Bank may deem appropriate, any such security. The decree also authorised the Central

Bank to issue a new money-market instrument, the treasury certificates and to approve loans exceeding a certain amount.

Any commercial bank that refused to comply with any direction issued as regards the purchase of stabilisation securities shall be prohibited from undertaking new investments until full compliance, and shall be fined, and such fines shall not exceed £50 for every day during which the default continues.

Furthermore any commercial bank that furnishes false information to the Central Bank shall be guilty of offence and will be liable to a fine of £100 for the first day, and for the second day or subsequent offence, the fine shall be £200.

9. The Central Bank of Nigeria (Amendment) Decree 1969, No. 4

This decree has nothing new to offer except to re-emphasise that the Bank is the only power to approve certain loans and advances, and place ceilings as the case may be.

10. Central Bank of Nigeria (Amendment) Decree 1970, No. 40

This decree dealt with the internal administration of the Bank. It made it mandatory for the board of the Central Bank to disclose any general policy it intends to pursue with special reference to staff, persons, salaries and other allowances as they apply to monetary and banking policy.

11. Central Bank of Nigeria (Amendment) (No. 2) Decree 1970, No. 59

This decree created the post of two deputy governors instead of one as contained in the Central Bank Act.

12. Central Bank of Nigeria (Amendment) Decree 1972, No. 46

This decree directed the Bank to ensure that before it ever declared an operating surplus, it should first ensure that it had met all its current expenditure for the year and also had made provision for depreciation in its assets and contribution to staff and superannuation funds as approved by its board.

From the various amendments of the first Act one can say that the main Act has witnessed eight amendments since 1968. This confirms the views expressed by a number of scholars and bankers that the Act was deficient in the context of the rapid economic development of Nigeria. A growing economy such as Nigeria's must be kept on an even keel by the use of a variety of monetary weapons which the principal Act failed to provide. As the economy continues to grow more amendments may become pertinent.

Notes

1. R.O. Ekundere, *An Economic History of Nigeria* (Methuen, London, 1973), p. 325.
2. Federation of Nigeria, *The Central Bank of Nigeria Ordinance*, 1958.
3. Federation of Nigeria, *Central Bank (Amendment) Act*, 1962, Nos. 17 and 19.
4. *Laws of Federal Republic of Nigeria, 1968, Decrees and Subsidiary Legislations*, p. A. 177.

4 FUNDAMENTAL PROBLEMS OF BANKING IN NIGERIA

N.O. Odoh

1. Introduction

Banking in Nigeria is essentially orthodox, and orthodox banking is a process whereby the banker sits cosily in his armchair waiting for the business which certainly comes. An orthodox banker has rigid ideas about bankable projects and assets. In contrast an unorthodox banker is dynamic. He goes in search of bank business and is not tradition oriented as to the type of bank business and collateral. The unorthodox banker is therefore venturesome and innovative.

Orthodox banking in Nigeria manifests itself in the rules and regulations that govern every facet of Nigerian banking operations. It can be traced to the colonial days but appears to be firmly entrenched in the Banking Decree of 1969 (as amended in 1970 and 1972) as well as in the credit guidelines issued every fiscal year. The Banking Decree incorporates types of bankable projects and assets, types of acceptable collateral and the types of loans and advances (mainly short-term loans) which should be granted. It further manifests itself in the empowering of the Central Bank of Nigeria to vary the interest rates, the discount and rediscount rates, the composition of specified liquid assets and the credit ceiling or guidelines. The body of rules and regulations which the banking system, particularly the commercial banks (and the merchant banks as from the 1976/7 fiscal year), is made to comply with is a strong evidence of the orthodox foundation of the Nigerian banking system which has been difficult to dislodge. The system has rather perpetuated itself.

Indigenisation of businesses in Nigeria tends to place more emphasis on indigenous ownership and participation in particular than on structural and operational transformation of the economic and financial bases of the economy. Pius Okigbo's Committee on the Nigerian Financial System has observed similarly in Section 2 of the Report and made far-reaching recommendations which will transform the Nigerian financial system from its orthodox rigidities to a dynamic setting. The social and economic costs of orthodox banking in Nigeria have been very great indeed.

70

The orthodox banker services rather than finances industries. Rigid ules of eligibility and liquidity restrict him to the archaic principle of self-liquidating loans. The banking laws prohibit the commercial-banking industry in Nigeria from engaging in medium- and long-term loans and from investing in industrial stocks. The argument is that 'since his stock-in-trade is a liability repayable on demand and at very short notice, he must correspondingly lend short'.[1]

Both the orthodox banker and the unorthodox banker are profit oriented but the unorthodox banker can finance a project or enterprise with long-term growth potentials even though in the short run profitability may not be assured. Orthodox banking is a luxury in a developing economy. It thrives in a developed economy which possesses a highly sophisticated financial environment with multiple financial channels which are prepared and willing. Britain is probably the only advanced country still operating an orthodox banking system though some innovations are currently taking place as a result of the influx of foreign banks into the UK. The influence of the American banks' flexible operational system has excited the British banks into some adjustments.

Banking is a dynamic industry which changes with and adapts to the changing conditions of the economy. Nigerian businesses are changing from sole proprietorship or simple partnership forms of businesses to corporate forms of business. The banking mode of operation should also shift. In the thirties, the teething period of banking business in Nigerian indigenous banking was essentially sole proprietorship or simple partnership, such as the National Bank of Nigeria which was founded in 1933 by Chief Akinola Maja and two others, and the African Continental Bank (ACB) Ltd which was established in 1947 and was for several years under the direct control of Dr Nnamdi Azikiwe.[2] The pattern has since changed. All the 18 commercial banks (ten of which are indigenous) currently operating in Nigeria are corporate entities.

But apart from the changes in legal status commercial banking in Nigeria is still basically orthodox. Bankers wait for depositors as well as borrowers. They do not scout for their customers as the insurance companies, for example, search for customers by engaging agents and brokers. The Nigerian Banking Decree of 1969 which has been amended several times does not explicitly or implicitly prohibit banks from canvassing for customers as the insurance companies do. Apart from the use of occasional advertisements to win more urban customers, the banks are unwilling to spread to the rural areas where some liquidity could be mopped up and mobilised. The Central Bank's directive that the opening up of banks' branches in urban centres can only be permitted if branches are opened up simultaneously in rural areas is aimed at the banks' traditional and orthodox practice of aiming only at the urban population, where the business pulse is stronger.

Another factor which fosters banking orthodoxy in Nigeria is the absence of a developed money market, where those who have funds surplus to their immediate requirements could dispose of them. The first major step to establish a money market in Nigeria was taken in April 1960 when the first treasury bills were issued in accordance with the Treasury Bills Ordinance of the previous year. Another new money-market instrument in the form of treasury certificates was introduced in 1968. The introduction of the Bill Market Scheme in 1962 added to the efforts of the Nigerian authorities to establish a money market in Nigeria, but a money market has not fully matured. For example, there is no discount house in the sense of the London money market and unlike that money market the Nigerian one is mainly aimed at the mobilisation of resources for government financing and development as indicated by the nature of the debt instruments. Because of the lack of a developed money market the banks are the only major avenue for depositing money.

Equally important for the explanation of the orthodoxy of banks is the inadequacy of the capital market. The only sources of long-term credits in Nigeria are the Nigerian Industrial Development Bank Limited, Investment Company of Nigeria Limited, Nigerian Stock Exchange, the Nigerian Mortgage Bank, insurance companies, pension and provident fund institutions, the Nigerian Bank for Commerce and Industry and the Nigerian Agricultural Bank Limited. These sources of long-term credit are grossly inadequate for a growing economy such as Nigeria's.

There is also a paucity of investment analysts and business advisers. Some of the financial institutions in the capital market are new and are not strongly staffed with a cadre of analysts and advisers. The apparent vacuum has led to an outcrop of feasibility consultants and investment analysts who charge exhorbitant fees. A good number of prospective investors are small-scale industrialists who are unable to pay the heavy charges of feasibility consultants. They prefer the commercial banks which provide free over-the-counter information. Because businessmen have a pressing need to go to the banks, the banks themselves are not motivated to search for their customers. This one-sided relationship between customers and banks has led to the banks stipulating stiff conditions for credit such as the acceptable collateral security. Until the mutualisation of the seventies, expatriate banks were the biggest culprits in this respect. In spite of their stiff credit conditions their ratio of loans and advances increased rapidly reaching 83.2 per cent in 1960 and 113.8 per cent in 1969. Although the loans and advances ratio has declined since 1970 because of the Central Bank's guidelines, it has still remained above the 70 per cent level. Bank investments have increased in Nigeria while the transfer of bank funds for investment in foreign financial markets has ceased. Other special services offered to customers by commercial banks include opening of letters of credit, selling of travellers' cheques, handling of personal remittances, advice to customers on investments of different kinds, carrying out of standing orders, storage of valuables for customers and information on foreign business.

2. Banking Density

Orthodoxy of operations is the main cause of the low banking density in Nigeria. The lopsided banking development is very apparent. There are too few offices in relation to the geographic area and population of the country. As of June 1976 there were only 450 bank offices, for a population of about 80 million in a land area of nearly 333 million sq. km (see Table 4.1). This works out to a ratio of one bank to 124,713 persons and to 739,361 sq. km. The total number of bank offices in Nigeria is less than half the number of branch offices of the Bank of America, the largest bank in the world, and which operates in the state of California only. The ratio of 1:124,713 contrasts sharply with 1:4,000 in the UK, 1:6,000 in the USA and 1:14,500 in Japan. A breakdown of these 450 bank offices according to states reveals a more disturbing picture. Lagos State with only 3,535 sq. km and a population of approximately 1.4 million people has as many as 93 bank offices or 21 per cent of the total number of banks in the country. Oyo State follows with 50 bank offices or 11 per cent, Bendel State has 46 bank offices or 10.3 per cent, Anambra State has 34 bank offices or 7.6 per cent. On the other hand, Gongola State with a land area of 102,067,210 sq. km and a population of nearly 3 million people has five bank offices or 1.1 per cent of the total. Niger and Bauchi States have six and seven bank offices respectively.

Table 4.1: Distribution of Bank Offices in Nigeria as at June 1976

State	No. of Banks	% of Total	Area in Sq. km	Estimated Population (1963)	Persons per Bank Office	Area per Bank Office
Anambra	34	7.6	15,770	2,943,483	86,573	464
Bauchi	7	1.6	61,813,790	2,193,674	313,382	8,830,541
Bendel	46	10.2	38,061	2,435,839	52,953	827
Benue	9	2.0	69,740	3,041,194	337,910	7,749
Borno	15	3.3	116,589	2,990,526	271,866	10,599
Cross River	17	3.8	29,164	3,600,000	211,764	1,715
Gongola	5	1.1	102,067,210	3,002,808	600,561	20,413,400
Imo	27	6.0	13,032	3,208,340	118,827	483
Kaduna	28	6.2	70,293	4,098,305	146,368	2,510
Kano	20	4.4	42,123	5,774,842	288,742	2,106
Kwara	14	3.1	73,403,503	2,309,339	164,952	5,243,107
Lagos	93	20.7	3,535	1,443,567	15,522	38
Niger	6	1.3	73,555,478	1,271,767	211,961	12,259,246
Ogun	15	3.3	20,241,204	1,557,946	103,863	1,349,414
Ondo	22	4.9	18,165	2,727,675	103,303	826
Oyo	50	11.1	42,862	5,158,884	103,177	857
Plateau	11	2.4	56,245	2,026,657	184,241	5,113
Rivers	21	4.7	21,172	1,800,000	85,714	1,008
Sokoto	10	2.2	94,588	4,538,800	453,880	9,459
TOTAL	450	100.0	332,712,524	56,120,655	3,855,559	42,139,462

Sources: *Quest, News Features of Nigeria, Politics, Economy and Culture*, no. 1 (August 1977), p. 118; *Business Times*, 5 October 1976, p. 16 and *Central Bank of Nigeria*, various publications.

About 223 bank branches or 49.5 per cent of the 450 bank offices in the country are concentrated in four states, namely: Lagos, Oyo, Bendel and Anambra. Even in these four states the bank offices are concentrated in the state capitals and the main trading and commercial centres. Within these states there are lopsided developments too. For example an analysis of the location of commercial-bank branches in Nigeria as at the end of December 1975[3] showed that out of the 93 bank offices in Lagos State, 35 are in Lagos City; out of the 50 bank offices in Oyo State 24 are in Ibadan; out of the 46 in Bendel State 12 are in Benin City and out of the 34 bank offices in Anambra State 12 are in Enugu.

The distribution is even more deplorable in most of the northern states. In the states of Gongola, Sokoto, Benue, Bauchi and Kano there are respectively 600,561, 453,880, 337,910, 313,382, and 288,742 persons per bank office. This compares very unfavourably with 15,522 persons per bank office in Lagos State and 52,953 persons per bank office in Bendel State.

Analysis of the distribution of bank offices on a town-village basis reveals that out of the several hundred towns and several thousand villages in the country only 144 towns and villages have the privilege of having bank office(s).

The far-reaching implications of this lopsided banking development in Nigeria are quite obvious. The development of banking habits and the mobilisation of savings are hindered. This in turn limits the amount of demand deposits in the banking system and the money-creating capacities of the commercial banks. Since a large part of the currency with the public cannot be converted into demand deposits, commercial banks' credit multiplier operates on a much narrow deposit base.

One of the three c's of banking is convenience (The three c's of banking are: confidence, convenience and cost). Banking is a service industry which must be marketed. For an effective marketing, the services must be made convenient and accessible to the public. Unfortunately it is not the case currently in Nigeria, where 124,713 persons compete for one bank office and have to traverse an average of 73,361 sq. km to reach it. In some parts of Nigeria, such as in Gongola State, 600,561 persons have to compete for one bank office and have to cover an average of 20.4 million sq. km to reach it.

Under the circumstances, it will certainly be a very difficult task to try to infuse banking habits into the populace. Even if such an infusion were to take place through public enlightenment it becomes difficult to practice because of the absence of banks. Moreover, where a person may have to travel thousands of kilometres to use a bank, he is entitled to expect prompt service, but he may have to queue for hours before being served. Other factors such as the inefficiency of some bank officials, impoliteness and bureaucratic bottlenecks discourage some people from developing banking habits.

3. Fraud and Infrastructural Problems

An important element in banking is the use of cheques. Because of misuse by some bank clients, confidence in the use of cheques continues to diminish instead of increasing. The lack of confidence in cheques (commercial banks' book money) is analogous to the lack of confidence in paper money in the early days of the currency notes. The reluctance to accept cheques has contributed in no small way to the low development of banking habits in many developing countries. This lack of confidence stems principally from the drawers of cheques rather than from the payee – the banking system. In order to enhance the acceptability of cheques a decree was enacted which made the issue of dud cheques a criminal and punishable offence. Still there have been hundreds of cases of cheques bouncing as a result of the drawer not having any credit balance in his account, or cheques being drawn simply to defraud the bank – all culminating to the public's lack of confidence in a payment system based on cheques. This does not augur well for the development of banking business in Nigeria. It has not been possible to enforce the decree as the legal apparatus is grossly inadequate to cope with the hundred-plus cheques that bounce in each bank's branch every business day.

The clearing time for cheques is unnecessarily long because of the Central Bank's few and unmechanised clearing-houses. It can take up to two months to clear a Lagos cheque paid in at Enugu, a distance of less than 800 km. Obviously this is not the case in the advanced countries where clearing-houses are well-established institutions and banking habits well advanced.

Another critical issue in the development of banking in Nigeria is that of communication. In Lagos, for example, it can take up to six hours to drive from one end of the city to the other, the same time it takes to fly to London from Lagos. Heavy traffic in Lagos has not been effectively controlled. The entire telephone network is paralysed and at times it is easier to telephone London or New York from Lagos than to telephone any other Nigerian town from there. Letters travel very slowly, it may take up to two to three weeks for letters to travel from Kaduna to Lagos or Port Harcourt, distances of less than 1,000 km. It is not surprising, then, that the clearing of cheques can take weeks to materialise. The transfer of accounts from one bank office to another may even take months. It may take days to obtain the necessary information about a customer's credibility. Communication is the energiser and the appetiser in banking and it is of paramount importance in linking bank customers. Without effective communication, good banking is impossible. Until communication and the mechanisation of banks are improved the development of banking awareness will continue to be an illusion.

Another hindrance to the development of banking habits is the outright disregard of financial obligation by many customers. It has been mentioned earlier that one of the three c's of banking is confidence. Confidence should exist between the banker and the customer. Unfortunately some bank customers have abused confidence reposed in them and absconded, only to surface at another bank where the betrayal of confidence is again repeated. The third of the three c's is cost. Bank costs rise as a result of bad debts. The high rate of bad debts has contributed to the high cost of banking operations in Nigeria.

Equally of importance in the long march to modern banking is bank management. Bank managers are at times not given a free hand to manage their branches. There are cases of branch managers rejecting loan applications considered insecure from facts and figures available, but are countered by their headquarters because the customer has appealed to a bank director who may be a friend or a relation. The director uses his 'big stick' and forces the loan facility to be extended. It often happens that a branch manager who rejected a loan application is confronted on his return to his home by either his mother- or father-in-law or his own parents waiting to pressurise him to grant the loan facility because he (the loan applicant) is 'we we'.[4] There have also been reports of managers approving loans on the basis of some 'cola'.[5] Banks have not been able to bring many defaulting customers to book for fear of revelations and in this way a bank is blackmailed into keeping quiet.

The last but not least obstacle on the way to modern banking in Nigeria is staffing. There is a shortage of skilled bank manpower with the proper executive capacity. The Indigenisation Decree of 1973 (as amended in 1976) led to an efflux of expatriate manpower in the banking industry in Nigeria. The decree directed that management positions in industries revert to indigenous Nigerians. The banking industry, like other industries, was faced with an acute high-level manpower problem and the problem of long-term training of the right calibre of staff. The staffing problem is further endangered by the conflict between the new 'elite' bankers and those without adequate qualifications but who have grown up in the job. The rate of expansion of the banks both in the urban and the rural areas is not matched by an equal rate of turnover of bank manpower. The transfer of staff from existing branches to new branches has compounded the manpower problems of the banks.

To inculcate the habit of banking in a developing country like Nigeria the banker must recognise that he must provide a good service to his customers. Efficiency and satisfactory service must constitute his cardinal virtues in the provision of financial accommodation to his customers. It is important, however, that where the accommodation cannot be granted the banker should make it firmly clear to the customer. To discharge his obligation without fear or favour and efficiently, the banker must possess common sense, and he must be firm.

4. Conclusion

Before the transition from orthodox to modern banking can be fully achieved in Nigeria the perennial problems of banks must be tackled from the grass-roots. They have been discussed already and they include the problems of efficient system of communication, intensive and extensive manpower training programmes for bank personnel and the mass education of Nigerians through public enlightenment programmes on the use of services offered by banks. Section 27(2) of the Banking Decree of 1969 which requires banks to '. . . deliver to the Central Bank the text of the proposed advertisement . . .' should be reviewed. Applied to the letter that section of the decree can hinder any effective public enlightenment programme through advertisement.

There is no doubt whatsoever that the Nigerian banks still have a number of bottleneck problems to overcome. Some of them are infrastructural, others administrative and some human. It is encouraging to note that all these problems notwithstanding, the banking system has made significant progress as evidenced by the growing number of branches, increase in the ratio of loans and advances to deposits and the increase in the number of bank customers. If the monetary authorities should dismantle those administrative directives which may be superfluous in terms of the proper performance of banks, banks may make greater strides than now. There is a broad optimism that by the turn of the century Nigerian banks will be fully modernised to face squarely those challenges which the growing economy will certainly pose.

Notes

1. G.O. Nwankwo, 'New Dimensions in Banking in Developing Countries', mimeograph of collected essays, Lagos, 1974, p. 41.
2. C.V. Brown, *The Nigerian Banking System* (George Allen and Unwin, London, 1966), pp. 27-9.
3. Central Bank of Nigeria, *Monthly Report*, March 1976, pp. 18-21.
4. A Nigerian expression corrupted from the English word 'we' and literally means 'one of us'.
5. Implies bribery or some percentage share (commission) for approving the loan.

5 COMMERCIAL BANKS' DEPOSIT LIABILITIES AND CREDIT GENERATION

J.K. Onoh

1. Introduction

The ability of commercial banks to create credit money in a free enterprise economy will depend on a number of factors, such as:

(a) the eligible assets of the commercial banks,
(b) the excess reserves of the banks,
(c) the instruments of monetary control available to monetary authorities,
(d) the effective application and direction of such instruments,
(e) the monetary behaviour of the non-banking public with respect to deposits, and
(f) political factors.

In the early years of the Nigerian Central Bank *moral suasion* was the classical instrument most frequently used in the control of credit. Appeals were directed to the banks to apply greater discretion in the granting of loans and advances. The instrument proved impotent. In the mid-sixties selective credit measures coupled with credit ceiling were used to back moral suasion in the control of credit. They also proved inadequate especially for the transformation of the economy from a consumption economy to a production-oriented economy.

Quantitative restriction, selective credit and credit ceiling were certainly helpful to anti-inflationary measures, to balance of payments and reserve policies but inadequate for the avowed policy of industrialisation. To achieve the latter objective the Nigerian monetary authorities re-enforced the available instruments with the policy of quantitative direction of credit to the productive sectors of the economy.

A hybrid credit policy christened *credit guidelines* was born and came into force for the first time in 1969 aimed at achieving a reasonable degree of industrialisation and reducing inflationary pressures through the local provision of goods and services.

This paper will study the developments in commercial banks' deposits and credit generation. The study will examine the following areas:

(1) developments in the deposit liabilities of the commercial banks;
(2) developments in the ratio of loans and advances to deposits;
(3) developments in the ratio of demand deposits to money supply;
and
(4) developments in the credit allocations to the various sectors of
the economy.

2. Developments in Deposit Liabilities

Deposit liabilities for the purpose of this study are defined to mean
demand, time and saving deposits of commercial banks. The growth of
deposit liabilities depends to a large extent on the behaviour of the non-
bank public, the prevailing lendings and deposit rates, the propensities
to consume and to save in the economy, the degree of speculative or
productive business, the nature of inflation, the degree of political
stability, government spending in the economy and other factors. These
quantifiable and unquantifiable factors have no doubt influenced both
the level and the rate of increase of bank deposit liabilities in Nigeria.
Most of the quantifiable factors themselves are directly influenced by
monetary and fiscal policies.

Table 5.1: Deposit Liabilities of Commercial Banks (N'000)

End of Year	Demand (1)	1 as % of 7 (2)	Time (3)	3 as % of 7 (4)	Savings (5)	5 as % of 7 (6)	Total (7)
1960	82,234	60.0	17,908	13.0	36,882	27.0	137,024
1961	83,316	54.0	28,136	18.0	42,376	28.0	153,828
1962	90,592	46.0	34,840	26.0	48,448	28.0	173,880
1963	97,546	59.0	37,896	12.0	56,374	29.0	191,816
1964	115,662	50.0	46,166	20.0	68,262	30.0	230,090
1965	123,902	47.0	60,670	23.0	80,330	30.0	264,918
1966	135,640	46.0	73,186	24.0	89,330	30.0	298,156
1967	110,374	48.0	79,378	30.0	51,864	22.0	241,616
1968	146,918	44.0	108,810	33.0	74,742	23.0	330,470
1969	185,532	46.0	120,720	30.0	94,678	24.0	400,930
1970	289,048	46.0	207,006	33.0	129,712	21.0	625,766
1971	285,340	43.0	211,380	33.0	160,382	24.0	657,102
1972	336,908	42.0	255,960	33.0	200,906	25.0	793,774
1973	430,743	43.0	357,816	35.0	224,464	22.0	1,013,023
1974	720,714	43.0	686,525	40.0	286,687	17.0	1,693,926
1975	1,266,819	45.0	1,051,050	37.0	521,306	18.0	2,839,175
1976	2,185,200	52.0	1,270,000	31.0	709,200	17.0	4,164,400
1977	2,853,614	55.9	1,324,993	25.9	930,100	18.2	5,108,707

Source: Central Bank of Nigeria, *Economic and Financial Review* of various years.
The percentage computations are those of the author (results are rounded).

To study the extent of the influence of these factors on the development of the Nigerian commercial banks' deposit liabilities three phases have been deliberately chosen. The first phase covers the period 1960-6. This was the immediate post-independence period, the teething period of the banking system. The second phase covers 1967-9. This was the period of civil commotion, of adverse balance of payments, of shaky external reserve base and intensive military activities with their accompanying heavy capital and recurrent military expenditure. The last phase, 1970-8, is the post-civil-war period. In this period there were a number of reconstruction and development activities, oil production reached its highest peak, new internal and external monetary policies were devised and the external reserve position improved significantly.

(a) Period 1 (1960-6)

This period was marked by relative political calm. Financial infrastructure was still at the stage of infancy. The population had developed few financial habits, least of all that of depositing money with financial institutions. Subsistence economy was preponderant. The monetised sector of the economy was mainly commerce. Between 1960 and 1963 the growth of demand, time and savings deposits was gradual but steady. Inflationary pressure was mild and speculative business was very limited. Between 1960 and 1963 developments of the various deposits could be described as gradual, except for the sudden jump of time deposits in 1961.

In 1964, however, there was a sudden increase in the various levels of deposits, which cannot be described as gradual. The sudden increases in the various deposits in 1964 does not defy explanation. In 1963, Nigeria's foreign-exchange reserve level had dropped to a critical point. Nigerian monetary authorities took a number of measures such as quantitative and selective credit measures and credit ceiling to reduce the volume of credit money which the commercial banks could generate.[1] The above measures reduced Nigeria's imports and domestic borrowing. Businessmen had no other alternative but to leave much of their deposits unutilised. Others who had no chequeable, time or savings accounts had to open them instead of hoarding their money. The slow trend in deposit liabilities continued till 1966. It reflected the new tight monetary policy which the authorities pursued at the time and which was a complete break from the past reliance on moral suasion.

As the computations suggest, the ratio of demand and time deposits to aggregate deposit liabilities for the period showed some severe fluctuations. From a 60 point position in 1960 demand deposits declined to the 46 point level in 1966. From a 13 point position time deposits increased to the 24 point level in 1966, after declining to an all-time low of 12 in 1963. In sharp contrast, savings progressively increased from the 27 point position in 1960 to 30 in 1966. The fluctuations of both demand and time deposits cannot be attributed to changing rates structure. In the period in question deposit and lending rates did not vary significantly. The increase in the ratio of savings to aggregate deposit liabilities may be attributed to the difficulty of withdrawal of savings rather than to an increase in deposit rates which remained almost at 3-3.5 per cent level in the period. Savers sometimes had to be identified before they could withdraw, and an advance notice was required sometimes before a certain amount could be withdrawn.

(b) Phase 2 (1967-9)

This was the civil-war period. From the available statistics developments in demand deposits did not show any significant change. However, one has to comment cautiously on the development of deposit liabilities during this period, as it was virtually impossible to obtain monetary statistics of the Eastern Region after the banks submitted their June 1967 returns. With the outbreak of the civil war at the beginning of July 1967, no further monetary statistics were obtainable from the war areas of Eastern Nigeria. It can be safely assumed that the deposit liabilities statistics of the period excluded those of the Eastern Region. This assumption is necessary, if the poor development in deposit liabilities is to be explained. In this period an overall increase in deposit liabilities was expected in view of the enormous recurrent military expenditure and the tight commercial and monetary policy. From the available statistics it would appear that deposit liabilities were indifferent to these important factors. One possible explanation for the lack of increase in deposit liabilities may be the preference to hold large cash balances. The speculative forms of businesses that prevailed during the war period warranted large cash balances for quick disposal by the non-bank public.

Time deposits, however, increased progressively in this period, while savings deposits which increased progressively in Period 1 declined. There appears to be an inverse relationship between the developments in time and saving deposits. The apparent absence of deposit liabilities statistics of the Eastern Region during the period makes a meaningful conclusion impossible.

(c) Period 3 (1970-8)

The Nigerian civil war ended in January 1970. The early part of the period was characterised by reconstruction, tight commercial policies and speculative businesses. In the latter part of the period, import was liberalised. Until the latter part of 1973 the war-devastated Eastern States were still busy reorganising and reconciling their bank documents affected by the Currency Conversion Decree and the token exchange of the Biafran money for the Nigerian currency. The Eastern States, especially the former East Central State (now partitioned into Anambra and Imo States), only started experiencing some economic recoveries in 1973. Development of deposit liabilities was therefore very gradual.

Between 1970 and 1973 the various deposits stagnated relatively, between 1974 and 1976 they grew rapidly. The ratio of demand deposits to aggregate deposit liabilities, however, dwindled between 1971 and 1974. In 1975 the trend was reversed. The ratio of time deposit to total deposit liabilities stagnated at the 33 point level between 1970 and 1972. It rose in 1973 and 1974 and has been on the decline since 1975. It reached its lowest ebb in 1977.

Monetary, fiscal and income policies of the Federal Government can explain to a large extent the development in deposit liabilities during the latter part of this period. The monetisation of petrol assets in 1974, when Nigeria had excess reserves adequate to support 24.5 months of imports, resulted in expanded money supply in the course of implementation of government projects of the second phase of the 15 Years' Development Plan. The increase in money supply in 1974 as a result of the government's programme was re-enforced in 1975. In 1975 wages and salaries were in some cases revised upwards by as much as 100 per cent. In addition a total arrears of over N0.5 billion was awarded to the workers in the public and the private sectors in 1975. As a result of this unexpected and unplanned income a number of workers opened various deposit accounts. This explains the astronomic rise in the volume of the various deposits, although the ratio of the individual deposits to total liabilities did not rise correspondingly.

Monetary policy of interest rate may have also influenced the movement of the various deposits in the latter part of the period. In the 1974/5 fiscal year the interest rate structure was drastically revised. Lending rates had a spread of between 6-10 per cent, depending on whether the loan was for the productive sector or for the sector classified as less productive. Loans for the productive sector attracted a lower rate, while those for the less productive sector attracted rates of up to 10 per cent. The new lending-rate system was aimed at supporting the credit guidelines. The new rate policy may have discouraged borrowers (especially borrowers of loans which attracted the maximum lending rate).

The ratio of time deposits to total deposit liabilities has been on the decline since 1975. The decline may be attributed to the new monetary policy which started in the 1974/5 fiscal year, and which allowed banks to negotiate the various rates for time deposits of different maturities.[2] The rates acceptable to banks, which had long complained of excess liquidity, may not have been attractive to time depositors. This may have accounted for the decline in the ratio of time deposit to total deposit liabilities in the years 1975 and 1976 respectively. In 1977 it reached 25.90 for the first time in ten years.

The new rate policy also affected savings. Although the savings rate was raised from 3 to 4 per cent, a ceiling was placed, which permitted banks to receive a maximum of N20,000 per saver. Beyond N20,000, banks were free to negotiate the interest rate. The ceiling was placed to protect banks from threatening excess liquidity. The ceiling no doubt discouraged big savers, and increased demand deposits. The point gains in the demand deposit ratio to aggregate deposit liabilities, that is, from 42 point level in 1972 to 43, 43, 45, and 52 point positions in 1973, 1974, 1975 and 1976 respectively, may be attributed to the drops in the ratios of savings deposit to aggregate deposit liabilities in the corresponding years. From 25 point level in 1972 savings ratio dropped to 22, 17, 18 and 17 positions for the years 1973, 1974, 1975 and 1976 respectively. It recovered slightly to 18.20 position in 1977.

3. Developments in the Ratio of Loans/Advances to Deposits

(a) Period 1 (1960-7)

Two phases have been chosen for this aspect of the study. The first phase covers 1960-7 while the second phase covers 1968-76. The first phase corresponds with the era of liberal monetary policy. In this period major bank customers were mainly foreign business houses based in Nigeria, which borrowed with relative ease from foreign commercial banks. Foreign-owned banks controlled over 80 per cent of the country's banking activities in the period. The growth in the ratio of loans and advances to commercial-bank deposits in this period was the highest ever achieved in Nigerian monetary history. The growth in the loans/advances – deposit ratio may be explained by the growing reliance of commerce and industries on domestic credit sources for working capital needs. Commerce in particular borrowed more from the banks. The high ratio in this period may also be explained by the fact that some newly established banks had not attracted enough deposits and depended on their capital and borrowed funds from their overseas head-quarters to finance their lending activities. The astronomic loans/ advances – deposit ratios between 1961 and 1968 may be explained by the last fact. The importation of funds for lending was made possible by the liberal monetary policy of the time. Before 1960 the ratio of loans/advances to deposits was low because of the lack of domestic investment outlets. Banks invested their surplus funds in London money-market assets. This was discouraged by the 1962 amendment of the Central Bank of Nigeria Act of 1958, which required banks to explore avenues for domestic investments. The increase in the ratio especially from 1963 is attributed to the amended Act which directed banks to look for investment outlets in Nigeria. The increase in the ratio may also be attributed to the gradual withdrawal of the large ex-patriate firms from retail trade, agricultural marketing and produce buying to investment in industry. As a result of the shift in operations from commerce to industry a vacuum was created for Nigerian business-men who, unlike the expatriate firms, were not to a very large extent self-financing and depended mainly on the banks for finance. The demand for durable consumer goods also helped to increase the ratio of loans to deposits, which reached highest peaks in 1963, 1964, 1965, 1966 and 1967.

Table 5.2: Ratio of Commercial Banks' Loans and Advances to Deposits (Computed figures are the rounded average of each year)

Year	Ratio in %	Year	Ratio in %
1960	58	1968	79
1961	72	1969	57
1962	73	1970	51
1963	89	1971	68
1964	92	1972	74
1965	94	1973	70
1966	93	1974	62
1967	98	1975	51
		1976	48
		1977	60

Source: Central Bank of Nigeria, *Economic and Financial Review* of various years.

(b) Phase 2 (1968-78)

The second phase covers the period 1967-78. The war which began in 1967 and ended in January 1970 warranted the application of a tight monetary policy. The result of the policy during and after the war was the decline in the ratio of loans and advances to deposits. Borrowing declined relatively during the war years especially from 1968. The rise in bank credit in 1972 and 1973 may be attributed to a slight increase in government borrowings to carry out government programmes and to private borrowings to purchase shares from foreigners as a result of the Indigenisation Decree. The decline in the ratio of loans and advances to deposits in 1974, 1975 and 1976 which reflects reduced borrowing may be attributed to the reimposition of cash-reserve ratio in the 1975/6 fiscal year and credit guidelines which were toughened in 1974 and re-enforced in subsequent years. The increase in the ratio in 1977 is an evidence of greater lending to the productive sector. In 1977 the lending target for 'production' was exceeded, a situation considered desirable (see Table 5.5). In addition to the above the decline in 1976 may be further explained by the new discriminatory interest rates spread of between 6 and 10 per cent, which favoured the productive sector and discriminated against the less productive sector. Most affected was commerce which had become the preoccupation of many Nigerians. Lending for 'commerce' dropped from 32.80 per cent in 1975 to 25.10 per cent in 1976 and reached its lowest ebb of 23.50 per cent in 1977. The increase in the ratio of loans and advances to deposits in 1977 was also the result of the increase in the aggregate loans and advances for the year 1977. Loans and advances for 1977 increased by 48.9 per cent over the 1976 level.

Decree No. 50 of 1968, which stipulated that 40 per cent of all bank lendings must be reserved to Nigerian businessmen, did not appear to have had any apparent expansionary effect on the ratio, even after it was later raised to 50 per cent. The anticipated expansionary effect of the measure on the ratio was neutralised by other anti-inflationary measures which restricted credit. The absence of deposit statistics from the war-affected areas significantly reduced the ratio in 1968 and 1969 respectively. The lack of economic activity in those areas immediately after the war also contributed to the low reports in 1970 and 1971. Last but not least is the Federal Government's acquisition of 60 per cent of all commercial banks' equities in 1972. The action made it impossible for Nigerian-based foreign banks to import capital and funds from their overseas headquarters to support domestic lending in view of the equity holding of 40 per cent to which they were restricted.

4. Developments in the Ratio of Demand Deposits to Money Supply

Table 5.3 reveals a slow development in the ratio of demand deposit to money supply. Money supply is here defined in the conventional narrow sense to mean currency outside banks plus current demand deposits with the banking system minus governments' demand deposit (Federal and State) at the commercial banks.

The slow development, especially in the pre-civil war years, is an evidence of the relative low-level income of the period and naturally the corresponding high rate of consumption and low level of savings and deposits expected from such an economy. The tight commercial and monetary policies of the war years and after, reduced consumption and domestic borrowing and increased relatively the ratio of demand deposits to money supply. The increase in money income resulting from government expenditure during and after the war years and the booming economic activities have contributed to a progressive increase in the propensity to save and to the opening of more chequeable accounts. The increase in the ratio of demand deposit to money supply is an evidence of the rate of monetisation of the economy and an increase of public confidence in the banking system.

Table 5.3: Ratio of Demand Deposits to Money Supply

Year	Ratio in %	Year	Ratio in %
1960	34	1969	41
1961	35	1970	44
1962	37	1971	44
1963	37	1972	45
1964	38	1973	47
1965	37	1974	52
1966	37	1975	50
1967	34	1976	59
1968	44	1977	60

Source: Central Bank of Nigeria, *Economic and Financial Review* of various years.

The encouraging developments in the ratio of demand deposits to money supply in the seventies may also be attributed partly to the public's growing financial awareness of the usefulness of financial institutions for business and economic development and partly to the expansion of banking facilities in the urban and rural areas. By March 1976 commercial banks operated in 144 centres throughout the Federation and with 433 branches.[3] This contrasts with the situation in the

prewar yeɛ   banks serving mainly the urban centres and the rural
areas only ˴   lly. The activities of the men of the underworld have
also encouraged bank deposits. Since the end of the war they have constantly terrorised people in their homes and in many cases have made
away with large sums of money leaving behind them death and destruction. Although the effect of these people's activities is not quantifiable,
there is no doubt that the psychological fear their presence generates in
the Nigerian communities encourages business and non-businessmen
alike to deposit their money with the banks.

5. Developments in Commercial Banks' Credit Allocations

The control of credit has been a major preoccupation of the Nigerian
Central Bank. In the earlier period of the Central Bank the accent was
on credit restriction. Moral suasion was the classical instrument employed for the purpose. In the course of time it dawned on the authorities that the quantitative and relative credit measures might be helpful
in stemming inflationary pressure and keeping non-fiduciary and fiduciary issues in proper proportion, but were certainly inadequate for
long-term economic growth objectives. A change in credit policy became imperative. From the policy of quantitative restriction of credit,
emphasis shifted to the policy of quantitative credit direction. Quantitative credit restriction through the policy of credit ceiling continued to
be applied but it was re-enforced with the policy of quantitative credit
direction as contained in the credit guidelines.

The years 1960-8 were the period in which liquidity ratio, moral suasion and credit restriction were the main instruments of monetary
policy. The period covering the years 1969-76 was one of active monetary policy. The Banking Decree No. 50 of 1968 added seven additional
instruments to the monetary arsenal of the Central Bank with the aim
of directing credits to the more productive sectors of the economy.
Developments in the credit allocations of the commercial banks operating in Nigeria can better be examined in two phases. Phase 1 covers the
years 1960-8 while Phase 2 covers the years 1969-78, a period of active
monetary policy.

(a) Phase 1 (1960-8)

This was a period of credit restriction rather than direction. Monetary
policy did not have clearly defined economic growth goals. As this was
the teething period of the Nigerian Central Bank, all monetary efforts

were channelled to ensure that the new financial institution (Central Bank) did not engage in excess generation of credit money to the government especially through ways and means advances. Experts had already viewed critically the idea of establishing a Central Bank in a developing economy such as Nigeria's. The fear rested squarely on the ground that in the absence of developed money and capital markets monetary instruments of control may be paralysed thereby paving the way for an inflationary monetary situation, which may be difficult to contain in view of Nigeria's limited instruments of fiscal control. In this phase, the objective of monetary control was merely to dampen inflationary pressure and to generate outside confidence in the Nigerian currency. The orthodox policy of keeping the marginal velocity of money as low as possible was rigorously pursued with the available limited tools of monetary control.

Commerce received on the average the highest allocation of credit in this phase. The average credit awarded the department between 1960 and 1968 was 35 per cent of the aggregate credit to the economy in the period, as the computation of Table 5.4 clearly shows. Credit allocation to commerce reached its highest levels during the civil war years. In 1968 almost half of the year's allocation went to commerce. Agriculture apparently had the second highest allocation; however, the computation is grossly misleading. Agriculture received one of the lowest allocations in the period. What actually inflated the average figure for agriculture, forestry and fishery is the loan provided to the marketing boards and other agents to enable them purchase exportable cash crops from producers. The trend in credit allocation to agriculture and allied departments starting from 1966 reflects the proper agricultural credit trend. The takeover of direct discount of cocoa bills by the Central Bank in 1964, as a result of the refusal of a consortium of commercial banks to finance the Western Nigerian marketing board, because of the absence of cocoa-sales contracts to act as collateral, and the direct discounting of ground-nut bills for the Northern Nigerian marketing boards for the same reason in 1967 removed entirely from the consortium of commercial banks the financing of exportable cash crops. Figures for agriculture from 1966 no longer reflected commercial bank loans for agricultural-produce financing. The low figures reveal gross neglect of agricultural and natural resources development. The third largest allocation was for 'Miscellaneous'. Until 1965 miscellaneous included transport and communications, personal and professional and call money outside the Central Bank. The amalgam of a number of departments into miscellaneous contributed apparently to the relatively high allocation for the department. The separation of credits grouped under miscellaneous starting from 1966 leaves a clearer image of the situation for appropriate monetary policy actions. Bills discounted count as a part of *general commerce*. If added to it, general commerce was allocated 61 per cent of all credit to the economy in 1966, 60 per cent in 1967 and 52.6 per cent in 1968. No developing economy would accept such a trend, if the goals of the economy are that of long-term relative self-reliance, rapid economic growth rate, higher standard of living and high level of employment of all the country's resources — human and material. The active monetary policies pursued in Phase 2 were aimed at reducing the degree of dependence on commerce and enhancing local productivity. The extent to which the 'new' monetary policies influenced credit allocation in the Nigerian economy with the objective of attaining the above enumerated goals will be examined in Phase 2.

(b) Phase 2 (1969-78)

In this phase monetary policies were aimed at countervailing inflationary pressures and accelerating economic growth rate. Monetary policies were pursued in the belief that if credit were directed to the more productive sectors of the economy more goods and services would be produced, inflation would be contained and Nigeria would achieve some degree of self-reliance. How monetary policies succeeded in suppressing inflation, in increasing the rate of economic growth and in committing Nigerian resources warrants a separate study. We shall be concerned here with analysing how far monetary policies physically influenced the quantitative direction of credit to the various sectors with the hope of attaining the various social and economic goals.

While monetary policy instruments such as liquidity ratio, cash reserve ratio, moral suasion, bank rate, open-market operations, stabilisation securities, special deposits, credit ceiling, variation of the composition of specified liquid assets and the approval of special loans by the Central Bank only may have restricted credit, it is the credit guidelines embodied in the monetary policy circulars of the Central Bank of Nigeria which have made spirited efforts to redirect credit.

In 1969 when the measure was first introduced the mechanism of the policy was not as refined or detailed as it is today. Although the Central Bank demanded an increase of 10 per cent in commercial banks' lending over the preceding year's bench-mark and directed that the increase in lending be directed to the more productive sectors and that loans and advances that fall under 'Others' be kept constant, commercial banks defied the directive and on the contrary increased lending in that sphere; this was also the case in 1970 when banks were required to increase lending by 20 per cent over the 1969 bench-mark and to direct the increase to the productive sectors. A tougher guideline for the 1972/3 fiscal year, for the first time, imposed specific sectoral allocation of loans and advances on the banks. The specific sectoral allocations expressed in percentages continued until the 1975/6 fiscal year when they were changed from 45, 11, 32 and 12 for *production, services, general commerce* and *others* to 48, 10, 32 and 10 respectively. In the 1976/7 period the percentage distributions were varied to 48, 10, 30, and 12 respectively. In 1978/9 the percentage distributions were raised for the productive sector and further lowered for the less productive sector.

Table 5.5 is clear about the performance of the commercial banks in respect of the target sectoral allocations of loans and advances and gives an insight as to how the new monetary policy of credit guidelines has succeeded in the quantitative direction of credit to the more productive sectors.

Figures in parentheses are the actual performances of commercial banks before and after 1972 with regard to the distribution of loans and advances between April and December of each year while figures to the left of the parentheses are the percentage target distributions as specified by the guidelines.

6. Conclusion

There is no doubt that the credit guidelines have proved a formidable instrument of monetary control in Nigeria. The prescribed target distributions for the productive sector were exceeded in 1976 and 1977 as indicated by the April to December performances. This is evidence of the Central Bank's tighter hold on the commercial banks' lending activities. The acquisition of 60 per cent of the equity of all the commercial banks by the Federal Government gave it a control over the banks' managements. This helped in the effective direction of banks' loans and advances towards the desired goals of the guidelines. The penalty imposed by the Central Bank in 1976 on the commercial banks for excessive lending to the less productive sector has also had its desired effects. But the penalty measures have not deterred some banks from excessive lending to the sub-sector classified as others. The lending rate for activities under 'others' is the highest but the penalty prescribed is much lower than the interest gained and the commercial banks can pay the small fines comfortably. An effective policy would be one that will force the banks to forfeit to the Central Bank all the interest earned by the unauthorised lending, in addition to the penalty.

The new 1978 regulations whereby any shortfall in loans and advances, earmarked for agriculture and building constructions, should be deposited with the Central Bank as a non-interest earning deposit will obviously force the commercial banks to comply with the directive of the guidelines. The rough edges of the guidelines are still being smoothened. In a few years hence all the loose nuts of the instruments will be effectively tightened. If that is achieved the Nigerian monetary authorities would have one of the finest weapons in their monetary arsenal from which many developing countries will certainly benefit.

Table 5.4: Percentage Computations of Loans and Advances of Commercial Banks by Departments

Departments	Phase 1									Phase 2									Per. Average in %		
	1960	1961	1962	1963	1964	1965	1966	1967	1968	1969	1970	1971	1972	1973	1974	1975	1976	1977	60-68	69-77	60-77
1. Government	2.00	1.00	1.10	0.80	0.80	0.70	0.40	0.60	1.70	2.00	0.40	0.70	1.50	2.30	3.40	2.40	2.20	2.90	(1.00)	(2.00)	(1.50)
2. Public utilities	1.00	0.80	0.20	1.00	0.60	1.00	0.40	1.30	1.00	0.70	0.20	0.70	0.80	1.50	0.80	1.00	1.40	1.40	(0.80)	(1.00)	(0.90)
3. Credit and financial institutions	5.00	4.00	1.00	1.50	3.00	1.00	2.50	3.30	4.00	2.00	0.80	1.60	2.30	1.60	2.30	3.40	2.80	3.20	(2.80)	(2.20)	(2.50)
4. Agriculture, forestry and fishing	20.00	21.00	23.00	22.00	25.00	25.00	1.60	1.40	1.70	1.80	2.00	1.90	3.00	2.90	2.90	2.40	2.50	4.50	(15.00)	(3.00)	(9.00)
5. Mining and quarrying	1.00	0.80	0.70	0.70	0.50	0.50	0.50	0.70	0.50	1.00	1.90	2.30	1.60	2.40	1.30	1.00	1.20	1.20	(0.60)	(2.00)	(1.30)
6. Manufacture	4.00	5.50	8.00	10.00	11.00	11.00	13.00	14.40	16.00	17.00	21.70	23.80	23.00	0.80	27.60	26.70	27.20	27.20	(10.00)	(22.00)	(16.00)
7. Real estate and construction	6.00	9.00	7.00	7.00	5.00	5.00	9.00	8.20	8.80	7.90	7.40	7.40	8.00	10.00	10.40	13.80	13.60	21.50	(7.00)	(11.11)	(9.05)
8. General commerce	37.00	32.00	26.00	34.00	27.00	21.00	41.00	47.00	49.90	50.30	46.00	42.00	34.60	35.00	28.90	31.00	30.70	22.40	(35.00)	(36.00)	(35.00)
9. Bills discounted	2.00	2.00	4.00	8.00	12.00	16.00	20.00	20.00	13.00	2.70	1.80	1.70	2.00	1.30	0.50	1.50	1.80	0.80	(8.80)	(2.00)	(5.40)
10. Transport and communications	–	–	–	–	–	–	3.40	3.00	4.00	4.00	5.40	5.00	7.20	6.70	7.00	5.30	5.60	7.60	(2.00)	(0.10)	(4.05)
11. Personal and professional	–	–	–	–	–	–	1.90	2.60	3.00	4.70	6.60	3.60	10.20	5.70	6.60	5.50	5.80	4.50	(2.50)	(6.24)	(4.37)
12. Miscellaneous	22.00	24.00	19.00	14.00	15.00	19.00	6.00	4.40	6.80	6.00	5.00	5.50	6.50	8.60	7.30	5.50	5.10	2.80	(14.50)	(6.00)	(10.25)
Total in %	100.00	100.00	100.00	100.00	100.00	100.00	100.00	100.00	100.00	100.00	100.00	100.00	100.00	100.00	100.00	100.00	100.00	100.00			

Note: Until 1965, transport and communications, personal and professional, and call money outside Central Bank were included in miscellaneous; agriculture included loans for financing exportable agricultural produce.

Figures have been rounded and may not add up exactly. Computations are based on end-of-year figures of relevant statistics of the Central Bank of Nigeria's *Economic and Financial Review* of various years.

Table 5.5: Recent Sectoral Credit Distributions and Actual Achievements by Banks in %

	1969[a]	1970[a]	1971[b]	1972[b]		1973[b]		1974[b]		1975[b]		1976[b]		1977[b]		1978[a]
A. Productive Sector/Sub-Sector																
(i) Production	(27.60)	(33.00)	(35.45)	45.00	(38.10)	45.00	(38.30)	45.00	(43.60)	48.00	(44.00)	48.00	(52.10)	48.00	(53.40)	50.00
(ii) Services	(4.70)	(5.60)	(7.49)	11.00	(7.70)	11.00	(8.10)	11.00	(7.50)	10.00	(6.40)	10.00	(9.20)	10.00	(9.20)	10.00
Total A	(32.30)	(38.60)	(42.94)	56.00	(45.80)	56.00	(46.40)	56.00	(51.10)	58.00	(50.40)	58.00	(61.30)	58.00	(62.60)	60.00
B. Less Productive Sector/Sub-Sector																
(i) General Commerce	(52.20)	(47.70)	(44.06)	32.00	(35.70)	32.00	(34.40)	32.00	(30.00)	32.00	(32.80)	30.00	(25.10)	30.00	(23.50)	28.00
(ii) Others	(15.50)	(13.70)	(13.00)	12.00	(18.50)	12.00	(19.20)	12.00	(18.90)	10.00	(16.80)	12.00	(13.60)	12.00	(13.90)	12.00
Total B	(67.70)	(61.40)	(57.06)	44.00	(54.20)	44.00	(53.60)	44.00	(48.90)	42.00	(49.60)	42.00	(38.70)	42.00	(37.40)	40.00
Total A + B =	(100.00)	(100.00)	(100.00)	100.00	(100.00)	100.00	(100.00)	100.00	(100.00)	100.00	(100.00)	100.00	(100.00)	100.00	(100.00)	100.00

Notes: [a] June-December figures.
[b] April-December figures.

Source: Central Bank of Nigeria, *Annual Report and Statement of Accounts* of various years.

Notes

1. Heinz-Guenther Geis, *Die Geld-und Banksysteme der Staaten Westafrikas* (Weltforum Verlag, Munich, 1967), p. 153.
2. See Central Bank of Nigeria, *Developments in the Nigerian Economy During the First Half of 1975* and also of *1976*, pp. 35 and 28 respectively.
3. Central Bank of Nigeria, *Monthly Report*, March 1976, pp. 15-22.

6 COMMERCIAL BANKS' LOANS AND ADVANCES: A DECOMPOSITIONAL ANALYSIS OF STRUCTURAL CHANGES

Ibi Ajayi

1. Introduction

We can look at loans and advances from two perspectives. The first is from the angle of the commercial banks and the second is from that of the economy. As profit-making concerns, loans and advances are important items for commercial banks. Over the past decade, loans and advances have consistently accounted for about one-third of banks' total assets. For the economy, the injection of funds can be important for the development of infrastructural facilities, industries, etc. The rate as well as the direction of the credit facilities have implications for the growth of the money supply and price stability for the economy.

The aim of this paper is to determine and analyse the structural changes of commercial banks' loans and advances for the period 1970-7.

2. Category of Loans and Advances

There are essentially four broad sectors of the Nigerian economy where bank loans and advances are injected. These are:

(a) *Production* – agriculture, forestry and fishing; manufacturing; mining and quarrying; real estate and construction.

(b) *General commerce* – bills discounted; domestic trade; exports and imports.

(c) *Services* – public utilities; transportation and communication; and

(d) *Others* – credit and financial institutions; governments; personal and professional; and miscellaneous.

3. The Model

Many methods can be used to test for structural changes. One method is the use of regression analysis. After obtaining the necessary coefficients, one can test for consistency of the entire regression coefficient or test for changes in different parts of the regression period. A second method uses the analysis of variance. A third method is the use of decomposition analysis. The last method is specially designed for allocation problems. While the total item is given, there may be compositional changes within the item that need to be closely examined. For the purpose of this study the decomposition analysis will be used. Structural changes of the entire loans and advances and the structural changes within the sectoral classifications will be analysed.

The matrix of the structural changes to be used is shown as follows:

Asset type	Absolute t	Values $t+1$	Relative values t	$t+1$
1	A^o_1	A'_1	$P^o_1 = \dfrac{A^o_1}{A^o}$	$P'_1 = \dfrac{A'_1}{A'}$
2	A^o_2	A'_2	$P^o_2 = \dfrac{A^o_2}{A^o}$	$P'_2 = \dfrac{A'_2}{A'}$
3	A^o_3	A'_3	$P^o_3 = \dfrac{A^o_3}{A^o}$	$P'_3 = \dfrac{A'_3}{A'}$
4	A^o_4	A'_4	$P^o_4 = \dfrac{A^o_4}{A^o}$	$P'_4 = \dfrac{A'_4}{A'}$
Total	A^o	A'		

From the above matrix, the decomposition measure for the period $t/t+1$ can be defined as:

$$I_{DA} = \sum_{i=i}^{n} P'_i \, \log \frac{P'_i}{P^o_i} \qquad \ldots \quad (1)$$

For subsequent years, the superscripts are replaced with 1 and 2. For the period t+1/t+2 for example, the decomposition measure is:

$$I_{DA} = \sum_{i=1}^{n} P_i^2 \ \log \ \frac{P_i^2}{P_i^1} \quad \ldots \quad (2)$$

For n assets for k years, we would have a data set with nk elements, k-1 decomposition measures.

To analyse the structural changes within each of the sectors, we use similar equations. To differentiate it from the aggregate loans and advances, the index for each sector is defined as follows:

$$I_p = \sum_{i=1}^{n} P_i' \ \log \ \frac{P_i'}{P_i^0} \qquad n = 4 \qquad (3)$$

$$I_{GC} = \sum_{i=1}^{n} P_i' \ \log \ \frac{P_i'}{P_i^0} \qquad n = 4 \qquad (4)$$

$$I_s = \sum_{i=1}^{n} P_i' \ \log \ \frac{P_i'}{P_i^0} \qquad n = 4 \qquad (5)$$

$$I_o = \sum_{i=1}^{n} P_i' \ \log \ \frac{P_i'}{P_i^0} \qquad n = 4 \qquad (6)$$

where I_p =   Index of decomposition in the production sector

I_{GC} =   Index of decomposition in the general commerce sector

I_s =   Index of decomposition in the service sector

I_o =   Index of decomposition in the 'other' sector.

4. Analysis

Following the procedures described earlier, Tables 6.1 and 6.2 show the results of the calculations using equations (1) and (3) to (6).

Table 6.1: Aggregate Decomposition Measures

Year	1970/1	1971/2	1972/3	1973/4	1974/5	1975/6	1976/7
I_{DA}	.0016	.0121	.0034	.0030	.0005	.0097	.0034
Sample size	16	121	34	30	5	97	34
Rank Order	6	1	3	5	7	2	3

Table 6.2: Sectoral Decomposition Measures

	1970/1	1971/2	1972/3	1973/4	1974/5	1975/6	1976/7
Production (I_p)	.0029	.0018	.2161	.1597	.0020	.0038	.0024
General commerce (I_{GC})	.0017	.0044	0	.0070	.0115	.0048	.0020
Service (I_s)	.0132	.0027	.0009	.0009	.0053	.0016	0
Others (I_o)	.0051	.0059	.0102	.0053	.0128	.0147	.0111

Table 6.1 suggests that aggregate loans and advances have changed structurally over the period under investigation. The rank order column of Table 6.1 shows the rank of the structural changes that have occurred over years.

We find the year 1971/2 was one in which the greatest structural changes occurred. The other years were 1975/6, 1972/3, 1976/7, 1973/4, 1970/1 and 1974/5. The last year, that is, 1974/5 witnessed the least structural change.

A number of explanations can be offered for these structural changes by looking at the Central Bank's Reports and circulars and trends of key indicators in the economy. There are two explanations for the 1971/2 changes. The first is that after the end of the civil war, the policy orientation was one of massive reconstruction. Consequently, through encouragement from the authorities, the level of loans and advances increased to different sectors of the economy. Second, during the Nigerian civil war, the banks in the Eastern part of the country were not functioning; afterwards, however, they started functioning; By 1971/2 many of them were operating with the same efficiency as in the prewar period. These two factors adequately explain a significant proportion of the high structural change in 1971/2. Looking at the figures on loans and advances to the economy, we find that in 1971/2, the growth rate of loans and advances to the economy was 96.9 per cent. The growth rate was slower in 1972/3, it grew at a rate of about 15.9 per cent. 1973-5 was a period of high price rises. Attempts were made by the authorities to minimise the growth rate of loans and advances. By 1975 for example, the inflation rate had risen to 34 per cent over its previous level of 13 per cent. Attempts by the government to stop the inflationary trends have led to directives being given to commercial banks to decrease their loans and advances especially in the non-productive sector. Between 1974 and 1975, this has led to slight but noticeable structural change in loans and advances.

Calculations of the structural changes in the sectoral groupings using equations (3)-(6) are shown in Table 6.2. We can now take each of the sectors in turn. For the production sector we find that structural changes did occur throughout the period with the greatest change occurring in 1972/3. This was the year in which the Central Bank dropped credit ceilings as a means of controlling inflation because of their ineffectiveness and instead introduced allocative shares. Target percentage shares for each of the four categories of loans and advances were introduced. The production sector, for example, was allocated a share of 45 per cent. It ended up, however, having 38 per cent in 1972 and 1973. The lowest structural change for the period 1971/2 has its explanation again in the aftermath of the war. Production took some time to pick up, especially agriculture and manufacturing. The share of production, which was only 37 per cent in 1971, rose to 43 per cent in 1975.

Looking at the general commerce and services sectors together, we find that structural changes occurred in both sectors during the period under review. The similarity of the two sectors is that no structural changes occurred in the general commerce sector in 1972/3 and none for the services section in 1976/7. In the case of the services sector, its share in total loans and advances remained unchanged in 1976/7 while that of general commerce also remained virtually unchanged.

The 'others' sector which consists of the sub-groups previously discussed, also witnessed structural changes. Despite the fall in loans going to the Government in 1975/6 the rise in the personal and professional, and the credit and finance sections overcompensated for the fall in other sectors to cause a general structural change. The yearly percentage change of this sector has not only been fantastic but also unsteady. It is then not surprising that structural changes occurred throughout the period.

5. Summary and Conclusions

We found that structural changes have occurred in loans and advances for the period 1970/7. We also found that structural changes existed for all the sectoral groupings of loans and advances — the only exceptions being general commerce 1972/3 and the service sector in 1976/7.

These structural changes have been brought about partly because of the decisions of the Central Bank and partly by the state of general economic conditions. The fact that economic conditions have important roles to play implies that when attempts are being made to control the directions of loans, care has to be taken to bear in mind commercial banks' profit maximisation behaviour. Loans will inevitably go to the sector where demand is very strong. Sectoral share allocation may therefore not work when the primary objectives of banks are being sacrificed.

Directives of the Central Bank or any other authority for that matter are likely to work when directed at goals that create the least friction between national interest and the profit-maximising behaviour of commercial banks.

7 MERCHANT BANKING IN NIGERIA

J.K. Onoh and F.E. Anisiuba

1. Introduction

The term *merchant bank* is sometimes applied to banks who are not
merchants, sometimes to merchants who are not banks and sometimes
to houses who are neither merchants not banks.[1] This statement is not
true in Nigeria where merchant banks are required by the Banking
Decree 1969 to be incorporated and to be licensed as banks. This, *ipso
facto*, places merchant banks under the control, supervision and the
guidelines of the Central Bank of Nigeria.

Merchant banks are financial institutions. They engage in banking
operations of long-term nature. Primarily they are banks because they
accept deposit liabilities and own liquid assets like commercial banks.
Unlike commercial banks, merchant banks *cannot* create credit money.
Traditionally they finance foreign trade. But in recent times their
activities have widened. They can now issue and underwrite new securities and engage in such other miscellaneous activities like counselling,
feasibility and viability appraisals.

A large percentage of merchant banks' assets are kept in liquid form.
This is necessary if they are to meet their obligations such as paying
promptly the bills they had accepted. In Nigeria they are empowered to
maintain chequing deposit accounts for their corporate customers. The
maintenance of deposit accounts for corporate customers does not
however entitle them to generate credit money from such accounts.
The lack of credit-creating capacity distinguishes them from commercial banks.

Before the advent of institutionally established merchant banks in
Nigeria, the commercial banks performed the functions of merchant
banks and still perform those functions today. Compared with the
commercial banks, the volume of their activities is relatively small. The
low-activity rate of merchant banks reflects the state of the Nigerian
economy at present. Merchant banks engage in long-term activities and
the volume of long-term investment in real assets and heavy industries
has not increased significantly. These are the major areas of operations
of merchant banks. Most of the transactions up to date have been of a
commercial nature; primarily buying and reselling activities.

The primary objective of this chapter is to examine this relatively new institution in the Nigerian scene and to analyse its activities and its relative impact on the Nigerian economy. The statistical data provided by the Central Bank of Nigeria will form the foundation for the analysis.

Any comparison of the activities of merchant banks in Nigeria with those of other countries, especially those countries with well developed, efficient and really competitive financial market systems, will reveal a number of differences. For example, a Nigerian Federal Government body, the Nigerian Security Exchange Commission, values and prices the shares of public companies. In developed financial markets it is the job of the merchant and investment bankers. Merchant bankers in developed financial markets seek out buyers of securities and stand by to take up any unpurchased securities. In Nigeria securities are oversubscribed; investment bankers are not disturbed by the fear of unsold stocks.

In spite of the absence of a mature financial market, merchant banks in Nigeria have a part to play in new securities' issue. The public company whose security is to be priced makes a representation to the commission during a pricing session. Sometimes a company may not possess qualified people who are sufficiently versed in the technicalities of finance to make a meaningful representation. In situations of that nature merchant-banking services are called in. The investment bank will then argue along those lines it considers proper, fit and favourable in the fixation of the price of the stock. Primarily stock prices reflect an individual company's performance. An investment bank which is called upon to represent a company before the Nigerian Security Exchange Commission does not aim at inflating the price of the share but rather at bringing into focus the company's performance which will help to ascertain the real value of the share.

2. Historical Development of Merchant Banking in Nigeria

The history of the development of the business of merchant banking in Nigeria is a short one. Although there have been some forms of merchant banking activities in Nigeria as far back as 1960 when Philip Hill (Nigeria) Limited was established, the actual impact of this brand of banking is considered a phenomenon of the seventies.

As of now, there are six such banks in business in Nigeria. The Nigerian Acceptances Limited came into being through the merger of

Philip Hill and the former Nigerian Acceptances in 1969. The Nigerian civil war which lasted from 1967 to 1970 may have discouraged merchant banks from incorporating. In 1972 two more merchant banks incorporated probably to participate in the oil-boom economy which forecasters said was imminent. These were the UDT Bank (Nigeria) Limited, formerly the Union Dominion Corporation (UDC), reconstituted and licensed as a merchant bank in 1973, and the First National City Bank of New York (Nigeria) Limited. Both banks were incorporated and opened for business in 1974.

In the wake of businesses arising from the implementation of the Indigenisation Decree such as the increasing take-overs, pricings, bids, amalgamations, divestitures and the heavy turn-out of shares by companies attempting to meet the Indigenisation Decree provision, two more merchant banks were attracted into the Nigerian scene. These were the ICON Merchant Bank (Nigeria) Limited and the Chase Manhattan Merchant Bank. They were incorporated and opened for business in the first half of 1975.

Merchant banks originated in England in the eighteenth century. They served English merchants who engaged in relatively large-scale international trade in building up their businesses and images by lending their names to trade bills readily discountable by financial institutions. Gradually these 'merchant banks' specialised in foreign trade — export and import trade. Funds deposited by their clients were applied in foreign-trade activities and the clients received interests that varied with the profitability of foreign trade. Since the end of the civil war in Nigeria merchant banks compete with the commercial banks in the finance of foreign trade instead of supplementing such activities. Before the war they financed the exports of the marketing boards' produce. Such financing was considered risk free. But with the demand for forward sales contract of produce at the London market, before marketing boards could be financed, the Federal Government requested the Central Bank in 1968 to take over the financing of the marketing boards' produce. The consortia of merchant and commercial banks lost a lucrative business. With the loss of marketing board finance, merchant banks had to fall back to foreign trade finance in competition with the commercial banks.

The two areas in which the merchant banks have left impacts in the middle seventies are plant leasing and the floating of shares. The experience of Nigerian Acceptances in the provision of funds for industrial re-equipment has encouraged the emergence of an associated company, NAL Securities Limited which has the principal function of leasing facilities to customers.

3. Activities of Merchant Banks

(a) General Services of Merchant Banks

Whether in Nigeria, the United States of America or in the UK, merchant-banking operations are essentially the same. There may be some minor operational adjustments to reflect the historical experience and the realities of the environs where merchant banks may be located. Basically merchant banks (even where they are called investment banks) perform the same functions such as:

(i) Risk Bearing. Underwriting connotes risk-bearing. By presenting an issuer with a cheque for an agreed amount of shares, a merchant bank frees the company from the burden of finding investors for its offering. It also assumes the risk of adverse price developments during the distribution period. In principle merchant bankers charge fees for underwriting bonds. The full amount for the value of bonds so underwritten is never paid. If a merchant bank underwrites bonds with N20 million it may issue a cheque to the value of N19.7 million and retains N300,000 as service charge. If the prices of bonds so underwritten 'fall out of bed' during the distribution of the purchased securities the bank sustains losses. Underwriting involves risks. Merchant bankers analyse any bond they may wish to underwrite studiously before committing themselves.

(ii) Pricing of Securities. This is a thorny and sensitive job. Issuers usually want the lowest possible rate to attach to their debt issues, but investors want maximum yields. Similarly issuers would want the highest naira proceeds for their stock offering but investors would like to bargain prices. Merchant bankers strive to reconcile these conflicting objectives by gauging markets accurately.

(iii) Marketing Support. Not all security offers in which merchant bankers participate are underwritten. In some cases merchant banks confine their contributions to marketing support. This means that they agree only to use their skills in finding investors willing to purchase the securities being offered. They do not guarantee the successful placement of the issue. This kind of arrangement is employed by merchant bankers especially when marketing the securities of small or new unproven companies.

(iv) Price Stabilisation Function. This is normally carried out during the distribution phase. Merchant banks place an order to purchase any of the underwritten securities at a fixed price usually at or near that at which the issue is being offered publicly. By pegging the price at which they stand by to purchase the securities being distributed, merchant bankers hope to achieve two objectives:

(i) to ward off any precipitous drop in the securities' prices and the concomitant underwriting loss that would ensue, and
(ii) to maintain favourable publicity for the issue and thereby encourage its acceptance among investors.[2]

(v) Advice on Capital Structure. Determining just what percentage of their total capital structure should consist of long-term debt instrument is a problem for some companies. Merchant bankers have a lot to advise in this respect. The capital structure of a company will depend on the nature of business and on other factors which may be of analytical interest to merchant bankers.

Research into industry conditions and investor requirements enables them to advise on optimal capital structure. The merchant banks' knowledge of money and capital markets enables them to devise financing strategies to make companies achieve desired mixes of debt and equity in their capitalisations.

(vi) Feasibility Studies. Often investment bankers investigate the practicability of setting up a capital finance subsidiary for a company. For a group of companies contemplating a joint project, they will present financing options and point out the benefit of each, as well as its pitfalls.

(vii) Acceptance of Bills. A bill of exchange ordinarily (not technically) is a document drawn by a seller on a buyer in the international (or even domestic) market by which the buyer undertakes to pay the stated amount in the bill either at sight or at a given time.

To the sellers, the bill represents an acknowledgement of indebtedness by the buyer. But the lenders or investors of funds or even the seller of goods would not take such a bill as a good security for a loan or good investment security unless it is 'accepted' by a reputable finance house. Here the merchant banks come in.

As acceptance houses, they endorse bills of exchange arising from foreign trade as 'accepted' with their corporate seal and signature, thus making those bills very liquid and carrying low discounting charges.[3]

(viii) Counselling and Financial Services. The investment bankers (especially in the United States) have provided services in all phases of corporate finance, including advice on capital structure, issuance of short- and long-term securities, acquisitions, proposing and structuring of complex financial transactions.

They make comprehensive evaluation of the operations and financial posture of companies, conduct merger negotiations and prepare financial restructuring plans. Investment bankers provide counselling services, usually for a separate fee, in the following areas: acquisitions, divestitures, take-over defences, merger partners, fair market valuation and sinking fund purchases of public bonds.

The training and experience of investment bankers make them uniquely qualified to handle the above functions expertly. They have been continuously exposed to such activities and can draw on their wealth of experience and understanding of conditions of money and capital markets, especially the latter, to provide the services to their clients.[4]

4. Merchant Banking in the Nigerian Economy

(a) Credit Guidelines as Applicable to Merchant Banks

Under normal circumstances merchant banks, even though they come under the Nigerian Central Bank's supervision, are not supposed to be as strictly controlled as the commercial banks. However, because the merchant banks have trespassed into the areas traditionally considered to be of interest to the commercial banks they have provoked Central Bank directives and credit guidelines which differ slightly from those of commercial banks. In fact they now perform most commercial banks' functions except money creation.

Merchant banks have been granted licences in the hope that they will fill the credit gaps in the economy by adapting their operations to reflect the changing structure of the economy towards increased industrialisation. A dynamic economy requires wholesale banking, project development underwriting, medium- and long-term financing, equipment leasing and other specialised functions.

Contrary to these expectations merchant banks have operated as commercial banks in terms of projects financed, and the maturity pattern of their loans. It therefore became necessary to prescribe the following sectoral distribution and maturity pattern of merchant banks loans and advances.[5]

Table 7.1: Merchant Bank Sectoral Distribution of Loans and Advances

A. Productive sectors/sub-sectors	Share %		
	1976	1977	1978
(i) Production	60.00	60.00	64.00
Agriculture	6.00	6.00	4.00
Mining	2.00	2.00	2.00
Manufacturing	36.00	36.00	40.00
Real Estate and construction including owner-occupied buildings	16.00	16.00	18.00
Residental building	(-)	(5.00)	(5.00)
other	(-)	(11.00)	(13.00)
(ii) Services	10.00	10.00	6.00
Transportation and communication	8.00	8.00	4.00
Public utilities	2.00	2.00	2.00
B. Less-productive sectors/sub-sectors			
(iii) General Commerce	23.00	23.00	23.00
Exports	5.00	5.00	5.00
Imports	11.00	11.00	11.00
Domestic trade	5.00	5.00	5.00
Bills discounted	2.00	2.00	2.00
(iv) Others	7.00	7.00	7.00
Credit and financial institutions	3.00	3.00	3.00
Government	2.00	2.00	2.00
Miscellaneous	2.00	2.00	2.00
Total	100.00	100.00	100.00

The prescribed guidelines for the maturity of loans and advances and the distributions of the portfolio assets of merchant banks are as follows:

(a) A minimum of 50 per cent of total loans and advances shall be of medium- and long-term nature with maturities of not less than three years.

(b) A maximum of 10 per cent of loans and advances shall be of short-term nature maturing within twelve months.

(c) A maximum of 15 per cent of total assets shall be in equipment leasing business.

(d) Further, a minimum of 30 per cent of total funds raised from other banks shall be in liquid assets.

The directives took effect from April 1976. In 1977 there was no change in the sectoral distribution of loans and advances of merchant banks except that the guideline was specific about the percentage to be allocated to residential buildings. The aggregate loan and advances was increased in the fiscal year 1978/9. Lending to agriculture was reduced because of the Central Bank's new Agricultural Credit Scheme. Lending to manufacturing increased by 4 per cent and construction by 2 per cent.

(b) Development of the Assets of Nigerian Merchant Banks

The assets of Nigerian merchant banks include the following:

(a) Cash balances with the Central Bank;

(b) Balances held with banks and offices within and outside Nigeria;

(c) Loans and advances to banks in Nigeria and to other customers; under loans and advances fall also such items as money at call outside Central Bank, bills discounted and payable in Nigeria and factored debts, and

(d) Merchant banks' investments in Nigeria which include treasury bills and certificates, balances with call money fund, bankers unit fund, stabilisation securities, certificates of deposit and equipment on lease.

Table 7.2 Merchant Banks' Assets (N'000) (End of Year Figures)

Year	Cash balances with the Central Bank (1)	Balances held with banks and offices in Nigeria and abroad (2)	Loans and advances (3)	Investments in Nigeria (4)	Other assets (5)	Total assets (6)
1968	—	56	2,464	1,390	682	4,592
1969	175	3	1,562	2,757	516	5,013
1970	92	6	1,292	5,064	1,380	7,834
1971	42	78	7,702	3,484	5,087	16,394
1972	73	408	13,994	6,620	8,114	29,210
1973	—	625	13,988	9,614	7,103	31,330
1974	1,147	4,593	23,483	16,123	14,998	60,344
1975	14,410	5,801	80,684	18,253	18,253	186,138
1976	6,153	1,984	77,974	44,622	37,367	168,100
1977	18,581	10,419	109,543	82,319	98,064	318,926

Source: Compiled from Central Bank of Nigeria, *Economic and Financial Review* of various years.

Table 7.2 reveals the trend in the development of merchant banks' assets in the last ten years; it can be seen that they have increased astronomically. From N4.5 million at the end of 1968 the value of assets reached an all-time high of N318.9 million in 1977, an increase of about 70 per cent. The value of assets of merchant banks is equal to the liabilities in the balance sheet.

The increase in the merchant banks' total assets is closely associated with the growth of the Nigerian economy, especially with the oil boom which started to register positive impacts on the Nigerian economy from 1974. Between 1973 and 1974 the assets of merchant banks almost doubled. From a modest N31.33 million in 1973 their total assets rose to N60.34 million in 1974, an increase of almost 100 per cent. This was the year that Nigeria's external reserves could support about 25 months of imports. The reserve level was unprecedented in the annals of Nigeria's external reserves. The increase in government revenue, a consequence of the petro-money, led to an expanded government programme and a general stimulation of the economy. All financial institutions especially the merchant and the commercial banks benefited from the stimulated economy and expanded their activities.

Until 1976 the merchant banks were not restricted in their operations. But having failed to undertake activities in the areas of long-term financing, project development underwriting, equipment leasing and other specialised functions, the merchant banks rather engaged in those activities traditionally reserved for commercial banks and attracted the Central Bank's credit guidelines (Table 7.1).

Before the credit guidelines came into force in 1976 merchant banks distributed their assets and liabilities in those activities considered to be most convenient and profitable; any meaningful discussion of the distribution of merchant banks' assets therefore must examine the assets' distribution pattern before and after the mandatory guidelines. Before the credit guidelines came into force in April 1976 merchant banks' assets were mainly distributed in cash balances with the Central Bank, loans and advances and unnamed assets classified as 'other assets' in their balance sheets.

In 1976, the merchant banks' loans and advances dropped from the N80.68 million position to N77.97 level. The merchant-bank guidelines of 1976 stipulated that not less than 50 per cent of total loans and advances should be of medium- and long-term nature with maturities of not less than five years, while a maximum of 10 per cent of total loans and advances of merchant banks was imposed on lendings of short durations, that is, twelve months. The restriction as to the nature of loans and advances and the percentage ceilings on maximum and minimum lendings was expected to influence the percentage of the merchant banks' total lendings in terms of their assets. The objectives of the merchant-bank guidelines do not appear to have been achieved completely especially in terms of the restructuring of the maturity patterns of loans. As Table 7.3 reveals the maturity pattern of loans and advances did not change significantly after the guidelines came into force.

Table 7.3: Structure of Loans and Advances of Merchant Banks

	May 1976		June 1976	
Structure of loans	N	%	N	%
Loans maturing in not more than twelve months	64.6	70.2	63.3	65.7
Loans maturing between one and three years	12.6	13.7	21.0	21.7
Loans maturing after three years	14.8	16.1	12.1	12.6
Total	92.0	100.0	96.4	100.0

Source: Central Bank of Nigeria, *Monthly Report* (June 1976).

The distribution of loans and advances for the month of June 1976 in favour of lendings of short-term duration (twelve months) did not meet the 10 per cent ceiling of all loans and advances imposed by the guidelines. The decline from 70.2 per cent for short-term lendings in May 1976 to 65.7 per cent for the month of June 1976 was not substantial and exceeded by far the 10 per cent limit imposed for short-term lendings. While medium-term lendings increased from 13.7 per cent in May 1976 to 21.7 per cent in June 1976, long-term lendings declined from 16.1 per cent to 12.6 per cent in the corresponding period. The percentage of loans and advances for medium- and long-term lendings for the month of June 1976 totalled 34.3 per cent as against the prescribed minimum of 50 per cent for both short- and long-term lendings. Generally as indicated in Table 7.2 there was a general decline in loans and advances in the year 1976, the year the merchant-bank guidelines came into force, as against the level which prevailed in 1975. Although loans and advances rose to N109.5 million at the end of December 1977, the total assets which reached the level of N318.93 million, increased at a faster rate than loans and advances.

An aspect of merchant banks' assets which experienced a phenomenal rise was cash balances with the Central Bank and balances with banks and offices in Nigeria and abroad. The balances abroad are certainly in foreign exchange or in easily monetisable foreign securities or bills. At the end of 1977 merchant banks' cash balances with the Central Bank amounted to N18.58 million as against N6.15 million in 1976, an increase of 200 per cent. Balances with banks and offices in Nigeria and abroad increased from N1.98 million in 1975 to N10.42 million in 1977, an increase of nearly 500 per cent.

The volume of acceptance business handled by the merchant banks and classified under 'loans and advances' has declined considerably over the years. The percentage of acceptance business in terms of the total loans and advances has been on the decrease. The decline in the use of bills reflects the increase in the use of cheques for settling indebtedness. Restrictions on foreign trade influence domestic businesses adversely and this has its consequence on bill generation and acceptance and discount businesses. Generally the merchant banks handle only a small fraction of the country's total acceptance and discounting businesses. Commercial banks have been engaged in the business of acceptance and discounting over the years and have consolidated their position on account of their comparative number and accessibility.

Merchant banks' investments in Nigeria appear to have received a strong stimulus from the merchant-bank guidelines. Before the guidelines came into force in 1976 merchant banks' investments amounted to N18.25 million in 1975. When the guidelines came into force the investment level rose to N44.6 million, an increase of over 100 per cent. In 1977 it rose further to N82.32 million. The increase in the merchant banks' investment level is attributable to the introduction of merchant bank money-market instrument, the Bankers Unit Fund, which the merchant banks invested in heavily from the beginning of 1976. The enforcement by the guidelines of equipment-leasing business on the merchant banks explains further the significant increase in merchant banks' investments.

Other unspecified assets of the merchant banks as shown in column (5) of Table 7.2 form a large component of merchant banks' assets. Investment in 'other assets' is sensitive to fluctuations and does not maintain a predictable trend.

(c) Developments of Merchant Banks' Liabilities

The liabilities of Nigerian merchant banks include the following items:

(a) capital accounts,

(b) balances held for banks within and outside Nigeria,

(c) money at call from banks in Nigeria,

(d) certificates of deposits issued by merchant banks,

(e) loans and advances from banks within and outside Nigeria and from other sources,

(f) deposits – demand and time, and

(g) other liabilities.

The merchant banks' total liabilities have grown considerably over the years. Table 7.4 shows the growth in their liabilities and reveals the major sources of their funds.

Table 7.4: Merchant Banks' Liabilities (N'000) (End of Year Figures)

Year	Capital accounts	Balances held for banks in and outside Nigeria	Money at call from banks in Nigeria	Certificate of deposits Issued	Loans and advances from other banks in Nigeria, banks outside Nigeria and others	Demand, time and savings deposits	Other liabilities	Other liabilities
	(1)	(2)	(3)	(4)	(5)	(6)	(7)	(8)
1968	1,500	–	–	–	79	2,169	844	4,592
1969	1,500	–	–	–	72	2,655	786	5,013
1970	1,530	–	–	–	9	4,386	1,909	7,834
1971	1,550	–	760	–	–	7,175	6,909	16,394
1972	1,641	4,820	–	–	–	10,796	11,980	29,210
1973	2,285	4,040	–	–	1,144	14,448	9,413	31,330
1974	7,000	12,994	3,500	–	52	22,049	16,749	60,344
1975	11,178	12,250	25,200	–	2,000	63,449	74,717	188,794
1976	9,795	10,000	8,630	18,750	10,250	61,737	48,938	168,100
1977	10,891	7,484	16,802	32,358	8,500	85,896	156,995	318,926

Source: Compiled from Central Bank of Nigeria, *Economic and Financial Review* of various years.

The merchant banks' ability to acquire new assets will depend on their incurring new liabilities. Their ability to incur liabilities has widened especially in the seventies. Since 1971 three new sources of funds have been added. They are (b), (c) and (d) of the items listed above as liabilities.

However deposits (demand and time) still constitute the greatest single and steady source of fund (liabilities) of the merchant banks. What at first sight appears to be the major single item of funds is but an amalgam of spread-out liabilities of various maturities and classified under 'others' in Table 7.4. The certificate of deposits introduced recently is gaining in strength; it was first applied in 1976 and by the end of 1977 it ranked second and constituted roughly 10 per cent of the aggregate of merchant banks' liabilities. Money at call, balances held for banks and loans and advances are prone to cyclical financial disturbances arising from both monetary and fiscal policies and they cannot be relied upon by the merchant banks as steady sources of funds. Capital account has experienced a reasonable increase especially since 1974 but still it contributes less than 3 per cent of merchant banks' funds as of 1977.

5. Problems and Prospects of Merchant Banking in Nigeria

(a) Problems. Although the number of merchant banks in Nigeria is relatively small, merchant-banking business is very limited both in volume and diversity. The lack of sufficient business to justify their existence has forced them to invade those areas which traditionally are reserved for the commercial banks.

In 1962, a consortium of banks, including merchant banks, financed the produce bills of the Northern Nigerian marketing board. In the following year the banks began to finance those of the Western Nigerian marketing board. In 1968 this activity was taken over by the Central Bank because of the demand for advanced sales contract by the consortium of bankers before any produce bill could be financed. It is believed that the commercial banks which formed the bigger partner of the consortium influenced the decision to demand sales contract before produce bills' financing. The consequence of that demand affected the merchant banks at a time when they were about to find their feet.

Before the establishment of merchant banking in Nigeria commercial banks conducted operations of merchant-banking nature. They accepted and discounted bills and they helped in the distribution of bonds and stocks of public limited liability companies during the indigenisation exercise. The pricing and valuation of stocks which is traditionally the concern of merchant banks were taken over by the Capital Issues Commission in 1973, a Nigerian Federal Government body (now called the Nigerian Security Exchange Commission). This was a serious encroachment into the functions of merchant banks. The argument of national economic interest has been used to justify the encroachment but the fact is that the action has helped to cripple the development of the capital market. The capital market should be encouraged to operate freely under the mechanics of demand and supply forces.

Nigerian merchant banks suffered another set-back in 1977. In accordance with the Nigerian Enterprises Promotions Decree of 1977, many firms were required to sell additional stocks to the public. It was feared that not only would the Lagos Stock Exchange be unable to handle the issues within the stipulated deadline but that shares might be undersubscribed. This fear later proved unfounded. Financial institutions were asked to form a contingency underwriting consortium to mop up whatever shares that may remain unsold. The idea was that of the Capital Issues Commission. The Nigerian Industrial Development Bank, Nigerian Bank for Commerce and Industry, National Provident Fund and National Insurance Corporation of Nigeria were to form the consortium to the exclusion of merchant banks which should have been called upon to lead the underwriting consortium; underwriting is the job of merchant banks. It may be argued that the funds of the merchant banks were grossly inadequate for such a large-scale underwriting operation but they could have borrowed funds from the commercial banks through the use of certificates of deposit.

Another impediment which frustrates merchant banks' operations is the Nigerian Stock Exchange's rigid regulations on the listing of stocks. This has affected the volume of business handled by the merchant banks as only very few corporations have so far qualified for listing. The development of the capital market has been correspondingly hampered. It often has been argued that the rigid listing conditions of the Stock Exchange are meant to ward off the participation of disreputable firms and to preserve investors' funds. The argument is good but there is no zero risk in investment. The investor has to take a modicum of risk when he is laying out his funds. He must balance risk, safety and yield. He should not expect 100 per cent safety and a sizeable return on his investment at the same time.

In addition to the above impediment poor financial habits in Nigeria have contributed to the merchant banks' low volume of activities. The average businessman in Nigeria still prefers a small business over which he alone presides as the 'chairman/managing director'. He is reluctant to incorporate his company even though he may be aware of the advantages of such an incorporation. An incorporated business attracts more funds from the capital market and debt instrument of longer term duration from merchant banks. The average Nigerian businessman is reluctant to take advantage of the benefits of incorporation if it will mean an erosion of his power over the management of the company so incorporated.

(b) Prospects. With the creation of the Economic Community of West African States (ECOWAS), there is every likelihood of increased trade within the sub-region. In addition, since Nigeria has been chosen as the headquarters of ECOWAS, Lagos will be a major financial centre where settlement of bills arising from transactions within ECOWAS will take place. Lagos will become a financial centre and will play the dominant role Antwerp played at one time in Europe or the present financial roles of Wall Street and London. There is a bright future for merchant banking in Nigeria especially in the areas of acceptance and discounting of bills arising from increased trade between the ECOWAS countries.

Recently, the government has accepted the recommendations of the Financial System Review Committee that the merchant banks be empowered to operate chequeing accounts for their corporate customers. The government also has restored dealership in foreign exchange to the merchant banks and it also has accepted in principle that special tax incentives in the form of special scale of capital allowances should be given to merchant banks for equipment leasing to make it a regular feature of merchant-banking activity.[6] These are recent developments which augur well for the future operations of the merchant banks.

Other developments which favour merchant-banking business in Nigeria are the reorganisation of the Stock Exchange and the newly acquired powers of the State and local governments and parastatal corporations to float securities. These new securities will need handling and the merchant banks will have a major role to play in this respect. Moreover, with the rapid increase in industrialisation and its attendant increase in the export and import business, the volume of acceptances and discounting is bound to rise to the comfort of the merchant banks.

Notes

1. T.M. Rybczynci, 'The Merchant Banks', *The Banker's Magazine*, vol. CCXVI, no. 1557 (London, August 1973), pp. 240-54.

2. 'Investment Banking Services', *Management in Nigeria* (Lagos, December 1975), p. 48.

3. R.S. Sayers, *Modern Banking*, 7th edn, (Oxford University Press, London 1972), p. 50.

4. R.P. Kent, *Corporate Financial Management*, 3rd edn (Richard D. Irwin Inc., Homewood, Illinois, 1969), p. 436.

5. Central Bank of Nigeria, *Monthly Report* (Lagos, June 1976).

6. Federal Ministry of Information, *Federal Military Government's Views On The Report Of The Committee On The Nigerian Financial System* (Lagos, 1977), p. 10.

8 THE NIGERIAN MONEY MARKET

J.K. Onoh and N. Diala-Ukah

1. Introduction

A money market could be described as a market for short-term credits. The precise meaning or definition of the compound adjective 'short-term' is not very definite. The usual tendency is to define money-market instruments as having a maturity of three months or under. In practice, however, instruments of longer duration are found in many of the world's money markets. In the London money market, for example, bills vary in currency from one to six months.[1] The commercial papers in the New York money market have lives of three, four or six months; while there are also United States treasury bills which run for three, six or twelve months.[2] In Nigeria the treasury certificate offers an example of an instrument which could have more than three months' currency. Section 5 (1) of the Treasury Certificate Decree 1968 states that:

The Treasury Certificates are issued in sums of five hundred pounds or a multiple of it and shall be payable at par at a date not more than twenty-four months from the date thereof.[3]

This means, therefore, that treasury certificates could have a currency of up to two years. What is short term, therefore, and what is not, can be said to be a function of both conventions and statutory definitions.

Short-term credit in itself must be as old as human society. An economic unit which is 'resource short' at a point in time goes to a surplus unit for some consideration to obtain short-term accommodation. In the money market, the commodity traded is money. This exercise will concern itself more with the organised money market, as opposed to the unorganised and informal one.

The organised money market came into existence as a result of the need to finance domestic and international trade and other economic activities. There was always the need for purchasers (especially importers) of a commodity to defer payment until the goods ordered were received, and the conflicting wish of the suppliers (especially exporters) of those commodities to receive payment immediately they parted with

118

the items in question. The gap so created was bridged by someone[4] undertaking to pay the seller immediately the face value of a bill of exchange (drawn on and accepted by the purchaser) less some consideration,[5] and keeping the bill or note till the maturity date when the purchaser, according to the agreement, would be able to pay. As time went on, specialised acceptors, known as accepting houses, emerged and added more credibility to the bills. To make for orderly transactions in these instruments, statutory provisions were introduced in various countries which helped to develop the use of commercial papers.

Government short-term debt instruments came into vogue originally as a means of securing funds from the public. In the United Kingdom, for example, the treasury bill was introduced through the advice of Sir Walter Bagehot who suggested that for the government to succeed in raising loans from the public on a commercial basis, its debt instrument should be as short as the popular bills of exchange. Hence the treasury bills were fashioned accordingly. As the market developed, the monetary authorities saw in the treasury bills a valuable weapon for monetary control.

Money-market instruments can be grouped into two broad groups:

(a) commercial papers – which are those instruments originating from non-government institutions such as bills of exchange, promissory notes, etc., and

(b) treasury papers – issued by the government, such as treasury bills, treasury certificates, etc.

The money market does not only embrace the purchasers and suppliers of short-term credits, it also includes those institutions or organisations that bring them together. Here again, the lines of demarcation between the demanders, the suppliers and the intermediaries in the money market cannot be drawn so sharply. In fact, they need not be drawn at all since every member of the market could be found on any of the three sides at any moment.

On the demand side the following are engaged in money-market operations:

(i) Central Government:[6] when it sells treasury bills in the open market,

(ii) Local governments: (depending on the laws) – when they sell short-term debt instruments,

(iii) Individuals and corporate bodies: when they discount a bill of exchange or note, or when they borrow short from banks, and

(iv) The banks and discount houses: when they rediscount treasury bills or certificates and eligible commercial bills at the Central Bank, or when they borrow short. Discount houses are habitual borrowers on call from the banks.

On the supply side we again find:

(i) Central Government: when it buys bills in the open market,

(ii) Local governments: when they invest in treasury bills or certificates (if allowed by the law),

(iii) Individuals and corporations: when they buy treasury bills or certificates and

(iv) The banks and the financial intermediaries: when they discount commercial bills, buy treasury papers or lend short.

The role of intermediation in the money market is normally the job of financial intermediaries. In the United States, for example, treasury bills are subscribed to by a few dealing banks and finance houses who later sell to both banks and non-bank buyers. The structure of the intermediaries in a country's money market depends on its history and laws. There are no special discount houses in either Nigeria or the United States but they exist in the United Kingdom.

2. The Development of the Nigerian Money Market

The main argument of the opponents of the establishment of the Nigerian Central Bank was the nonexistence of a developed money market in Nigeria. Mars was of the opinion (during the Second World War) that a central bank in Nigeria could play a significant role in stabilising the economy. But he cautioned that a central bank could only be effective if a market for government securities existed. Such a market takes a long time to develop.[7]

In their study of 1953 Newlyn and Rowan rejected completely the argument of Mars in favour of a central bank in Nigeria: 'The view that a Central Bank can (in Nigerian circumstances) promote economic stability by monetary management, is, to put matters tersely, nothing but an illusion.'[8] They argued strongly that a central bank in Nigeria would not be able to achieve economic stabilisation since the Nigerian economy was a very dependent one, where destabilising forces frequently originated abroad and where lack of developed financial institutions made central bank control ineffective. They argued that private investment in Nigeria was low and that the expatriate banks in Nigeria would not depend on the Central Bank as the lender of last resort since they had access to the London money market. They therefore advocated the establishment of an economic development-oriented central bank in Nigeria.

The issue was also debated in Parliament. In reply to a motion introduced by the Hon. K.O. Mbadiwe in the first session of the House of Representatives on 21 March 1952, for the establishment of a central bank in Nigeria, the then Financial Secretary stated that the government was opposed to the idea for certain reasons, one of which was the absence of a stock and money market.[9] The Fisher Report which came up as a result of this motion also rejected the idea of a central bank for various reasons including the absence of a Nigerian money market and good access to the London money market. On the other hand, the Report of the mission from the 'International Bank for Reconstruction and Development' (IBRD) rejected Fisher's report and recommended the establishment of a central bank in Nigeria with limited powers which would help in economic development and the establishment of a money market. It can, therefore, be said that it was the establishment of the Central Bank of Nigeria in 1959 which brought about the existence of a Nigerian money market.

3. Nigerian Money Market Instruments

(a) Treasury Bills

The treasury bills were introduced in Nigeria by the Treasury Bills Ordinance of 1959 which came into force on 19 March 1959. Under the Ordinance, the Government of Nigeria was empowered to borrow money by issuing treasury bills through the Central Bank. The maximum permissible issue to be outstanding at any time was limited to 10 per cent of the estimated revenue of the Federal Government during the year then current.[10] They were to be issued in multiples of £1,000 and a subsidiary legislation[11] provided for issue either by tender or at a fixed rate of discount. In practice, treasury bills are issued for three months[12] at a fixed rate of discount after four days' notice has been given in the gazette. The Treasury Bills Ordinance, 1959 also stated that the treasury bills should be denominated in Nigerian pounds after Sections 16 and 18 of the Central Bank of Nigeria Ordinance 1958 came into operation, and until that date should be denominated in currency issued by the West African Currency Board.[13] The Ordinance also specified the Regulations guiding the issue of treasury bills and the powers of the Minister of Finance in this connection. For example:

> The Minister of Finance, after consultation with the Central Bank may make regulations to prescribe or provide for —
> (a) the preparation, form, mode of issue, mode of payment and cancellation of Treasury Bills;
> (b) the issue of a new Bill in lieu of one defaced, lost or destroyed;
> (c) such other matter as may seem to him necessary for the purpose of carrying this Ordinance into effect.[14]

Therefore that the issue of treasury bills by the Central Bank of Nigeria in the form prescribed by regulations made under Section 10 shall be sufficient evidence on behalf of any holder thereof that the authority of the Minister of Finance has been given for such issue in accordance with Section 3, and that such issue has been made in accordance with this Ordinance.

Several amendments to the Ordinance have taken place. For example:

(a) The Treasury Bills (Amendment) Act, 1961, increased the upper limit of issue to 20 per cent of government revenue,

(b) The Treasury Bills (Amendment) No. 2 Act, 1961 gave the minister the right to loan the proceeds from the treasury bills to regional governments,

(c) The Treasury Bills (Amendment) Act, 1962 repealed the Treasury Bills (Amendment) Act, 1961, and increased the upper limit of treasury bills to 40 per cent of expected government revenue,

(d) The Treasury Bills (Amendment) Decree 1967 increased this limit further to 50 per cent,

(e) The Treasury Bills (Amendment) Decree 1968 repealed the above and extended the limit to 85 per cent,

(f) The Finance Decree 1969 made the outstandable amount of treasury bills equal to the estimated revenue of the Federal Government in the year current but not exceeding it; that is, 100 per cent of it. This decree repealed the 1968 Decree,[15]

(g) The Treasury Bills (Amendment) Decree 1970 amended this provision further by substituting the words 'One hundred and fifty per cent of the estimated revenue retained by the Federal Government and gross revenues of the States'.[16]

4. Issues and Subscriptions

The first issue of treasury bills was for £4m in April 1960. A further £2m were issued in the next month and £3m in June bringing the total issue outstanding to £9m. Thereafter sufficient new bills were issued each month to replace those maturing, leaving the total unchanged until June 1961, when the total issue was successively increased until it reached the £18m mark in November of that year.

Table 8.1: Treasury Bills — Issues and Subscription (N'000)

Year	Issues (total for each year)	Central Bank	Commercial banks	Individual	Savings institutions	Statutory boards and corporations	State and local governments	others[a]
(1)	(1)	(2)	(3)	(4)	(5)	(6)	(7)	(8)
1963	194,000	876,706	35,816	556	35,664	23,432	11,600	3,432
1964	261,000	125,266	53,054	638	31,200	24,756	16,336	11,338
1965	292,000	153,406	51,356	1,170	31,200	48,740	2,120	4,008
1966	404,000	221,858	54,692	1,548	45,956	61,876	14,040	4,030
1967	592,000	456,792	38,980	1,260	36,296	30,976	20,304	7,392
1968	810,000	432,518	287,842	1,090	37,590	34,710	9,482	7,410
1969	1,150,000	376,040	608,848	3,430	29,298	4,420	30,502	97,462
1970	1,878,000	769,612	771,572	9,974	46,648	37,854	35,196	203,736
1971	2,640,000	1,516,172	553,930	8,950	37,580	86,736	60,410	200,736
1972	2,464,000	1,674,156	445,366	10,454	44,906	110,760	41,722	138,636
1973	2,464,000	1,318,898	700,237	16,344	66,255	142,944	13,138	189,876
1974	2,464,000	694,590	1,413,891	16,384	65,752	84,718	45,545	132,016
1975	2,464,000	358,178	1,602,173	12,192	110,754	37,232	14,734	328,827
1976	2,510,000	328,236	1,699,826	13,491	72,612	32,962	65,466	297,397
1977	3,471,603	513,261	2,170,376	20,382	141,042	57,774	67,786	176,982

Source: *Economic and Financial Review* of various years.

[a] Others include federal, state, local government and companies.

From Table 8.1 it can be seen that the issue of treasury bills has been on the increase. A number of factors influence treasury bills' issues. They include:

(a) The government revenue level which is the base for calculating the amount of treasury bills to be issued,

(b) The percentage stipulations of the amended Treasury Bills Ordinance, 1959, and

(c) The effects of the civil war.

From 1972 the level of issue of the treasury bills was kept constant until 1975 (see Table 8.1). It is not difficult to guess at the reason for this change in policy. By 1972 the Federal Government was experiencing a sudden 'boom' from oil revenue coupled with the attendant problem of managing the money. The policy was therefore designed to save the monetary authorities some trouble in monetary management and debt servicing. The oil boom reached its climax in 1974.

Table 8.2: Treasury Bills — Issues and Subscription in %.

(Figures have been rounded and may not in some cases add up to 100)

Year	Issues	Central Bank	Commercial banks	Individuals	Savings institutions	Statutory boards and corporations	State and local govts.	others
1963	100	45.2	18.5	0.3	16.3	12.0	6.0	1.2
1964	100	47.8	20.2	0.2	11.7	9.4	6.0	4.3
1965	100	52.5	17.6	0.4	10.7	16.7	0.7	1.4
1966	100	54.9	13.5	0.4	11.4	15.3	3.5	1.6
1967	100	77.2	6.6	0.2	6.1	5.2	3.4	1.2
1968	100	53.4	35.5	0.1	4.6	4.3	1.2	0.9
1969	100	32.7	52.9	0.3	2.5	0.4	2.7	8.5
1970	100	41.0	41.1	0.5	2.5	2.0	1.9	10.8
1971	100	57.4	21.0	0.3	1.4	3.3	2.3	7.6
1972	100	67.9	18.1	0.4	1.8	4.5	1.7	5.6
1973	100	53.5	31.7	0.7	2.7	5.8	0.5	7.7
1974	100	28.2	57.4	0.7	2.7	3.4	1.8	5.4
1975	100	14.5	65.0	0.5	4.4	1.5	0.6	13.3
1976	100	13.0	67.0	0.5	3.0	1.0	2.6	12.0
1977	100	16.3	68.9	0.6	4.5	1.8	2.1	5.6

Table 8.2 is of much more interest to us. It allows a quick picture of the important purchasers of treasury bills. From the data available the most important buyer of treasury bills is the Central Bank of Nigeria with an average consumption of 48.16 per cent over the years. It is closely followed by the commercial banks, which include the Bank of Commerce and the NIDB with an average of 30.7 per cent. Therefore an average of about 79 per cent of the treasury-bills market is dominated by these two groups. This has earned them the title of the 'big two' in the market. The statutory boards and corporations are the third

most important group with an average share of 6.89 per cent; followed by savings institutions with 6.06 per cent; the 'others' with 5.3 per cent; State and Local Governments with 2.5 per cent and individuals with 0.38 per cent. There is some inverse relation between the Central Bank's and commercial banks' holdings of treasury bills. When the holdings of commercial banks increase that of the Central Bank decreases and vice versa.

5. Treasury Certificates

(a) Legal Provision

The treasury certificate came into existence during the Nigerian civil war as an additional debt instrument for financing the war. It was created by the Treasury Certificates Decree 1968 (Decree No. 40) which came into effect on 6 August 1968. Sub-section 1 of the Decree states that:

> The Commissioner is hereby authorised to borrow by the issue in Nigeria of Federal Government Treasury Certificates, and the Central Bank of Nigeria, when authorised in writing by the Commissioner, may for the purpose issue in Nigeria, within the terms of the authority and subject to any direction given by him, such Federal Government Treasury Certificates together with such further Treasury Certificates as shall be required to pay off at maturity Treasury Certificates already lawfully issued.[17]

Under the Decree the principal sums represented by any treasury certificates outstanding at any one time shall not exceed 50 per cent of the estimated revenue of the Federal Government during the year then current.[18]

The treasury certificates are issued in sums of £500 or in multiples of that sum and are payable at par at a date not more than 24 months from the date thereof.[19] This means therefore that treasury certificates can have a currency of up to two years.

The Finance Decree 1969 amended the provisions of S.1 (2) of the Treasury Certificates Decree 1968 by substituting the word 'sixty' for 'fifty' with effect from 16 March 1969. There were no other amendments in the Decree until 1975 when the Federal Government decided to phase out the treasury certificates outstanding in the market. Consequently from April 1975 there were no more issues.[20]

But as a result of the over-liquidity which this policy and other similar policies (such as keeping the issue of the treasury bills fixed at N2,464,000 per annum and the abolition of the call-money scheme on 1 July 1974)[21] caused among commercial banks and other investors in the market as well as the fall in oil revenue in 1976, the treasury certificates were reintroduced in 1976[22] to help solve the problem of idle cash in the hands of investors.

(b) Issues and Subscriptions

Treasury certificates were first issued in December 1968. Tables 8.3 and 8.4 reveal the developments of the treasury certificate issues over the years. Tables 8.1 and 8.3 reveal that treasury certificates are not as important in the money market as are treasury bills.

Table 8.3: Treasury Certificates — Issues and Subscription (N'000)

Year	Issues (total for each)	Central bank	Commercial banks[a]	Individuals	Savings institutions[b]	Statutory boards and corps.	Private Companies and acceptance houses	State and local govts/ 'others'
1968	20,000	198	19,194	8	–	200	600	–
1969	132,000	28	128,874	356	160	200	2,382	–
1970	170,000	16,920	148,400	182	298	100	1,900	2,300
1971	197,800	31,730	161,379	66	236	69	3,600	720
1972	208,000	58,490	144,771	106	–	–	4,139	494
1973	198,000	25,457	163,210	34	1,188	–	7,881	317
1974	208,000	32,623	170,886	62	1,255	–	2,718	456
1975	140,000	749	178,057	–	1	–	1,193	–
1976	600,000	51,243	540,845	18	1,200	–	6,444	250
1977	600,000	58,000	540,661	–	–	–	–	–

Sources: Central Bank of Nigeria, *Economic and Financial Review*, vol. 8, no. 1 (June 1970) p. 94 and vol. 13, no. 2 (December 1975), pp. 70-1.

Notes: [a]Commercial banks include Nigerian Industrial and Development Bank Ltd, Nigerian Bank for Commerce and Industry Ltd

[b]Savings institutions include mutual savings and loans groups, credit organisations, co-operative societies and insurance companies, Federal Savings Bank, pension and provident funds, schools, unions etc.

Table 8.4: Treasury Certificates — Issue and Subscription.
(% Distribution computed from Table 8.3)

Year	Issues	Central Bank	Commercial Banks	Individuals	Savings institutions	Statutory boards and Corporations	Private Companies acceptance houses	State and local Govts' 'other'
1968	100	1.0	96.0	0.04	—	—	3.0	—
1969	100	0.02	98.0	0.3	0.1	0.1	1.8	—
1970	100	10.00	87.3	0.1	0.17	0.05	1.1	1.3
1971	100	16.04	81.6	0.03	0.11	0.03	1.8	0.3
1972	100	28.12	69.6	0.05	—	—	1.98	0.2
1973	100	12.12	82.4	0.01	0.6	—	3.98	0.16
1974	100	15.68	82.2	0.03	0.6	—	1.3	0.2
1975	100	0.53	127.2	—	—	—	0.85	—
1976	100	8.50	90.1	—	0.2	—	1.10	0.04
1977	100	9.70	90.1	—	—	—	—	—

The highest issue of the treasury certificates amounted to N208m in 1972 and 1974 while the treasury bills went up as high as N2,640m in 1971. The lowest level of the treasury bills was £405,000 in 1968 as against the treasury certificates' level of £10,000 in the same year. One reason for the supremacy of the treasury bill over the certificates is the greater legal backing it enjoys from the Federal Government. The amount of treasury bills outstanding at any point in time is far greater than that of the treasury certificates. Treasury bills outstanding are over 100 per cent of expected revenue of the Federal Government,[23] while treasury certificates outstanding are only 60 per cent.[24] It is no wonder therefore that the Federal Government found the latter easier to phase out than the treasury bill.

Table 8.4 shows clearly that the treasury certificates' market is dominated by the commercial banks with an average subscription of 90.53 per cent, over the eight years of treasury certificates issue. This contrasts with the treasury bills market which is dominated by the Central Bank. Second in importance in the certificates market is the Central Bank with an average subscription of about 10.53 per cent between 1968 and 1977.

5. The Call-Money Scheme

The call-money scheme was a device introduced into the Nigerian money market in 1962 whereby commercial banks placed their idle cash at call with the Central Bank for which some interest was paid.

This interest was normally not declared by the Central Bank but in practice it was always 1 per cent below that on a treasury bill. The funds so collected were invested by the Central Bank in treasury bills. Through this means therefore, the Central Bank was able to make some profit out of the scheme which was the difference between the interest earned on the treasury bill and that paid on call money, less other expenses. Commercial banks found the scheme profitable since it provided an earning for their idle cash. The scheme grew into a force to reckon with in the money market especially in the early seventies (see Table 8.5). The amount deposited on call rose by about 52 per cent in 1970 while the amount withdrawn rose by about 50 per cent. Thereafter deposits and withdrawals continued to rise yearly. The figures for 1974 are for the half year till June. The scheme was abolished with effect from 1 July 1974.

Table 8.5: Call Money Fund with Central Bank (N'000)

Year	Amount received	Amount withdrawn	Operating balance December
1963			6,950
1964	938,360	392,810	9,710
1965	325,440	328,340	6,510
1966	292,310	292,242	6,720
1967	345,600	340,470	5,850
1968	388,280	385,260	8,830
1969	509,980	506,620	12,190
1970	773,290	757,240	28,240
1971	859,972	864,720	24,292
1972	961,174	949,997	34,200
1973	964,597	954,017	40,730
1974	763,298	709,116 [a]	309,658

Source: Central Bank of Nigeria, *Economic and Financial Review* of several years.
[a]Call Money Fund was abolished on 1 July 1974.

6. Money at Call Outside Central Bank

Beside the money at call with the Central Bank, commercial banks also placed money on call with other commercial banks and finance houses. Unlike the balances with the call money fund, money at call outside the Central Bank is classified under 'Loans and Advances' in the commercial banks' statement of assets and liabilities while the former is grouped under 'investments'. Statistics of money at call outside Central

Bank became available from 1963, although there was money at call outside the Central Bank before then. Like any other advance it earned interest for the lenders and became another profitable avenue for channelling idle cash. It should not be confused with 'balances with other banks'.

Table 8.6 gives some insight into the amount of business involved in money at call outside the Central Bank. It reveals only the upper and lower limits of the monthly deposits but says nothing about average deposits or skewness of the monthly distributions. It is, therefore, no adequate basis for comparison, but the very high upper limit of 1975 may be connected with the shortage of investment outlets which characterised the Nigerian economy in that year.

Table 8.6: Money at Call Outside the Central Bank of Nigeria

Year	Highest monthly balance	Lowest monthly balance
1963	2,170	100
1964	2,736	602
1965	4.482	1,618
1966	6,000	2,492
1967	5,560	2,430
1968	6,790	1,760
1969	7,130	1,220
1970	6,520	—
1971	5,870	530
1972	8,694	1,600
1973	4,824	467
1974	9,012	1,897
1975	33,500	1,764

Source: Central Bank of Nigeria, *Economic and Financial Review*, June 1970, pp. 42-4 and December 1975, pp. 28-9.

7. Produce Papers

The produce papers were an instrument created by the Nigerian Government in the early sixties for financing the marketing boards. In the fifties the Nigerian marketing boards secured funds by borrowing in London on the security of their sterling assets there. The sterling assets, however, were soon exhausted as a result of the use of the boards' funds for development projects by the Regional Governments.[25] As a result of the depletion of the sterling assets alternative means of finance was inevitable. The Western Region Marketing Board took the lead by raising part of its finance for the 1960/1 season by ways of bills from the British Bank for West Africa which in turn was financed by a consortium of twelve London banks headed by N.M. Rothschild and Sons. This arrangement was, however, a temporary measure. In the 1962 Budget speech, the Minister of Finance announced the introduction of the produce paper which empowered the Central Bank to finance the marketing boards.

The produce papers were bills drawn on the Nigerian Produce Marketing Company Limited, which was the only authorised seller of all marketing boards' produce. Under the arrangement the marketing boards met their requirements for cash by drawing 90-day commercial bills of exchange supported by a sales contract on the Nigerian Produce Marketing Co. Ltd. Upon acceptance by the company, the marketing boards would then discount the bills with their financing consortia of banks and acceptance houses. On its own part the Central Bank of Nigeria offered a rediscount facility for the produce bills so discounted. At the height of the produce bills' existence three different consortia involving the majority of both indigenous and expatriate banks in Nigeria financed the produce trades of Northern, Western and Mid-Western Region Marketing Boards.[26]

The produce-bills market was also short lived. By 1964 it became inactive following the cocoa crises in the Western Region. The Cocoa Producers Alliance withdrew cocoa from the world market because of the low price offers, a consequence of the forward contract method of marketing the produce. The leading foreign banks withdrew from the bill finance in the absence of a sales contract and because of the looming Nigerian political crisis. The Central Bank of Nigeria then stepped in and made direct loans of £15m to the Western Nigeria Marketing Board. In the 1965/6 and 1966/7 seasons the Central Bank made similar loans to the Northern Nigeria Marketing Board to finance the purchase of ground-nuts. By 1968 the Central Bank had made a credit of N69.2 million to the marketing boards. Produce bills were last re-discounted in June 1968. They died a natural death thereafter.

8. Certificates of Deposit and Bankers Unit Fund

These instruments were introduced in 1975 with a view to helping the banks out of their investment problems. The merchant banks appear to be more active in that area of investment. The merchant banks subscribed a total of over N51 million worth of Bankers Unit Fund, and

N13.8 million worth of certificates of deposits in the first half of 1976.

9. Stabilisation Securities

The stabilisation securities came into force as one of the monetary policy prescriptions of the 1976/7 Federal budget. Under this policy, the Central Bank of Nigeria, as part of the government's determined effort to reduce inflationary pressures in the economy and to mop up some of the excess liquidity in the banking system, is to issue and allocate to the banks an instrument known as the *stabilisation securities*. The amount to be considered in the allocation of stabilisation securities shall be the increase in *savings deposits* over the level outstanding on 31 March 1976, arising from deposits in individual savings accounts not exceeding N20,000 each. The stabilisation securities would earn an interest of 4 per cent or any such rate as may be determined from time to time by the Central Bank. The securities are nonnegotiable, nontransferable and do not count as part of commercial banks' liquid assets. There are no statistics as to their issues and allocations.

10. Commercial Bills

These include bills of exchange and promissory notes. Before the introduction of government securities they constituted the main lending system of the commercial banks. By December 1959 bills discounted by the banks stood at £606,000. At that time none of the instruments discussed above had been introduced. The Treasury Bills Ordinance came into effect only in 1959 but it was not issued until 1960. As can be seen from Table 8.7 bills payable in Nigeria form the bulk of the

Table 8.7: Bills Discounted (N'000)

Year	Amount by end of December	Percentage payable in Nigeria	Year	Amount by end of December	Percentage payable in Nigeria
1959	1,212	n.a.	1967	36,384	99.45
1960	2,542	n.a.	1968	5,114	83.65
1961	2,234	n.a.	1969	4,490	74.88
1962	6,196	n.a.	1970	5,854	73.39
1963	14,888	99.48	1971	10,024	70.29
1964	30,102	99.22	1972	8,006	50.89
1965	42,060	97.69	1973	11,098	58.67
1966	60,104	99.01	1974	14,011	79.72
			1975	28,215	95.23

Source: Central Bank of Nigeria, *Economic and Financial Review* of several years.

bills discounted by the commercial banks in Nigeria. There has been some decline in bills discounted especially during the civil war years. Merchant banks are also involved in the discounting of commercial bills. Table 8.7, however, does not include discounting by merchant banks but the greater part of the discounting is performed by the commercial banks.

11 Rediscounting Activities of the Central Bank of Nigeria

The treasury bills, treasury certificates and the produce papers are the only rediscountable instruments at the Central Bank. Rediscounting is a device through which the Central Bank lends to the commercial banks and discount houses who have liquidity problems. In practice, only the specified liquid instruments are rediscountable. Instruments such as stabilisation securities and long-term bonds etc. are technically not rediscountable.

Table 8.8: Rediscounting Operation of the Central Bank of Nigeria
(N'000)

Year	Treasury bills		Treasury certs.		Produce bills		Total
	Amount	%	Amount	%	Amount	%	
1963	26,766	27.4	−	−	70,832	72.6	97,598
1964	53,036	47.2	−	−	59,310	52.8	112,346
1965	78,416	70.0	−	−	33,540	30.0	111,956
1966	79,642	65.3	−	−	42,330	34.7	121,972
1967	113,220	44.3	−	−	142,290	55.7	255,510
1968	202,310	94.9	−	−	10,840	5.1	213,150
1969	414,706	98.3	−	−	71,000	1.7	421,806
1970	882,588	100	−	−			882,588
1971	1,735,384	97.7	41,076	2.3			1,776,460
1972	1,783,740	99.9	1,600	0.1			1,785,340
1973	2,321,166	99.5	12,127	0.5			2,333,293
1974	1,375,330	99.0	13,854	1.0			1,389,184
1975	395,939	100	6	0			395,945

Source: Central Bank of Nigeria, *Economic and Financial Review* of several years.

The rediscounting of produce and treasury bills at the Central Bank was a very important source of financing the seasonal rise in advances of the commercial banks in the early sixties. Until 1968 the two were the only eligible papers in Nigeria. In 1968 the treasury certificates were introduced but were not rediscounted until 1971. Produce bills were last rediscounted in 1968. It was the major rediscounted paper in 1963 and 1964 (about 73 per cent and 53 per cent respectively). After 1964 it became less rediscounted than the treasury bills until 1967 when it took prominence again; thereafter it diminished. From 1968 the treasury bills accounted for not less than 94 per cent of the rediscounted instruments in Nigeria. The treasury certificates which were first rediscounted in 1971 attained their highest percentage that same year (see Table 8.8), that is, 2.3 per cent. They form a minor instrument in the rediscount market.

12 Conclusion

The Nigerian money market, no doubt, is developing fast but not as fast as one would wish. The views of Fisher, Newlyn and Rowan and other critics that a central bank in Nigeria would not achieve economic stabilisation through monetary policies and that a central bank in Nigeria would be an expensive luxury has been disproved. For one thing, these critics saw the Nigerian Central Bank as one that would function exactly like the Bank of England or the federal reserve system in the United States, or perhaps underestimated the amount of support it would get. However, the first decade of the Central Bank witnessed the development of an active money market in Nigeria and the corresponding development of a capital market and a stock exchange. By 1960, some strong indigenous banks and financial institutions, such as the African Continental Bank, the National Bank of Nigeria, Agbonmagbe Bank, etc., had been established. Many others, like the Co-operative Bank of Western Nigeria, the Co-operative Bank of Eastern Nigeria Ltd, Pan African Bank Mercantile Bank, etc., sprang up in the different states of the Federation. These banks depended on the Central Bank as the lender of last resort and therefore could be controlled easily.

Considerable legislation controlling the financial intermediaries has been passed such as the Banking Decree of 1969, the Insurance Decree of 1976 and the credit guidelines. The seventies saw the Indigenisation Decrees of 1972 and 1977. These were attempts by the Nigerian Federal Government to transfer the control of the Nigerian economy to the hands of Nigerians. To this effect the Government has acquired about 60 per cent equity share (controlling shares) of all the expatriate banks and financial institutions in Nigeria. This has made the control of the Nigerian money market much easier by removing the danger of the foreign banks' non-compliance with regulations.

Again noteworthy in the annals of the Nigerian money market was the 'overliquidity fetish' of the finance houses between 1973 and 1975. The position of the banks was most notable. The monthly average volume of liquid assets increased by 29, 52 and 76 per cent respectively in 1973, 1974 and 1975. The liquidity level of 1975 was three times that of 1970. The liquidity ratio, on the average, was 66.0 per cent during the period compared with the mandatory 25 per cent. This problem was brought about by the decrease of investment outlets for the banks caused by the stopping of the call-money scheme in 1974 and the decision of the Government in the April 1975 budget speech to phase out the treasury certificates while keeping the issue of treasury bills unchanged. Another cause of this over-liquidity could be mentioned, that is, the unwillingness of the commercial banks to lend long or to comply with the credit guidelines by lending more to the 'production and services' sector, which to them would be more risky and less profitable. This over-liquidity of the banks not only meant that they had to maintain idle cash, but also that they would be a source of further monetary instability were they to expand their credit to anywhere near the full potential of their resources. That would be equal to pouring petrol on the already blazing fire of inflation in the country.

The Federal Government of Nigeria introduced a very unconventional policy in the 1975 budget speech, the objective of which has not been very clear. Thenceforth, 'commercial banks' holdings of Development Loans Stocks would be treated as part of their liquid assets and the Central Bank will guarantee the repurchase of such stocks at par on demand.'[27]

The money market, by nature, is an indicator of the degree of monetary stability in an economy, and contributes significantly to the achievement of such stability. The Nigerian money market therefore has still a major role to play in this direction.

Notes

1. R.S. Sayers, *Modern Banking*, 7th edn (Oxford University Press, London, 1967), pp. 46-7.
2. Ibid, p. 272.
3. Treasury Certificates Decree 1968, S. 5(1).
4. 'Someone', in the earliest days of the bill history, meant individual merchants. The businesses gave rise to some of the present day big finance houses in England.
5. Usually not less than the difference of the face amount and its present value calculated at the market rate of interest.
6. The Central Bank is seen as an agent of the government.
7. For Mars's views see C.V. Brown, *The Nigerian Banking System* (George Allen and Unwin, London, 1966), p. 127.
8. Ibid.
9. House of Representatives Debates, First Session, vol. 1, p. 377.
10. Ordinance No. 11 of 1959, *Laws of Nigeria*, 1959, S. 3(2).

11. Treasury Bills Regulations, 1960; Legal Notice No. 36 of 1960 commencing on 17 March 1960.

12. Treasury bills may be issued for up to twelve months (Treasury Bills Ordinance, 1959, S. 8(1).

13. Ibid., S. 8(1).

14. Ibid., S. 10.

15. Finance Decree 1969, *Laws of the Federal Republic of Nigeria*, 1970, S. 1.

16. The Treasury Bills (Amendment) Decree 1970, S. 1.

17. The Treasury Certificates Decree 1968, S. 1(1).

18. Ibid., S. (1(2).

19. Ibid., S. 5(1).

20. Central Bank of Nigeria, *Economic and Financial Review*, vol. 13, no. 2 (December 1975), p. 71.

21. Ibid., p. 63.

22. No new issues between April 1975 and September 1976.

23. Treasury Bills (Amendment) Decree 1970, S. 1.

24. Finance Decree 1969, S.1.

25. By 1955 the sterling assets amounted to £74m, but by 1962 they were only £0.5m.

26. The Eastern Region Marketing Board never benefited from the arrangement.

27. General Yakubu Gowon's Budget Speech, 1975/6, *New Nigerian* (2 April 1975), p. 11.

9 THE NIGERIAN CAPITAL MARKET

F.O. Okafor

1. Introduction

Capital inadequacy often has been identified as a major limiting factor in the industrial development of Nigeria.[1] The real nature of this limitation, unfortunately, has not been fully investigated. A feeling of capital inadequacy could arise from actual shortages of investment funds in an economy. It could however be illusory and merely epitomise frustrations occasioned by unnecessary impediments to the free flow of investment funds. Such impediments are indicative of underlying rigidities and imperfections in the capital market.

This chapter will attempt an in depth analysis of the structure, development and operations of the Nigerian capital market with the objective of establishing a basis for assessing the merits of the market in terms of facilitating the flow of investment funds in the economy or demerits in terms of hindering such flows. A section of the chapter will be devoted to a short comment on terminology. This will be followed by a detailed discussion of key institutions and facilities in the market for privately negotiated funds. Lastly, the Nigerian securities market will be analysed. The concluding section will explore possible institutional and regulatory reforms capable of improving the operations of the market.

2. Conceptual Framework

Some facilities usually exist within every economy for the creation, custodianship and distribution of financial assets and liabilities.[2] These facilities constitute the financial markets. The capital market is a subsection of the financial market. It deals with long-term investments and operations necessary for financing them. Discussions on the capital market very often have tended to be restricted to transactions connected with the issue and sale of long-term securities. A plausible explanation for this myopia is the fact that in advanced market economies, firms raise long-term funds mostly by issuing securities.

The feature of negotiability accounts for the popularity of securities

136

as media for raising long-term funds. A lot of transactions in long-term funds are however not covered by negotiable instruments even in the most developed market economies. In developing countries like Nigeria, only a negligible proportion of business enterprises issue marketable securities. A predominant percentage of firms raise funds through direct negotiation with potential suppliers of capital. In a broad sense therefore, the capital market covers all services rendered by institutions and facilities which exist for mobilising long-term funds and for channelling such funds to ultimate users. Two distinct segments of the market are therefore identifiable in Nigeria:

(a) Long-term securities market which is a market in titles to productive assets and constitutes the centrepin of the capital market. It includes the new-issue market and the stock exchange which exists for the resale of existing securities.

(b) Market for negotiated long-term finance (NLF) which is descriptive of all dealings in long-term funds not covered by negotiable instruments. Such dealings involve direct negotiation between suppliers and users of long-term funds.

Each segment of the capital market is given overt expression by the activities of individual/institutional users and suppliers of funds as they interact with financial institutions which intermediate in the investment process.

3. Negotiated Financing

The traditional market in Nigeria for privately negotiated funds found early expression in the operations of village credit societies and thrift (*esusu*) unions. These local institutions provided the bulk of financing for members and non-members for social and economic investments. Money-lending is part of the economic life of traditional society. The operating procedures of these early institutions were shrouded in secrecy. Loans of various maturities could be arranged, but there was no meaningful term structure in the rates of interest charged. The system is becoming less significant in the face of specialised modern financial institutions but will ever be remembered for the notoriety of its penal rates of financial charges.[3]

(i) Early Institutions

Modern institutions for term financing did not start in Nigeria until fairly recently. The late start is attributable to one major reason; before independence in 1960 and even till the early seventies, the economic life of the nation was dominated by foreign business interests. Most firms then in the country were essentially outposts of multinational corporations. The resident managers of the Nigerian outposts had very limited powers generally and no powers in particular to raise long-term funds locally. Major investment and financing decisions were taken at headquarters located in the metropolitan countries from where periodic appropriations were made to meet the long-term financing needs of the outposts. The Nigerian establishments therefore did not feel the need to develop local facilities for term financing.

Early attempts at establishing such facilities were therefore geared primarily towards servicing the public sector. The earliest institution established for this purpose was the Nigerian Development Loans Board which was inauguarated in 1945, to provide medium-term capital. Following constitutional developments, the board was decentralised in 1949 along regional lines. Regional Development Corporations were later established to provide long-term financing. The institutions which unfortunately were inadequately funded, were not sufficiently profit oriented and did not extend financing on purely economic considerations. They failed to provide the desired catalyst for economic development. Whatever financial accommodation they provided tended to be directed towards ailing government establishments or were converted into political instruments for the dispensation of party patronage.

(ii) Pressure for Development Finance

Demand for investment capital grew tremendously in both the public and private sectors of the Nigerian economy towards the approach of independence. By the end of 1959, both the Federal and Regional Governments had net deficites in their current and capital accounts and by 1963 the accumulated deficits in these accounts had grown to N454.8 million.[4] The growth in public sector deficit accounts was matched by an upsurge in private-sector demand for capital. Indigenous business enterprises were growing in number and scale of operations, a phenomenon which made self-financing more difficult. There were also perceptible changes in the attitude of foreign enterprises towards locally generated term financing. With the approach of political independence, expatriate firms started to perceive early warnings of the need to incorporate local interest in their capital structure. The pressure of demand for long-term capital was therefore very apparent and must have influenced the government's introduction of some measures between 1960 and 1964 which had far-reaching implications for the development of the Nigerian capital market. Two of such measures were directed to the market for securities while the third measure was directed to the introduction of development banking into the economy.

(Iiii) Institutions for Development Financing

Development banking, in the Nigerian context, is a generic term which is descriptive of all financial institutions that exist primarily for providing medium- and long-term financing for other enterprises. In addition to this primary function, most of them provide technical and managerial support or advice for client organisations if only to protect their investments. Most of these institutions in Nigeria are controlled either exclusively or to a great extent by government. Unlike their predecessors, however, they are usually incorporated as limited liability companies and consequently enjoy a large measure of autonomy in operations. Institutions for development financing in Nigeria fall into two broad categories. The first group comprises development or finance companies. The other covers the development banks. By the end of 1977, there were 19 of both types of institutions in Nigeria.

A. Development Banks

Development banks are specialised development finance institutions that cater for enterprises within specified sector(s) of the economy. All the four development banks in Nigeria are owned almost exclusively by the Federal Government and are generally better funded than the development finance companies. The premier institution is the Nigerian Industrial Development Bank (NIDB) which was incorporated in 1964 out of a reconstruction of the then Investment Company of Nigeria Ltd (ICON).[5] Following the reconstruction the Nigerian Government acquired controlling interest in the bank. Initially, the bank restricted its financing operations to large-scale industrial and mining sub-sectors. Gradually the scope of operations was expanded to accommodate public-sector establishments as well as business in such sub-sectors as tourism and furniture fabrication. In the case of public-sector establishments, the bank insists on dependable evidence that such enterprises are sufficiently profit oriented and independent of direct government control.

Three additional development banks were established in the seventies. Two of them, the Nigerian Bank for Commerce and Industry (NBCI) and the Nigerian Agricultural and Co-operative Bank (NACB) were set up in 1973. The NACB was set up to finance agriculture and agro-based industries – a very vital but stagnating sector of the Nigerian economy which curiously was not covered by NIDB operations. The bank extends financing to *bona fide* farmers either directly or through state government and/or co-operative associations for on-lending to such farmers.

The NBCI is authorised to finance a wide range of industrial and commercial enterprises and to undertake merchant banking and acceptance business. A primary motivation behind the establishment of the bank was to facilitate the smooth implementation of the Nigerian Enterprises Promotion Decree (NEPD) 1972. Hence the bank was expected to and did provide a lot of financial support to Nigerians for the take-over of enterprises affected by the provisions of the Decree.

In 1975, the Nigerian Building Society was reconstituted into a housing development bank – the Federal Mortgage Bank (FMB) by the Federal Government. Discussion on the FMB is limited to the foregoing passing mention partly because of the relative youth of the institution but mainly in consideration of its very specialised nature and limited scope of operations.

(i) Funding

Development banks require adequate funding in order to mediate effectively in long-term investment activities. They rely heavily on three main sources, equity capital, reserves and long-term loans from the Federal Government.

During the period 1973/4, which was the first year of combined operations, the resources available to the three development banks totalled N42.16 million, of which N40.91 or 97 per cent was from long-term sources. The breakdown of the figure is given in Table 9.1.

One striking feature of Table 9.1 is the intensity of the dependence on loans from the Federal Government. The loans are in most cases interest free, or are granted on very liberal interest and repayment terms. The relative importance of government loans to the capitalisation of the banks has increased over the period 1970-6. This development is illustrated by the capital structure of the NIDB. At the end of its first full year of operations following the reconstruction (31

December 1976) the NIDB had long-term loans of N4 million from the Federal Government against a long-term capitalisation of N8,990,574. Federal Government loans therefore constituted roughly 44.5 per cent of the bank's long-term resources in that year. The comparable figure for 1973 was 51.2 per cent. By 1976, the relative contribution had jumped to 83.1 per cent. Much as the bank is authorised to borrow up to three times the value of the sum of its share capital, reserves and subordinated loans, undue reliance on Federal Government long-term loans creates a false sense of sufficiency. This contention is underscored by the decreasing contribution of accumulated reserves to the finances of the banks. The relative youth of the NBCI and NACB may be responsible for the low contribution of reserves to the long-term funds of both banks. One is hard pressed to find any defence for the unimpressive performance of the NIDB in that regard. In 1966, some 5.5 per cent of the bank's long-term funds were internally generated. There was a brief period of sustained improvement up to 1971 when about 11.4 per cent of the bank's long-term funds derived from that source. Since then, the bank's dependence on internally generated resources has rather been marginal. In 1976, it was only 3.97 per cent.

Table 9.1: Sources of Funds for Development Banks in Nigeria for the 1973/74 Period.[a]

Source	NIDB (Nm)	NBCI (Nm)	NACB (Nm)	TOTAL (Nm)
Share capital	4.50	10.00	1.00	15.50
Reserves	1.89	−	−	1.89
Shareholder fund	6.39	10.00	1.00	17.39
Federal govt loans	13.27	−	4.00	17.27
Other loans	6.25	−	−	6.25
Total long-term sources	25.91	10.00	5.00	42.16
Other accounts[b]	1.24	.01	−	1.25
Total funds	27.15	10.01	5.00	43.41

Source: *Annual Report and Accounts* of the banks for the period.

Notes: [a] The year ending for the NIDB is 31 December, while that of NBCI and NACB is 31 March. The figures therefore refer to balance sheet figures for NIDB as at 31 December 1973 and for NBCI and NACB the figures are for 31 March 1974.

[b] Other accounts refer to current liabilities, future taxation, etc.

(ii) Operating Guidelines

In a sense significant interbank differences exist as regards operating policies. Such differences naturally arise from underlying peculiarities in the scope of operations and sectoral preferences of each bank. There are however a number of fundamental policy issues in which all the banks share an indentity of interest. The most significant of such issues are summarised below.

(a) Investment Criteria.[6] In general, the banks endeavour to invest in projects which are economically desirable, technically feasible and commercially viable.

(i) Economic Desirability

Projects are presumed to be economically desirable if they show clear evidence of developmental value to the country in such broad areas as employment generation, local raw material utilisation, and conservation of foreign exchange through import substitution. As a result of this consideration, the banks do not patronise projects whose activities conflict in any way with stated government policies on industrialisation, fiscal policies and policies in other areas.

(ii) Technical Feasibility

Technical feasibility refers essentially to the existence of environmental and intracompany conditions necessary for the implementation of a project such as the availability of requisite factor inputs, including managerial and technical manpower.

(iii) Viability

The banks do not measure commercial viability from the narrow viewpoint of making accounting profits. Rather they insist on a proven ability to generate enough cash from operations to enable a firm repay loans, build up reserves and pay reasonable dividends to the owners.

(iv) Sound Capital Structure

A sound capital structure requires a proper balance between the main components of the capital structure. Because of this consideration, the banks expect the promoters to provide a reasonable fraction of the risk capital of a business. Minimum equity participation expected from project promoters varies from 25 per cent in the case of the NACB to 40 per cent for NIDB. The policy of withholding financial support until a specified percentage of the prescribed promoter's stake is paid up is adopted by all the banks.

(b) Terms of Investment. Industrial finance could be provided in the form of loan or equity capital. A strong preference for loan financing has been demonstrated by the banks. Loans are granted for periods up to 15 years at more favourable rates of interest than prevailing capital-market rates. Repayment terms are sufficiently flexible to accommodate varying interests and circumstances of clients. In most cases, a period of grace is allowed and very rapid repayment schedules are discouraged except where rapid cash accruals justify special consideration.

(c) Security Requirements. Conservatism permeates the approach of the banks to loan management. Most of their loans are secured on tangible assets. In addition, they generally insist on having first legal mortgages or floating charges on the assets. In the absence of such protection, they insist on third-party guarantees from financial institutions or government agencies. Some form of security requirement is definitely necessary for term loans if only for the psychological feeling of protection which they engender. However, the most dependable form of security is the ability of a client to create a repayment capacity through a judicious utilisation of the funds. Unless security is defined in this broader perspective, the banks will not only deny funding to viable projects but will continue to be obsessed with the bogy of risk aversion which is mainly responsible for the preponderance of loan capital in their investment portfolios.

(iii) Performance

The performance of the banks in promoting industrial development is summarised in Table 9.2.

Table 9.2: Cumulative Sanctions and Disbursements of the Nigerian Development Banks up to 1976

Bank	Sanctions[a]		Disbursements[a]		Disbursement ratio[b] (percentage)
	No. of projects	Value (Nm)	No. of projects	Value (Nm)	
NIDB	na	186.08	na	76.10	40.9
NBCI	77	76.00	28	7.00	9.1
NACB	99	103.00	76	22.80	22.1
Total		365.08		105.90	29

Source: Extracted from the *Annual Reports and Accounts* of the various banks for the period up to 1976.

Notes: [a] The naira values of sanctions and disbursements are in some cases gross values. Some sanctions which eventually lapsed were converted or fully liquidated. Consequently, net sanctions and net disbursements ought to be less than the figures given above.

[b] Disbursement ratio is derived by dividing the value of disbursements by the corresponding value of sanctions.

Table 9.2 shows that the impact of the banks has not been very impressive. Cumulative value of sanctions (approvals) up to 1976 for the three
institutions was only N365.08 million which by that year was less than
N5 *per capita.*[7] Apart from the low value of sanctions, the disbursement ratio has been deplorably low. A low disbursement ratio is indicative of one of two situations. It could indicate avoidable lapses in the
initial selection of projects. It could underscore the existence of bureaucratic rigidities in the release of funds. Whatever the reason, the practice
ultimately forces the banks to hold a very substantial part of their
assets in low income yielding short-term assets. This practice in combination with limited involvement in equity financing has been largely
responsible for the unimpressive profit performance of the NIDB.

B. Development Companies

Development companies complement the activities of the development
banks. Like the latter they supply equity and loan capital for financing
new and existing enterprises. Many of them started operations in the
mid-seventies. Their operating policies in such vital areas as precondi-
tions for financial assistance, terms of investment, disbursements, supervision and security requirements are very similar to those of development banks.

Unlike the development banks, however, they cater for a wider range
of industrial groups in both the public and private sectors. Figures of
total investments by these companies are not available. A quantitative
evaluation of the promotional impact of their activities therefore is not
attempted. There is no doubt, however, that some of them are making
impressive contributions.

Up to March 1976, one of these companies, the New Nigerian Development Company (NNDC) made a total investment of N25 million in
64 different projects. Its net profit before tax for the fiscal year 1975/6
was N3.8 million compared with N2.1 million in the preceding period.

The importance of investment companies does not, however, lie
necessarily in the nominal size of industrial finance provided by them.
Their importance in the Nigerian economy derives more from the fact
that they cater for medium-scale enterprises which have neither developed the financial stature necessary for successful issue of securities
nor satisfied some of the stringent conditions prerequisite for consideration by the development banks. In addition some of them render other
developmental services like serving as holding companies for State

government business enterprises. They are more in touch with and render continuous managerial and technical assistance to their clients in all stages of project formulation and implementation.

C. Securities Market

A passing mention was made earlier to important measures which the Federal Government took in the early sixties that facilitated the development of a market for long-term securities in Nigeria. The first of such measures was the introduction in 1959 of the government's novel experiment of floating loan securities; the other was the establishment of the Lagos Stock Exchange. Before discussing these developments, the difference between the new issue and the secondary market for securities will be explained.

Transactions in the new-issue market involve activities connected with the issue or sale of new securities by government or corporate enterprises. The stock exchange is typical of the resale market, which exists for the sale or purchase of existing securities. Operations in the stock exchanges do not therefore normally result in a new accretion of funds to organisations whose securities are being traded. New issues are marketed through public offers or by private negotiation with potential buyers. In the resale market, only securities which are listed on an exchange can be traded in that exchange.

(i) Development of the New-Issue Market

Public issues of securities were very rare events in Nigeria before 1960. Private transfers of securities by companies then existing in Nigeria may conceivably have taken place. Such transfers however must have been very severely limited. The first public issue was the 3¼ per cent Nigerian Government Registered Stock 1956-61 valued at N600,000.[8] The issue was essentially a stopgap measure by the colonial authority. Regular issues of Federal Government bonds started in 1959 with the floatation of three securities valued at N4 million. The issue was such a huge success that it was oversubscribed by N1,712,000.[9] Since then, yearly issues have been maintained. The value of each issue is tailored to the treasury needs of the Federal Government.

(ii) Range of Securities Offered

Apart from Federal Government bonds a limited range of industrial securities are offered in the new-issue market. These include industrial

146   *The Nigerian Capital Market*

bonds, preference stock and equity stock (shares). In 1978 the first state government loan stock was floated. This was the N20m, 7 per cent First Bendel State of Nigeria Loan Stock 1988. Though the overall success of that offer has not been assessed, there are indications more State governments and parastatal organisations are likely to take advantage of powers granted to them recently (1977) to float securities directly.[10]

Table 9.3 summarises the types and value of all public issues of securities in Nigeria from 1962-77. Within the period a gross total of 141 government and industrial securities was placed in the new-issue market for a total consideration of N2,092.06 million.[11] The dominance of Federal Government loan stock is evident from the table. Government loan securities accounted for a greater percentage of total value of new issues. Equity stock came second while industrial loan and preference securities accounted for the rest.

Table 9.3: Public Issues of Securities 1961-77

Year of issue	Government stock		Industrial Securities				Total value
			Pref. stock and bonds		Equity stock[a]		
	No.	Value (Nm)	No.	Value (Nm)	No.	Value (Nm)	(Nm)
1961	3	20.00	–	–	–	–	20.00
1962	2	14.00	3	5.47	3	10.00	29.47
1963	3	30.00	1	0.60	1	1.05	31.65
1964	4	40.00	1	0.50	3	4.002	44.502
1965	3	30.00	1	2.60	1	0.30	32.90
1966	3	28.00	1	1.40	–	–	29.40
1967	4	40.00	–	–	–	–	40.00
1968	4	40.00	–	–	–	–	40.00
1969	3	30.00	–	–	1	1.75	31.75
1970	4	40.00	1	0.50	3[b]	4.58	45.08
1971	3	60.00	–	–	5	27.40	87.40
1972	3	60.00	–	–	7	9.46	69.46
1973	6	120.00	–	–	12	14.30	134.30
1974	3	60.00	–	–	11	16.70	76.70
1975	6	450.00	1	8.00	1	1.41	459.41
1976	2	400.00	4	28.00	4	13.34	441.34
1977	3	415.00	–	–	17	63.70	478.70
TOTAL	59	1,877.00	13	47.07	69	167.992	2,092.062

Source: Extracted from the Central Bank of Nigeria, *Annual Report and Statements of Account* (1961-77).

Notes: [a] The number and value of equity issues given above include both new offerings and supplementary issues.

[b] One of the securities, the ordinary shares of New Nigeria Bank, was not listed on the Lagos Stock Exchange.

In developed market economies, industrial bonds dominate the new-issue market in terms of frequency and value of issues. The experience in Nigeria has been contrary to this norm. Between 1961 and 1970 only six industrial bonds were issued through public offer. The frequency of such issues has not increased even in the wake of the country's drive towards indigenising the ownership of the economy. Within the 16-year period (1961-77) the average annual frequency of public issues of industrial loan securities was less than one. The apparent lack of popularity of industrial loan securities could be attributed to two main reasons.

(i) The very concept of public offerings is relatively new in the country. Offers of securities are mainly geared towards broadening the equity base without which successful issues of loan stock cannot be embarked upon.

(ii) Returns on equity securities have been very high in the country. The incidence of corporate failures, on the other hand, has been relatively low.

As a result of the fixed and relatively low rate of returns industrial bonds have very limited appeal. Nigerian investors have not fully appreciated the lower risk exposure inherent in bond ownership.

(iii) Dominance of Government Loan Stock

The dominant position of government loan securities in the Nigerian capital market is evident from Table 9.4. This is due partly to the frequency of government new issues of securities but mainly to the existence of legislative measures which support the market for government securities. Among these legislative measures are: the Income Tax Management Act, 1961 which confers tax-free status on pension and provident funds that maintain at least one-third of their total investment in government securities (50 per cent for those approved after 1961); the Trustee Investment Act, 1962 which empowered trustees to invest in Government stocks and in industrial securities provided such securities are quoted on the exchange. Since very few industrial securities were quoted until recently the Trustee Investment Act, 1962, had the ultimate effect of forcing all trust funds to be invested in Government stocks. The other public policy measure is the Insurance (Miscellaneous Provisions) Act 1964 which requires insurance companies to invest at least two-fifths of all funds from risk premium in Nigerian securities, one-quarter of which must be held in Government stocks.

As a result of these measures, the demand for Government loan bonds comes mainly from financial institutions and government agencies. A large proportion of such bonds has continued to be held by provident and pension funds as well as other savings type institutions. Holdings by individual investors have been very negligible in proportionate terms. However, in absolute terms, they have grown from N0.35 million in 1970 to N1.65 million in 1977. The growth reflects the increasing avidity of Nigerians for opportunities to invest in securities. Up to the end of 1970 public issues of industrial securities were very limited. In relative terms, issues of equity shares were more substantial than industrial bond issues both in terms of value and in terms of frequency. Public offering of equity securities was given a big boost by the Enterprises Promotions Decree (NEPD), Phase 1, 1972 and NEPD, Phase II, 1977. Though companies affected by provisions of the decree had some options, many sought compliance through public offers of their equity stock. As a result and/or in anticipation of the decrees, a total of 57 equity securities valued at N146.31 million was unloaded on the Nigerian new-issue market between 1971 and 1977 (Table 9.3). Of this amount, 31 securities valued at N66.18 million were new issues. The rest represented supplementary offerings, which accounted for about 55 per cent of total value of all issues of equity shares made during the period.

(iv) Marketing of New Issues

Demand for industrial securities, particularly shares, has been very strong in Nigeria. The need to develop elaborate marketing organisations for new issues has therefore not been very apparent. Before 1970, only three industrial securities offered for public subscription in Nigeria were not fully subscribed.[12] When the NEPD 1972 was promulgated there was some apprehension within the country and outright scepticism in the foreign press about the ability of the investing public in Nigeria to absorb the anticipated volume of new securities to be issued, but the response to the issues failed to justify the initial scepticism. Almost all new issues made in compliance with NEPD 1972 were oversubscribed. Public response has continued to be strong with respect to the increased volume of new issues made in compliance with NEPD Phase II (1977).

(v) Issuing Houses

Public issues are handled on behalf of companies by merchant banks that undertake issuing business. There were by the end of 1978 five merchant banks in the country.[13] Three of them, ICON Limited (Merchant Bankers), Nigerian Acceptances Limited and Nigeria Merchant Bank Limited (formerly UDT) are issuers for most public offers of securities. Their primary job is to provide technical advice on new issues, serve as receivers and assist in the process of share allotment. They have not been hard pressed for underwriting facilities probably as a result of the underlying strength in public demand for securities. Where undue pressure is anticipated, the merchant bank in question usually arranges for part of the commitment to be sub-underwritten.

(vi) Pricing of New Issues

The most important service provided by Nigerian issuing houses appears to be that of representing client companies before the Securities and Exchange Commission (SEC) in the process of fixing offer prices for new issues. Under efficient capital-market conditions, free-market forces are relied upon to determine rational prices for both new and existing securities. The Nigerian situation is different. Apart from overt imperfections in the capital market, the majority of the investors are ill-equipped to appreciate the technicalities of the market. As a result the government intervenes in setting offer prices for all public issues of securities. The price-fixing authority is the SEC which was established in 1978 following a reorganisation of its predecessor, the Capital Issues Commission (1972).

The Commission adopts one of two approaches in determining the appraised offer prices for securities. Under the first approach, the maintainable profit per share of the issue company is capitalised at a rate considered adequate for the industry. In general, prices are set to give earnings yield in the range of 20-30 per cent. Technically, the Commission works on the premise that the maintainable profit of a company is equivalent to the average after-tax profits made by the company during the five-year period preceding the offer. Alternatively, the net asset value per share of the company is ascertained. This is done by deducting total liabilities outstanding at the time of issue from the realisable value of all assets and dividing into the total number of shares to be fully paid following the offer. The Commission uses the lower of the two methods but feels free to make whatever adjustments it can justify on the basis of any peculiar environmental or intracompany factors which are expected to affect the current or future operations of the company.

(vii) The Nigerian Stock Exchanges

The existence of a resale market for securities is preconditional to sustained and rapid development of the new-issue market. Before 1961 such a facility did not exist in Nigeria. The only facility that existed was that which the Central Bank provided between 1960 and 1961 for the transfer of Government bonds.

The Lagos Stock Exchange (LSE) was incorporated on 15 September 1960. Dealings on the exchange started on 5 June 1961. It was the first security exchange in black Africa and the only one in Nigeria until 1978 when it was reorganised. Following the reorganisation, the Nigerian Stock Exchange was created with branches in Lagos, Kaduna and Port Harcourt. Because of the newness of the other branches however, a discussion of the Nigerian Stock Exchange is bound to concentrate almost exclusively on the Lagos Stock Exchange.

(a) Organisation of the Lagos Stock Exchange. The exchange was established under the Lagos Stock Exchange Act of May 1961. Under the Act, transaction in relation to any security quoted on the exchange is restricted to members of the exchange. The exchange is not a government agency but rather is a non profit-making company limited by guarantee. However due to the pivotal position which it holds in the economy, its activities are monitored closely by the government.

The exchange has three categories of members, council members, ordinary members and dealing members. Its articles of association provided for a minimum of seven council members including a chairman and deputy chairman of the exchange. Management of the exchange is vested in the council which operates through committees created for such responsibilities as the admission of new members, listing and delisting of securities, disciplinary functions and other functions incidental to the above. Membership of the council is drawn from ordinary and dealing members.

Ordinary membership is open to persons or firms whose applications are acceptable to the council of the exchange. Applications for membership must be supported by two current members. Ordinary members are required to take up a minimum of five shares of the exchange each of which was initially valued at N20.

(b) Dealing Members. In advanced stock exchanges there is a clear-cut separation of functions between brokers who transact business on behalf of clients and jobbers who deal on their own account. In such exchanges both jobbers and brokers pursue fine lines of specialisation.

Established brokers could, for instance, concentrate on big orders for institutional investors who transact business in round lots, that is, orders of 100 units and multiples thereof. They are therefore known as *round-lot brokers*. Other brokers concentrate on small unit orders and are known as *odd-lot brokers*. In the same way jobbers could either handle all securities or specialise in industrial groups in which case they are called specialists.

The Nigerian Stock Exchange does not operate on a clear-cut separation of functions. Dealers combine stockbrokerage and jobbing functions and handle both odd-lot and round-lot orders. Apart from stockbrokerage functions, the dealers paddle their clients through the intricacies of security transfers and registration.

There were (by 1977) five dealing members of the Exchange: CTB Stock Brokers (Nigeria) Limited, ICON Stock Brokers Limited, the Nigerian Stock Brokers Limited, City Securities Nigeria Limited and the Financial Trust Company (Nigeria) Limited. Each dealing member must in addition to being a member of the exchange:

(i) Deposit a stipulated amount of funds or acceptable security with the trustees of the exchange. The value of security was fixed initially at N3,000.

(ii) Pay annual dealership fees, the value of which is subject to change without notice. Up to 1977 the annual dealership fee was N300.

(iii) Maintain an effective presence in at least two branches of the Nigerian Stock Exchange.

Dealers are free to handle business in any quoted security at any time except that they serve in rotation for a period of one year at a time as Government brokers. All transactions in government stocks must be routed through the government broker. Dealing members are not allowed to canvas openly for business.

(c) Transaction Costs. Dealers' income accrues from two sources: profits made from trading on securities, and commissions. The rate of commission for different securities is fixed by the exchange. They vary from 1/32 to 3/8 per cent of total consideration for government securities and 1¼ per cent of 'total consideration or market capitalisation' whichever is higher, for industrial securities. The minimum commission on any transaction is N2.00. Dealers are not allowed to charge less than the prescribed commission. Contravention of this regulation attracts a fine of up to N200, suspension or expulsion as may be deter-

mined by the council.

(d) Financing of the Exchange. The initial share capital of the exchange
was fixed at N100,000 divided into 500 shares of N20 par value. The
main sources of income for the exchange however are dealing members'
annual fees, quotation fees, registered agents' fees and grants from
other organisations. Quotation fees are paid by companies whose securities are listed on the exchange. The rate varies but is based on a gradu-
ated scale according to the value of the authorised capital of the firm
whose securities are listed. The minimum and maximum fees payable are
currently fixed at N1,000 and N9,000 respectively. The exchange was
unable to pay its way during the initial stages and depended heavily on
grants and subventions from both the Central Bank of Nigeria and the
NIDB. During the nine-year period 1963-72, both institutions subsi-
dised the exchange to the tune of N38,000. In addition, the NIDB
provided free office accommodation for the exchange during the
period. The exchange has become financially more self-reliant as a
result of the massive all-round increase in the number of securities
listed, increase in fees charged and the introduction of quotation fees
for government securities.

(e) Operations of the Exchange. The Nigerian Stock Exchange adopts
the call-over system of operations. Under the system transactions in
each security must be completed within the period during which the
particular security is called up by the call-over clerk. This method
differs from the tick system. In the latter system, market participants
move around the floor of the exchange and negotiate business directly.
The tick system is indispensable in highly developed exchanges where
the volume of activity is such that individual call-over of securities
would not be practicable.

   Call-over at the Nigerian Stock Exchange starts at stipulated periods
and continues until the call-over clerk has gone through all listed securities. Dealers quote two different prices for each security in which they
are interested, the higher price (offer price) represents the price at
which they are prepared to sell. The lower price, on the other hand,
indicates the bid price at which the dealer is prepared to buy. Dealers
do not, however, disclose whether they intend to buy or sell at the time
they quote for any security. The higher offer made for a security
constitutes the *offer price* for it until changed. Conversely the highest
bid made will be the *bid price* until changed. The price at which the last
deal was made (business done) remains in force, that is, remains pasted

on the price board until changed.

The speed of price changes for securities indicates how active the market is. However only such price changes that result from round-lot transactions are recorded on the price board. Odd-lot transactions are not recorded even when they result in prices different from those at which the last business was done. Transactions involving more than 500 units of a given security are 'parcel' deals and brokers intending to make parcel deals are compelled to mention the number of units of security involved. Deals for more than 50,000 shares must be referred to the Securities and Exchange Commission for price determination.

(f) Listed Securities. The Lagos Stock Exchange until recently was very thin and sluggish: thin in the sense that very few securities were listed and sluggish on account of the irregularity of dealings on the securities. Another limitation of the exchange is the narrow range of securities offered by each quoted company. Apart from the Federal Government which had 49 listed securities as at 31 December 1978 only three firms — Guiness Nigeria Limited, BFN Limited and John Holt Investment Company Ltd — each had up to the three different listed securities at that date. One company, Thomas Wyatt Nigeria Limited had two listed securities while the remaining 41 quoted companies had only one listed security each.

Other aspects of transactions on the exchange are summarised in Tables 9.4 and 9.5. Table 9.4 gives the year-end figures of the number of securities listed and companies quoted for the period 1970-78. The subsidiary nature of the market for industrial bonds and preference stock is very apparent from the table. There is a striking parallel between Tables 9.3 and 9.4. An upsurge occurred within and around the fiscal years specified for compliance with both phases of the Indigenisation Decree in new listings of equity securities (Table 9.4) and new issues of securities (Table 9.3).

The impact of NEPD Phase I is evident from the fact that 20 industrial securities were listed for the first time within 1972-74. Similarly the upsurge in fresh listings in 1977 is attributable to the large number of companies which sought early compliance with NEPD Phase II. However the tables fail to highlight the full impact of Phase II because most companies affected complied during the 1978/9 period which is not covered by the table.

Table 9.5 summarises the number and value of transactions for the same period 1961-77. In 1961, there were a total of 334 transactions on ten listed securities, a yearly average of 33 transactions on each security. The market has broadened through the introduction of new securities. Consequently one expects substantial increases in both the total number of transactions and the frequency of deals per security. While the number of transactions has increased considerably between 1961 and 1977, the frequency of deals per security has fallen from 33 in 1961 to 17 in 1977. There is an encouraging development in the pattern of transactions. The average value per deal has decreased particularly as regards industrial securities. That change indicates a greater involvement of private investors in daily transactions.

Table 9.4: Lagos Stock Exchange — Cumulative Distribution of Securities Listed and Companies Quoted 1970-78

Year	Number of securities listed as at 31 December				Number of companies quoted as at 31 December		
	Govt. stock	Industrial securities		Total	Govt.	Ind.	Total
		Bonds and pref. stock	Equity stock				
1970	30	9	10	49	—	12	12
1971	32	9	15	56	—	18	18
1972	34	9	22	65	—	25	25
1973	38	8	26	72	—	28	28
1974	40	8	36	84	—	38	38
1975	42	7	36	85	—	38	38
1976	46	6[a]	34[a]	86	—	37	37
1977	47	8	35	90	—	38	38
1978	49	11	42	102	—	45	45

Source: Lagos Stock Exchange, *Daily Official List*.

Note: [a] Withdrawal of NIDB securities (one preference and two ordinary shares).

Table 9.5: Lagos Stock Exchange Transactions 1961-77

Year	Number of transactions			Value of transactions (Nm)		
	Govt.	Ind.	Total	Govt.	Ind.	Total
1961	92	242	334	1.42	0.10	1.52
1962	105	244	349	2.92	0.22	3.14
1963	296	415	711	9.74	0.64	10.38
1964	404	581	985	11.82	2.17	13.99
1965	391	627	1018	14.39	1.46	15.85
1966	501	595	1096	15.22	1.17	16.39
1967	336	427	763	12.10	0.39	12.49
1968	286	360	646	12.58	0.21	12.79
1969	307	246	553	16.19	0.18	16.37
1970	303	331	634	16.34	0.24	16.63
1971	204	748	952	32.68	3.51	36.19
1972	258	640	898	26.19	0.98	27.17
1973	285	537	822	91.86	0.53	92.39
1974	256	2807[a]	3063	48.37	1.30	49.67
1975	193	501	694	62.83	0.90	63.73
1976[b]	321	696	1017	111.28	0.56	111.84
1977[b]	337	1314	1651	178.78	1.22	180.00

Source: Derived from Central Bank of Nigeria, *Economic and Financial Review*, of various issues.

Note: [a] The abnormal rise in the number and value of transactions in industrial securities occurred in March 1974 when an all-time record of 1147 transactions valued at N412,900 was made.

[b] Figures for 1977 are provisional.

5. Concluding Remarks

Government has played a leading role in the development of the Nigerian capital market. The major consequence and possibly the objective of public policies have been to broaden the market through the introduction of more instruments and the provision of institutional support. Some fundamental reform is however necessary if only to remove some contradictions in existing government policies.

In the market for negotiated financing, new policies should be geared towards increasing the financing capability of the development finance institutions. Continued reliance on government loans and subventions cannot achieve this purpose. The institutions can have easy access to private and institutional savings through public issues of marketable securities. For this to happen, government's attitude towards public ownership of development finance institutions has to be reviewed. Another area of review concerns the operating scope of government-sponsored institutions. At the moment such institutions have a preponderance of loans in their investment portfolios which underscores unnecessary risk-averting tendencies. It implies also that their overall achievement in the area of industrial promotion has been very limited. The ideal role of development institutions should be to seek out and assist promoters who have sound bankable projects. Financing of ongoing concerns has limited developmental merit except where it is directed towards firms which cannot raise needed funds through direct issue of securities. In that light, there is perhaps more justification for extending financial accommodation to medium-scale than public companies which can and ought to be encouraged to issue marketable securities. The current policy of the development banks runs counter to this principle.

Regular issues of Federal Government bonds have succeeded because institutional investors are statutorily coerced into holding government bonds in their portfolios. The recent introduction of State government bonds calls for some reassessment of existing regulations. State bonds conceivably could achieve independent market appeal through high nominal rates of interest and the offer of low denomination securities. However they need part of the sheltered market which Federal Government bonds enjoy.

The euphoria in the market for industrial securities occasioned by the indigenisation programmes will soon die out. The tempo of activity in both the new-issue market and the stock exchange can however be sustained if more indigenous companies are encouraged to seek quotation on the exchange. Such a mutualisation policy has more chance of success if there is a progressive elimination of some of the stringent requirements for quotation and some form of direct tax incentive for companies seeking quotation for the first time. Since the economy suffocates with a lot of government business, the governments of the Federation ought to play leadership roles in the mutualisation programme by seeking quotations for most of their companies.

The continuation of government restriction on the rate of dividends payable by public companies in Nigeria is detrimental to the growth of the capital market. Dividend restriction was introduced in 1976 as part of the government's wages and income anti-inflationary package. Share ownership is not very widely diffused in Nigeria hence the inflationary effect on dividend payments, whatever the magnitude, is bound to be very minimal. The policy results in a lower risk-adjusted rate of return for Nigerian public firms relative to private firms. Consequently it constitutes a major disincentive for private firms which could have sought public quotation and for private investors who contemplate subscribing to public issues of equity stock. The motivation behind the current practice whereby expatriate firms prefer to seek compliance with the provisions of NEPD, 1977 through public offers for sale has to be investigated. It may be indicative of the hostility which restrictions on dividend payment have engendered among expatriate investors. Whatever happens, the policy is irrational since it bases dividends on nominal share capital and not on the performance of companies.

Two final points have to be made. The pricing formula adopted by the SEC does not do justice to young companies which have modest asset bases and past profit records. That class of firms constitutes a clear majority of Nigerian firms. They ought to be coerced or encouraged to seek quotation, but the pricing formula of the SEC fails to reward their growth potentials. A system of differential pricing by the SEC might therefore be effective in broadening the securities market and channelling public savings to desired areas in the economy.

While every effort is being made to encourage the maximum spread of share ownership of public companies, the allotment rules of SEC need enough flexibility to accommodate block purchases. A blind pursuit of equality in share allotment may result in the enthronement of minority control, which, in a majority of public companies in Nigeria, implies control by expatriate interests. Undue diffusion of share ownership discourages the healthy development of the secondary market.

Notes

1. See Federal Republic of Nigeria, *Second National Development Plan, 1970-74*, p. 65.
2. Financial assets are rights or claims on productive assets. Examples are cash, equity stocks, bonds, etc. Financial assets have to be distinguished from real assets.
3. Rates of interest are calculated on monthly or even weekly bases. Even in such circumstances, they could be as high as 50 per cent. The most obnoxious aspect of the system was the provision that the principal amount borrowed 'doubled' each time the borrower defaulted in interest obligations.
4. Central Bank of Nigeria, *Annual Report and Statement of Accounts*, 1963.
5. Following the reconstruction, the share capital was raised to N4m voting shares and N0.5m non-voting cumulative participating preference shares. Fifty-one per cent of the voting shares (Class A Shares) was held jointly by the Federal Government of Nigeria and the International Finance Corporation (IFC). The rest of the voting shares (Class B) were held by a consortium of American, British, German, Italian and Japanese bankers. As a result of the reconstruction, two subsidiaries of the NIDB emerged, ICON Securities Ltd and ICON Nominees Ltd. In 1975, ICON Securities was reconstructed into a merchant bank. See Nigeria Industrial Development Bank, *Annual Reports and Accounts* (1964 and 1975).

6. The criteria for investment are discussed in great detail in 'Guides to Applicants' issued by each of the banks.

7. A population figure (1976) of 76.8 million Nigerians is assumed, based on estimates prepared by the Central Planning Office, Lagos; see Central Bank of Nigeria, *Nigeria's Principal Economic and Financial Indicators 1970-1976*.

8. J.O. Ojiako (ed.), *Investors' Guide* (Caxton Press W.A., Ibadan, 1970).

9. Total subscriptions were worth N5,712,000 and allotments were made for N4,710,000.

10. The powers were granted following the Federal Government's acceptance of the recommendations of the *Financial System Review Committee*. The Committee recommended as follows:

1. each state be allowed free access to the capital market to issue and redeem its own bonds;

2. statutory Corporations and State-owned companies be empowered and encouraged to seek funds directly from the capital market through the issue of their securities.

11. Some of the supplementary offerings were 'offers for sale', i.e., sales of existing shares held by expatriate interests. Such sales should in normal situations have been handled directly on the stock exchange. However under existing regulations all block offers whether for sale or for subscription must be handled through public offerings at prices fixed by the Securities Exchange Commission.

12. There were the N2, Ordinary Shares of the Nigerian Cement Company Ltd, issued in 1959; the 50k Ordinary Shares of John Holt Investment Company Ltd (1960) and the N2 Ordinary Shares of the New Nigeria Bank Ltd (1970). The New Nigeria Bank did not seek quotation on the exchange.

13. The first merchant bank to be established was Philip Hill (Nigeria) Ltd (1960) which later in 1969 merged with the Nigerian Acceptances Ltd. Between 1973 and 1975, five others were established. These were the Nigerian Merchant Bank Ltd (formerly UDT) (1973), International Merchant Bank (Nigeria) Ltd (1974, formerly First National Bank of Chicago), Chase Merchant Bank (Nigeria) Ltd (1975) and ICON Ltd (Merchant Bankers). The sixth bank, First National City Bank of New York (Nigeria) Ltd started in 1974 but wound up in 1976.

Part Three

ASPECTS OF PUBLIC AND PRIVATE SECTORS' FINANCE

10 FINANCING THE NIGERIAN PUBLIC SECTOR

P.N.O Ejiofor and F.O. Okafor

1. Introduction

On 5 April 1976, in the height of a frightening two-digit inflation, the head of state addressed a hurriedly assembled panel of eminent economists and financiers[1] charging them with the task of revamping Nigeria's financial system. Eight months after, the panel submitted its report.

One of the highlights of its recommendations was that the right to raise funds in the Nigerian capital market through the issue of government paper should no more be a monopoly of the Federal Government. It therefore recommended that:

> Each State can be allowed free access to the capital market to issue and redeem its own bonds (7.31).

> Local governments whose areas of jurisdiction cover Nigeria's major urban centres should be allowed to publicly issue project-tied bonds . . . and that local governments would be exposed to the financial discipline generated by public flotation (7.39).

> That statutory corporations and state-owned companies be empowered and encouraged to seek funds directly from the capital market through the issue of their securities (7.47)[2].

These were radical recommendations.

The potential beneficiaries of the new measures were taken unawares. Financial independence was offered to them on a plate of gold. Hitherto, they were sponsored in the capital market by the Federal Government and this financial concession came as a shock. They were further paralysed into inactivity by the fact that, the offer came at a time when no programme of training in the area of management of securities had been undertaken. Consequently the Federal Government continued to enjoy its monopoly position in the issuing of government papers for the following 17 months.

Bendel State of Nigeria became the first state to plan the issue of papers. On 8 August 1978, arrangements were completed for the launching of the N20m 7 per cent First Bendel State of Nigeria Loan Stock maturing in 1988. The loan was project-tied to the building of

161

residential houses by the Bendel Development and Planning Authority
in eight urban centres of the state — Benin, Warri, Asaba, Auchi, Sapele,
Agbor, Uromi and Ughelli.[3] The Nigerian Acceptances Limited was the
issuing house.

The right granted to State governments and parastatal organisations
to float bond issues has far-reaching significance. This significance justi-
fies an in-depth appraisal of the implication of the issuing concession on
the Nigerian financial system and on the future ability of the organisations to stand on their own and honour their obligations. The appraisal
will consider the following areas: delimitation of public sector; traditional methods of financing the public sector; innovations in public
sector financing; and the role of banks in the new system.

2. Delimitation of Public Sector

The boundary between the public and the private sectors in Nigeria has
been receding over the years to the disadvantage of the private sector.
As Uzoaga and Okafor[4] put it, the 'increasing bureaucratization of
economic life has made it difficult to perceive only but a thin line that
separates the "real" private sector from the "operational" public sector
in Nigeria. This is because no particular sector of economic activity is
reserved exclusively for the play of private initiative.' The Udoji
Report[5] emphasised this 'increasing bureaucratization of economic life'
when it observed that:

> Today, the public services of Nigeria are involved in affairs that were
> beyond the imagination of our civil servants 15 years ago. We are
> now selling insurance and minting coins, we are sailing ships and
> refining oil . . . We are banking and building. Tomorrow, we shall be
> forging steel, and educating every young Nigerian through his
> primary years.[6]

The only constant feature in the historical evolvement of the public
sector in Nigeria is that its boundary has been expanding. A definition
of the public sector in Nigeria must therefore be made more in terms of
ownership than in terms of the field of operation of the organisations in
question. Accordingly, the public sector is defined here as comprising
all organisations run by employees of any of the governments, or in
which any of the governments has a majority of the equity holding.
These organisations fall into two broad groups: the civil service and

the parastatals.

The Nigerian civil service includes the Federal and State Government services, the Local Government services and regulatory service boards such as the state school boards and research organisations such as the Project Development Institute and the Federal Research Institute.

The parastatals include 'all Corporations, Authorities, Boards, Councils and Limited Liability Companies in which the Government has full or majority interest'.[7] They are of three types:

(i) The Utilities. These are 'infrastructural organisations, fundamental to the national economy [which] the government has decided to control to ensure proper balance between social and commercial aims'.[8] In terms of financial efficiency and output effectiveness, the emphasis is on *giving satisfactory service while minimising cost.* The Post and Telecommunications, the Water Boards and the Nigerian Ports Authority fall into this group.

(ii) The Corporations. These are public organisations engaged in productive services. Economically, they are expected to *break even while rendering service at reasonable cost.* The Coal Corporation, Airways and Railways belong to this group.

(iii) The Commercial and Industrial Enterprises (Government Business). These are 'concerned with the development, production, sale and maintenance of a wide range of goods and services for public consumption on a normal commercial basis'.[9] In other words, they are expected to *make profit while charging reasonable prices.* All Government financial institutions with the exception of the Central Bank, government trading organisations and manufacturing companies belong to this group.

Table 10.1: Typology of Nigerian Public Sector Organisations

Type of Organisation	Ownership		
	Federal (1)	State (2)	LGA (3)
A. Civil Service	A.1	A.2	A.3
B. Parastatals	B.1	B.2	B.3[a]
B_1 Utilities	$B_1.1$	$B_1.2$	$B_1.3$
B_2 Corporations	$B_2.1$	$B_2.2$	$B_2.3$
B_3 Commercial and industrial enterprises	$B_3.1$	$B_3.2$	$B_3.3$

Notes: [a] Local Government parastatals have not yet developed fully in all parts of Nigeria. But one easily foresees successful local governments operating all three categories of the parastatals.

Table 10.1 illustrates the typology of public sector organisation. By definition, organisations in B₃ (commercial and industrial enterprises) are profit-oriented. Their charter of incorporation should empower them to raise equity and funded debt from the financial market with the proviso that the proprietory interest of the 'state' should not be jeopardised.

In analysing the financing of the public sector through direct raising of funds in the capital market, these government businesses will therefore be excluded.

3. Traditional Methods of Financing

The public sector in Nigeria has two major sources of finance: the primary and secondary sources. The primary sources normally yield a net increase in transferred funds to the public sector from the private sector. There are three main sources of public finance, namely direct taxes, indirect taxes and loans.

Direct taxes comprise personal income tax, company income tax, petroleum-profit tax and other taxes including capital gains and casino taxes. Of these forms of direct taxes, petroleum-profit tax is the most dominant accounting for 89 per cent of revenues from direct taxes from January to September 1977 (see Table 10.2).

Indirect taxes are made up mainly of import duties, export duties, excise duties, sales taxes, mining (rent and royalties), fees, licences and other receipts. Table 10.2 shows the current revenue of the Federal Government for the period 1972-77.

Government can also raise funds through borrowing. Until recently public borrowing was the prerogative of the Federal Government. This was conducted through the sale of Government paper. Prior to the issue of Bendel State government papers, only the Federal Government issued these papers, and to date the Federal Government has a monopoly of external borrowing. Table 10.3 shows the total public debt holding of Nigeria for some selected periods.

Secondary sources do not result in a net increase in funds available to the public sector. They represent mere transfers of funds usually from an 'upper' arm of the public sector to a 'lower' one. Thus the Federal Government makes statutory and non-statutory transfers to State governments. The Federal Government also lends to the states part of the proceeds from the sale of government stocks. State governments in turn transfer funds to local governments as subventions in 'the form of a combination of revenue sharing, block grants and specific grants'. In turn both Federal and State governments transfer funds to parastatals both in terms of initial capital and in terms of operating funds.

Table 10.2: Current Revenue of the Federal Government 1972-77 (Nm)

Type and source	1972	1973	1974	1975	1976	1977[c]
Direct Taxes	624.4	852	3,031.1	2,990.2	3.852.4	3,597.4
Personal income tax		75.5	146.6	261.9	222.2	2.4
Company income tax	80.4	1.2	11.1	15.9	3.5	373.3
Petroleum-profit tax	540.5	769.2	2,872.5	2,707.5	3,624.9	3,197.1
Other tax revenue[a]	3.5	7.0	1.9	4.9	1.8	24.6
Indirect Taxes	48.1	516.2	498.2	760.7	882.7	838.2
✓Import duties	274.4	307.9	328.3	629.3	724.3	703.6
✓ Export duties	26.9	12.5	5.5	5.8	6.1	6.3
✓Excise duties	179.8	196.0	164.4	125.5	152.3	128.3
Interest and repayments	44.8	49.8	127.1	162.7	189.0	247.4
Mining (rent, royalties)	223.8	246.8	854.2	1,564.0	1,740.3	1,129.4
Miscellaneous[b]	30.7	29.6	25.4	37.1	101.5	30.8
TOTAL	1,404.8	1,695.3	4,537.0	5,514.7	6,765.9	5,843.2

Notes:

[a] Includes capital gains, casino and airport taxes.
[b] Includes earnings and sales, fees, and licenses, reimbursement and other receipts not elsewhere specified.
[c] Figures for January–September 1977.

Source: Central Bank of Nigeria, *Economic and Financial Review*, vol. 15, no. 2 (December 1977), Table 40, p. 79.

Table 10.3 Public Debt of Nigeria in N'000

Type of Debt	1960/61	1965/66	1970/71	1974/75	1976 Dec.	1977 Dec.
External	(40%)	(25%)	(15%)	(20%)	(.0007%)	(.008%)
Internal	(60%)	(75%)	(85%)	(80%)	(99.9993%)	(99.991%)
Total	200,000	500,000	1,200,000	2,000,000	1,419,711	1,815,711

Sources: Report on the *Financial System Review Committee*, para. 719; and Central Bank of Nigeria, *Economic and Financial Review*, vol. 15, no. 2 (December 1977), Table 39.

4. Problems of Public Sector Financing

The traditional methods of financing public-sector expenditure have recently run into serious problems. The most serious problems are discussed below.

(i) Fluctuations in Traditional Revenue Sources. There has been a dramatic fall in the amount of oil revenue accruing to the Federal Government and this development simply took the Government unawares. Earlier, the formulation of the gigantic *Third National Development Plan* was predicted on the projection 'that finance is unlikely to be a major problem during the Third Plan period';[10] the only constraints and bottlenecks which were expected to mar the full implementation of the Plan being 'lack of sufficient technical know-how, inadequate preparation, shortage of executive capacity and problems of material procurement and importation'.[11]

However, within a year of the operation of the Plan, experts warned that there were indications 'that the peak of current budget surpluses has been reached, and that they are likely to decline as the *Third National Development Plan 1975-80* runs its course . . . All these point to the emergence of an increasingly tight public financial situation during the remainder of the 1975-80 Plan period.'[12] The fall in traditional revenue sources as suggested by Table 10.2 has meant a tighter budget, smaller subsidies, delayed transfers, a more thorough exploitation of existing revenue sources and a frantic search for new revenue territories.

(ii) Big-Brother Relationship. The monetisation of oil assets increased the Federal Government's revenue in the first half of the seventies. The Federal Government extended financial assistance to the State Governments and parastatals indiscriminately. This resulted in overdependence of local governments and State parastatals on State governments, while State governments and Federal parastatals depended on the Federal Government.

Thus during the first half of the seventies, State governments relied for between 60 and 90 per cent of their current revenue on statutory revenue transfers from the Federal Government.[13] Local governments' revenue on the other hand depended by over 90 per cent on subventions from the State governments.[14] Federal and State governments' transfers constituted about 10 per cent of current expenditure and up to 25 per cent of capital expenditure of local governments. The greater part of the funds available to parastatals are also transferred by the Federal Government.

(iii) Stickiness of Government Expenditure. A cardinal principle of investment in private business is that good money should not be thrown overboard. In other words, irrespective of how far investment in a project has gone, no further expenditure should be made in the project if it is found that it is unlikely to be economically worthwhile. This principle should also apply to the public sector.

Much of government expenditure is socio-political in nature. Table 10.4 shows that 37.7 per cent of total planned government expenditure during 1975-80 is in the 'social', 'regional development' and 'administration' sectors. Even the so-called 'economic' expenditure which accounts for 62.5 per cent of total expenditure is not completely without political consideration since economic decisions of governments often have political overtones. As a result it becomes difficult to abandon unviable government projects midstream. They are notoriously sticky. The Nigerian sponsored FESTAC and the Trade Fairs come readily to mind.

Table 10.4: Summary of Public-Sector Capital Programme for all Governments 1975/76—1979/80 (in Nm)

Sector	1975/76	1976/77	1977/78	1978/79	1979/80	1975-80	1975-80 (%)
Economic	3,754.3	4,659.7	4,816.2	3,843.7	3,400.3	20,474.1	62.3%
Social	606.6	760.2	830.3	797.6	792.1	3,786.8	11.5%
Regional development	438.6	639.4	824.9	1,022.5	1,218.8	4,144.1	12.6%
Administration	561.9	778.2	904.5	1,044.1	1,161.0	44,449.6	13.6%
Total	5,361.4	6,837.5	7,375.9	6,706.8	6,572.1	32,854.6	100%

Source: Culled from the *Third National Development Plan 1975-80*, Tables 29.1-7

The net effect of the lack of rationalisation is that in the public sector particularly in Nigeria little concern is shown for self-liquidating financing. State governments and parastatals are the biggest culprits. They have long realised that they can always fall back on subsidies. State governments are mainly interested in securing adequate allocations of statutory and nonstatutory grants for their governments. Loans to State governments were usually not tied to projects. As the Financial

System Review Committee put it 'it is, perhaps, unrealistic to expect public corporations [and we add, Federal and State governments] to generate substantial internal funds when these bodies know that they have a ready source of financing in the Treasury'.[16]

5. Innovations in Public-Sector Financing

The undue reliance of the Nigerian public sector on traditional sources of revenue has been emphasised and problems attendant on the approach have been raised. In private-sector establishments, conscious attempts are often made to use a modest dose of debt in financing corporate activities. The strategy has salutary effects. Apart from enforcing a stricter sense of discipline on corporate financial management, debt financing opens up opportunities for deriving the benefits of financial leverage. In some cases, it may be the only means available for increasing the scope of operations.

Similar benefits could be derived through a judicious application of debt financing in the public sector. The success of the strategy would, however, depend on three major factors:

(a) the burden of the debt should fall directly on the beneficiary. Direct incidence instils a sense of responsibility for loan repayment and public accountability for the effective deployment of the funds;

(b) debt financing should be perceived as an integral part of public sector finances and not necessarily as a balancing item in the accounts. Consequently the maturity pattern and composition of public debt would be consciously managed within the overall framework of development goals and objectives; and

(c) public debt should be perceived as a dynamic instrument of financing control. This implies that the timing of the loans as well as the choice of debt instruments ought to mirror developments in the general financial system.

The factors outlined above provide a useful framework for analysing the implications of the recent right of direct access to the capital market which has been granted to State governments and statutory corporations. The analysis will better be appreciated if the basic difference between the new option and the former mode of entry to the capital market by State governments is further emphasised.

Under the former system the Federal Government issued long-term securities part of which was for on-lending to State governments. In the same vein, the Federal Government extended liberal guarantees on request for other long-term debts raised by some statutory corporations. One possible problem with this approach is that State governments and parastatals may be starved of needed funds. This however is not a major issue. The major issue is that the system violates the principles of direct incidence of financial accommodation and hence does not excite any feeling of urgency for prudent financial management on the part of the beneficiaries. Another pitfall in the old system deals with the timing of the issue of government paper. Securities were issued to raise money for balancing shortfalls in revenue expectations. As a result of this approach the involvement of the states in the capital market could neither yield any meaningful basis for financial control on the national level nor provide opportunities for the states to utilise market conditions to the greatest advantage. Thus between 1974 and 1975 when the financial system (particularly the banking system) was virtually overflowing with excess liquidity, the Federal Government initiated measures to phase out certain categories of government paper. A contrary decision could have been taken if government involvement in the loan market was regarded as an accepted instrument of financial control.

Direct access to the capital market creates immense opportunities for State governments and parastatals. It affords them ample chance to manage the composition and maturity pattern of their liabilities in line with their investment or developmental objectives. However a lot depends on the nature of their involvement in the capital market.

(i) Direct or Sponsored Involvement

State securities in different parts of the world may or may not be accorded Federal (central) government guarantees. The existence of a guarantee could be a major, if not a decisive, factor in attracting a ready market for State securities. This is so because potential holders of the securities could count on the ultimate commitment of the Federal (central) Government to redeem the obligation in the event of default by the borrower.

Federal Government sponsorship of all State issues is however likely to give rise to a number of problems. Apart from consolidating the big brother image, it will blur differences between the intrinsic investment worth of different State securities. A blanket sponsorship of State securities by the Federal Government will be attractive so long as the credibility of the Federal Treasury is not in doubt. But once a crack develops in the credit rating of the Federal Treasury, public confidence in State securities would be eroded. In that event, the spectre of doubt would extend to all State securities irrespective of the investment merits of individual issues. Blanket guarantees of State 'issues' are therefore likely to obliterate the distinctive features of such securities. In addition the system could lead to the same sense of indiscipline in the deployment of borrowed funds that formerly existed when the Federal Treasury assumed ultimate and final responsibility for all loans including State-originated bonds.

We are in favour therefore of the Federal Government's decision against sponsoring any State or parastatal issues. A contrary policy would have raised political issues for which the nation would have been ill-prepared, and the resulting Federal 'scholarship' to State governments would have brought the management of public-sector finances back to square one.[17]

An alternative approach which has not been adopted is to deny Federal government guarantees to securities issued by State governments or statutory corporations. In that case, the beneficiary will have the first and the ultimate responsibility for meeting all the financial obligations of all securities issued. Absence of Federal government sponsorship increases the risk congestion of potential buyers of the affected securities and hence reduces the market appeal of the securities. There is no evidence that the average investor in Nigeria would be rational in assessing the investment worth of State securities, as he is not a sophisticated investor. As a result, Nigerian investors could in the absence of Federal government guarantees underrate securities issued by State governments relative to competing securities in the market. Such a feeling may or may not be justified. A State issue could conceivably have more investment merit than a Federal issue. However we completely agree with the conclusion reached elsewhere[18] that confidence (and not rationality) will be the dominant influence on public reaction to State issues.

Public confidence in State issues could be bolstered by demonstrated ability on the part of states to manage funds. Such ability provides some guarantee that cash inflows from state issues would be so deployed as to generate enough cash to ensure the safety of both the principal and the periodic interest obligations arising from the issues.

Effective management of State issues poses two major problems. The first problem relates to the choice of proper investment outlets for the funds. The other problem deals with the selection of an appropriate package of incentives to create a broad and ready market for the securities.

(ii) Project-Tied Loans

In private-sector establishments project viability is a primary factor in the choice of outlets for borrowed funds. Such a selection criterion ensures that borrowed funds are tied to self-liquidating projects.

A strict interpretation of project viability cannot be enforced in the selection of investment outlets for the deployment of proceeds from State issues. This happens to be so because of the socio-political nature of State projects. They could be utilities which can hardly be self-sustaining. They could be service-oriented projects which, at best, can be expected to break even. It is however necessary that the proceeds of all State issues be tied to specific projects. The measure provides some assurance that loans are not raised for financing recurrent expenditure. Certainly projects which can generate more cash flows for debt-servicing should be given priority in the investment of funds realised from the issue of State securities. A good lead has been provided by the Bendel State Government in tying its first issue to the construction of residential estates. Other income-yielding but service-oriented projects which could qualify for similar treatment are the development of industrial estates, market development and the provision of fee-paying recreational facilities.

The principle of tying all the proceeds of State issues to specific projects provides one basis for timing the entry of State governments and parastatal organisations to the capital market. In that regard, the perception and proper articulation of potentially viable projects to be sponsored by the affected organisations would provide the needed signal rather than the current fund position of the organisations. Such a strategy ensures that investment decisions of the various arms of the government are not tied to the vagaries of the current budgetary positions of the various tiers of government.

(iii) Strategy for Debt Marketing

The market appeal of the issues could be substantially improved by the incorporation of reasonably attractive features in the issues. Three possible types of incentives could be considered:

(a) Financial incentives in the form of high coupon rates and tax exemption for bond interest could be incorporated in the indentures. Serial maturities could be made regular features of State issues.

(b) Some form of administrative authority may also be extended to bond holders. The trustee of the issues could be given the right to participate in top level decisions affecting projects in which the funds are tied.

(c) Policy measures could be formulated to ensure a ready resale market for State securities. One possible way of doing this would be to encourage (if not force) government savings and investment institutions such as the Provident Fund to incorporate State securities in their investment portfolios.

Market support for State and parastatal issues will be enhanced if the issues are directed to a wider market segment than alternative bonds in the Nigerian capital market. Federal issues are by virtue of unit size (N1,000) basically directed to a preferred class of corporate investors. Even existing corporate bonds in the market are denominated in units (usually N100 or N200) which are relatively high for the grass-roots investor. State bonds therefore have potential in the lowest level of the capital-market segment where low-unit size issues would be favoured. We therefore believe that the decision of the Bendel State Government to float N20 per value issue has a lot of merit.

6. Role of Banks

The banking system has a crucial role to play in the successful implementation of the new system. As a mobiliser of savings, the system could ensure that the economy is permanently in a desired state of liquidity necessary for absorbing new issues of State or parastatal securities. Banks are also in a privileged position to assist in the maintenance of a ready resale market for such securities. Both functions can be performed by every type of institution in the banking system. There are, in addition, specialised functions which each of the major types of banks in the Nigerian financial system has to perform.

(i) Central Bank. The Central Bank of Nigeria has been a major holder of Federal government issues of development stock. Apart from 1973/4 when the economy was suffering from an unexpected liquidity glut, the Central Bank has continued to account for over 25 per cent of the total holdings of Federal government bonds (see Table 10.5). A similar role is expected of the Central Bank in relation to State issues. The market support of the Central Bank is particularly necessary when new

issues of State securities encounter difficulties of initial acceptance by the market. Thereafter, the Central Bank should utilise its dominant percentage holdings of such securities to ensure that a steady and regular resale market is maintained for the securities, by freely trading in the security in the stock exchange to counter erratic movements in the market.

Table 10.5: Holdings of Federal Government Stocks — Percentage Distribution (End of Year)

	1970	1971	1972	1973	1974	1975	1976	1977
Federal Government	—	—	—	24.83	34.71	17.98	4.2	.002
State and local governments	6.29	5.10	5.17	2.50	0.54	0.35	.37	.19
Central Bank	25.38	28.60	29.60	13.30	0.01	30.23	41.79	47.80
Statutory corporations, marketing boards, other corporations and companies	6.67	4.56	3.91	2.85	2.36	1.71	1.60	1.40
National Provident Fund, other provident and pension funds and savings type institutions	55.76	56.06	54.97	51.20	56.69	38.75	34.60	31.56
Commercial banks	2.42	2.46	2.69	1.10	1.83	7.26	10.01	13.41
Insurance companies	3.25	3.00	3.11	2.71	3.20	2.87	2.73	3.15
Individuals	0.23	0.22	0.21	0.30	0.19	0.19	.13	.09
Miscellaneous	—	—	0.34	1.21	0.47	0.66	—	—
Others[a]	—	—	—	—	—	—	4.57	2.40
Total	100.00	100.00	100.00	100.00	100.00	100.00	100.00	100.00

Sources: Report of the *Financial System Review Committee*, para. 6.09; and
Central Bank of Nigeria, *Economic and Financial Review*, vol. 15, no. 2 (December 1977), p. 78.

Notes [a] The subhead includes holdings by merchant banks, and Central Bank of Nigeria sales not classified.

Apart from direct market support, the Central Bank could assist State issues in another way. It could encourage commercial and merchant banks to patronise the issues by according the status of 'preferred assets' to such securities, that is, State securities that could be accepted as part of the mandatory level of liquid assets required of the various institutions in the banking system. It should be recalled that during the early stages of Federal issues the Central Bank was permanently in a standby position to take up unsubscribed issues.

(ii) Commercial Banks. Traditionally commercial banks are not expected to hold 'long positions' in long-term securities. It is evident from

174 *Financing the Nigerian Public Sector*

Table 10.5 that commercial banks account for a very modest percentage of the holdings of Federal government bonds.

Admittedly, there is nothing special about State issues that would force commercial banks to alter their traditional attitude to long-term securities. However the commercial-banking system could provide some meaningful market support if the issues have serial maturities, high coupon rates and are of medium-term maturities.

Commercial banks could provide a lot of indirect but vital market support for the issues. Such desired indirect support requires that commercial banks:

(a) act as agents for the sale of the securities;
(b) act as registrars for the issues;
(c) increase the market appeal of such issues by readily accepting them as collaterals for commercial banks' loans; and
(d) extend liberal financial accommodation to individuals and organisations buying the securities.

(iii) Merchant Banks. The primary banking institutions around which much of the success of the system will depend are merchant banks, investment (development) banks and development companies. The traditional structure of their liabilities provides ample leeway for them to incorporate long-term securities in their investment portfolios.

In addition to direct market support, like outright purchase of the securities, these institutions are organised to perform other specialist functions in the marketing of the securities. The services of reputable merchant bankers would be indispensable in the origination, underwriting and pricing of the issues. Success in State issues will ultimately depend on the choice of packaging devices for marketing the issues, a function which can best be performed by reputable merchant/development banks.

7. Conclusion

The issuing and successful marketing of State bonds in Nigeria is likely to be a difficult and multifaceted task. Fortunately the opportunity created by the challenge has added a silver lining to the cloud of public-finance management in Nigeria.

Since the nation has not yet gone totalitarian, the kingship of the bond consumer − the investor − confers on him absolute freedom to choose whether or not to buy State or parastatal bonds, and the rational investor will buy bonds only if he perceives that his loan will be managed properly.

Many of the State governments and parastatals are severely handicapped by shortage of funds in the execution of worthwhile development projects. We have already shown in this chapter that traditional revenue sources have shrunk. Tax revenue cannot be augmented indefinitely. Direct borrowing by States and parastatals is one of the few revenue sources left untapped; and there lies the dilemma.

To refrain from bond flotation in the face of acute financial difficulties is to openly admit prodigality in State finance management. To float securities unsuccessfully is to dramatise this fact. On the other hand, successful issue of bonds by States and parastatals will surely open public finance management to the rigid discipline of debt financing. And sooner or later, a desirable multiplier effect in the form of higher level of public accountability in other sectors of public life will result.

Notes

1. Financial System Review Committee.
2. Paragraph references of the Committee's Report; the authors have access to a loose-leaf typed Report which may not necessarily agree with the format of the 'final' document.
3. See *Business Times*, vol. 3, no. 15, 8 August 1978, p. 1.
4. W.O. Uzoaga and F.O. Okafor, 'The Private Sector in the Nigerian Economy' (University of Nigeria, Enugu Campus, 1975).
5. *Udoji Report: Public Service Review Commission*, para. 28 (Lagos, 1975).
6. Ibid., para. 419.
7. Ibid., para. 420.
8. Ibid., para. 422.
9. *Financial System Review Committee Report*, paragraph 7.36.
10. Federal Republic of Nigeria, *Third National Development Plan 1975-80*, vol. 1 (The Central Planning Office, Federal Ministry of Economic Development, Lagos, 1975), p. 366.
11. Ibid., p. 341.
12. CNFS, para. 7.07.
13. Ibid., para. 7.24.
14. Ibid., para. 7.35.
15. Ibid., para. 7.41.
16. Ibid., para. 7.42.
17. The Committee recommended that 'Local Governments whose areas of jurisdiction cover Nigeria's major urban centres should be allowed to publicly issue project-tied bonds guaranteed by the Government', para. 7.39. The government accepted the recommendation provided 'the suggested guarantees are made by the relevant State government'.
18. P.N. Ejiofor, 'Nigeria States and Barriers to Entry into the Capital Market' in *Nigerian Journal of Business Management*, vol. 1, no. 5 (November/December 1977), pp. 199-203.

11 REVENUE ALLOCATION IN NIGERIA

E.J. Nwosu

1. Introduction

For the purpose of this chapter, we decipher three major principles which seem implicit in the concept and philosophy of a federal state. The first is that of a *covenant*, expressed or implied, but generally incorporating the idea of 'faith' of the component parts (states) in the alliance. The second, which indeed gives meat to the bone 'faith', is that of *common ideal and goal or purpose*. The third principle relates to what may be called the pull and push of self-interests in the functioning of federalism, namely, the principle of *give and take* which gives meaning and content to the first and second principles.

The idea of a covenant, if it is to have a legitimate stamp of authority as well as become a central guiding force must imply that component states of Nigeria must be *equal* partners — no more, no less. The principle of common ideal and purpose for Nigeria has found expression in the five principal national objectives which have been enunciated in the country's Second National Development Plan, 1970-74 and confirmed in the current Third Plan, 1975-80. These national objectives are to establish Nigeria firmly as:

(i) a united, strong and self-reliant nation;
(ii) a great and dynamic economy;
(iii) a just and egalitarian society;
(iv) a land of bright and full opportunities for all citizens; and
(v) a free and democratic society.

The third idea of give and take seeks to transform the naked self-interest of each component part into an *enlightened self-interest* for the purpose of achieving the common goal of all. This principle assumes, and correctly too, that each component part has intrinsically something to contribute as well as something to gain from the others, in one form or the other, material and non-material. Where one is weak, another may be strong and vice versa, and so on. In terms of gains, this means that no one component part or a group of component parts can have things always its way. Where, owing to some intemperate demonstration of sheer naked political or other pressure, one component part or a group of component parts succeeds in having things its way, over time, this must necessarily lead to the disintegration of the entire entity. The basis for the covenant must have been destroyed.

This way of looking at the federal question seems to me to provide the only sound basis for an enduring sense of national solidarity. It makes it futile in the context of federalism for one to argue that any component part is more important or contributes more than the others or that a 100 per cent input of material resources by a component part is a reason for that component part to earn exactly the net yield (less costs) from such resources. Because the other component part(s) may have contributed just those other factors, perhaps intangible, without which the material resources in question would not have been optimally utilised in the first place. If this point should be discounted, then there would certainly not be any need for federating. Each part would then better be sovereign and compete, or rather deal, with the others individually as sovereign entities.

Now that the concept and philosophy of a federal state have been briefly discussed the revenue allocation proposals of many years in respect of the Federal Republic of Nigeria will be examined.

2. Revenue Allocation Before the Seventies

Between 1949 and 1952, the central government had power over revenue and taxes even though the Report of Sir Sydney Philipson of 1947 had recommended greater revenue autonomy for the regions. The excess of its revenue over its expenditure was allocated amongst the regions on the basis of the principle of derivation.

In 1953 another Report, by Sir Louis Chick, was accepted by the Nigerian Government. But Chick's recommendations were strictly based on his major term of reference which already *a priori* tied his hands. Chick was required to provide to the regions and to the centre an adequate measure of fiscal autonomy within their own spheres of government and to lay emphasis on the importance of ensuring that the total revenues available to Nigeria are allocated in such a way that the principle of derivation is followed to the fullest degree compatible with meeting the reasonable needs of the centre and each of the regions.

The apparent imposition on Sir Louis of the principle of derivation left the impression that some powerful political groups whose interests at the time would be better protected via the derivation principle must have greatly and unduly influenced Chick's machinery and rendered the exercise dubious from the start.

⌡   The main recommendations of Chick's Report were as follows:

(a) 100 per cent of the import duty on motor spirit was to be returned to the regions in proportion to the estimated distribution for consumption in the regions;

(b) 50 per cent of the import duty on tobacco was to be returned to the regions in proportion to the estimated distribution for consumption in the regions;

(c) 15 per cent of the proceeds of other import duties other than import duties on motor spirit and tobacco was to be paid to the Northern Region, 20 per cent to the Western Region and 14.5 per cent to the Eastern Region;

(d) the Federal Government was to retain all taxes on companies while all personal income tax was to be returned to the region in which the tax payer was resident; and

(e) the mining rents and royalties levied and collected by the Federal Government were to be returned to the region from which minerals were extracted.

Chick unwittingly laid undue emphasis on the principle of derivation.

In 1958, another report by Sir Jeremy Raisman added other criteria to the principle of derivation. The new dimensions were:

(a) population;

(b) basic responsibilities of each regional government;

(c) the need for continuity in regional public services;

(d) the need for balanced development of the Federation;

(e) a grant of N1m in the 1958/9 fiscal year to the Northern Region to make up for shortfalls of the previous years;

(f) export duties on produce, hides and skins should be returned to region of origin;

(g) import duty on motor spirit and diesel oil should be distributed on consumption basis;

(h) mining rents and royalties should be allotted as follows:

(i) 50 per cent to the region of origin,
(ii) 20 per cent to the Federal Government, and
(iii) 30 per cent to the distributable pools account.

(i) The slightly enlarged distributable pools account (DPA) was to be distributed between the regions as follows:

(i) 40 per cent to the North,
(ii) 31 per cent to the East, and
(iii) 24 per cent to the West.

The DPA took the population of the regions into consideration.

After the submission of the Raisman Report and after due consultations with regional governments, it was agreed that the Federal Government should appoint, *from time to time*, a Fiscal Review Commission.

The 1963 Constitution examined further the problem of revenue sources and allocation. Tables 11.1 and 11.2 show the various decisions reached on both revenue sources and allocations.

Table 11.1: Tax Jurisdiction under the 1963 Nigerian Constitution

Federal	State
1. Import duties	1. Personal income tax[a] (administration)
2. Export duties	2. Sales and purchases taxes on produce and other commodities
3. Excise duties	3. Entertainment tax
4. Mining rents and royalties	4. Cattle tax
5. Petroleum-profits tax	5. Football pools and other betting taxes
6. Personal income tax[a] (legal basis)	6. Motor vehicle tax and drivers' licence fees
7. Company income tax	7. Capital gains tax (administration)
8. Capital gains Tax[a] (legal basis)	

Note: [a] Personal income tax (legal basis) originally under the state jurisdiction was transferred to the Federal in 1975 while the administration and retention of revenue remained with the State. The same applies to capital gains tax.

3. Revenue Allocation in the Seventies

In 1970 the formula for sharing the revenues among the states was radically changed as follows:

(a) 50 per cent of the distributable pools account fund to go to the states on the basis of equality of states; and

(b) 50 per cent to be shared on the basis of population.

Table 11.2: Allocation of Revenue under the 1963 Nigerian Constitution (%)

	Federal	Regions
1. Import duties		
a) Tobacco	–	100
b) Beverages – beer, wine and spirits	100	–
c) Motor spirit and fuel	–	100
d) Other imports	65	35
2. Export duties		
Produce, hides and skins	–	100
3. Excise duties		
a) Except tobacco and motor fuel	100	–
b) Tobacco and motor fuel	–	100
4. Mining royalties and rents	15	50
5. Rest (35%) of mining royalties and rent channelled to *Distributable Pool Account*[a] (distributed to the regions according to the Raisman formula)	–	35

Note: [a] 35% of mining royalties and rents came under the DPA, 15% to the Federal Government and 50% to the region of derivation.

Source: Extracted from the *Constitution of the Federal Republic of Nigeria, 1963.*

Two years after the 1963 Constitution allocation formula, it became necessary to re-examine the revenue-sharing formula. Accordingly, the Binns' Commission was set up in 1963. It recommended as follows:
(a) greater priority in the use of population as a basis for revenue allocation; and
(b) comparable financial positions among the regions so that they could carry out their capital development programmes.

In 1972, Decree No. 51, directed that tax paid by armed forces personnel, external affairs officers and pensioners overseas was to be channelled to the distributable pools account.

Decree No. 6 of 1975 amended some allocations as follows:

(a) 50 per cent of all excise duties were to be channelled to the Federal Government;

(b) 50 per cent to the State governments;

(c) 20 per cent of on-shore receipts (mining royalties and rents) were to be channelled to the region of origin (derivation);

(d) 80 per cent to the distributable pools account as well; and

(e) 100 per cent of all off-shore receipts were to be directed to the distributable pools account.

Thus far, this country has passed through various stages in the evolution of its revenue allocation. As the Constitution Drafting Committee's (CDC) Sub-Committee on Economy, Finance and Division of Powers aptly observed:

> The disposition of tax jurisdiction has remained substantially unchanged since 1963 but the allocation of revenue has undergone various changes since then, particularly with respect to the formula for allocation. At various stages in the evolution of our revenue allocation, different principles have been given more prominence than others: derivation (in the 1950s), need (in the early 1960s), equity and even development (in the 1970s).[1]

A. The Constitution Drafting Committee and Revenue Allocation

The Constitution Drafting Committee recommended the preparation of a new revenue allocation formula for submission to a Constituent Assembly for possible incorporation in the new Nigerian Constitution. To assist the Constituent Assembly, a committee of experts under the chairmanship of Professor O. Aboyade was appointed with the following terms of reference:

> Taking into consideration the need to ensure that each government of the Federation has adequate revenue to enable it to discharge responsibilities and having regard to the factors of population, equality of status among the States, derivation, geographical peculiarities, even development, the national interest and any other factors bearing on the problem, the Committee should:
>
> (a) examine the present revenue allocation formula with a view to determining its adequacy in the light of the factors mentioned above and representations from the Federal Government and the State Governments and other interested parties.
> (b) following from the findings in (a) above, recommend new proposals as necessary for the allocation of revenue as between the Federal, State, as well as the Local Governments, and also amongst the States, and the Local Governments.
> (c) make whatever recommendations are considered necessary for

the effective collection and distribution of Federal and State revenues.

B. Technical Committee on Revenue Allocation

The Aboyade Committee acknowledged in its Report[2] that under the military regime a *de facto* federal *superiority* emerged in the relationship between the centre and the states on the one hand, and between the states and the local governments on the other. Federal superiority was strengthened by the increase in revenue accruing to the Federal Military Government, especially from petroleum and company taxation. The wealth of the centre in the decade has resulted in a growing arbitrary appropriation of states' functions by the centre.

On the revenue side, the central government has considerably reduced the independent sources of states' revenue thus making them increasingly dependent on the statutory allocations and non-statutory grants from the centre.

(a) Observations of Aboyade's Committee

Aboyade's Technical Committee on Revenue Allocation studied in depth the past principles of revenue allocation in Nigeria. The Committee's observations may be summarised as follows:

1. The absolute, raw, unweighted and dubious *population* figures constitute poor measure in terms of relative fiscal or economic needs. Revenue sharing based on them creates the erroneous impression that 'sharing the national cake' is more important than producing it.

2. The principle of *derivation* is of little significance in a cohesive fiscal system for national political and social development. The use of the principle should be discontinued.

3. The principle of *need* as a basis for revenue sharing can only be meaningful if need can be disaggregated into a number of component parts instead of the acceptance of need as an omnibus concept.

4. The criterion of *even development* is analytically ambiguous and technically difficult to apply.

5. The states are neither equal economically nor in terms of their immediate budgetary and developmental requirements. The concept of *equality of states* is purely legal and has no merit whatsoever in revenue sharing among states.

6. The principle of *geographical peculiarities* defies definition and

there is no known single non-controversial index for its measurement for purposes of revenue sharing.

7. The principle of *national interest* is analytically capable of many interpretations. It can hardly be quantified and at best it can only be used qualitatively as a residual element of political judgement.

8. The present *grants system* currently in operation is too open to arbitrary administrative discretion. It hardly promotes the fiscal comparability to which it might have been directed as an objective.[3]

In the light of the above observations the Aboyade Committee dismissed the various past principles for allocation of revenue. They were considered less applicable in the more complex governmental and economic structure of Nigeria.

(b) The Technical Committee's Recommendations

The Committee noted with regret that the principle of taxable capacity and tax efforts had never been dealt with in past Nigerian revenue-sharing formulae.[4] For the structure of the new Revenue Allocation accounts, the Technical Committee recommended as follows:

1. All federally collected revenue (except the personal income tax from the armed forces, external affairs officers and the new Federal capital territory) to be consolidated into one account to be shared by the Federal, State and local governments.

2. The consolidated account should be shared in the following proportion:

	%
Federal Government	57
States' joint account	30
Local governments' fund	10
Special grants account[5]	
(administered by Federal Government)	3
Total	100

3. Each state to allocate, in addition to the share it may receive from the federally allocated local governments' fund, another 10 per cent of its own total revenue (that is, statutory receipts, the states' joint account plus its internal independent revenue) for redistribution among the local governments in its area.

In respect of revenue sharing from the states' joint account, it strongly recommended the adoption of the following five criteria:

(i) equality of access to development opportunities;
(ii) national minimum standard for national integration;
(iii) absorptive capacity;
(iv) independent revenue and minimum tax effort; and
(v) fiscal efficiency.

Considering the relative importance of the above five criteria, it recommended the adoption of the following statistical weights:

	%
(i) Equality of access	0.25
(ii) National minimum standard	0.22
(iii) Absorptive capacity	0.20
(iv) Independent revenue	0.18
(v) Fiscal efficiency	0.15
Total	1.00

The new allocation criteria applies only to the yearly incremental changes in the states' joint account and not to the total, absolute sum that goes into the account itself. This is in line with the need for each State Government to maintain a minimum continuity of services in the discharge of the responsibilities.[6]

It is against this utterly confusing background that an attempt will be made to examine some of the prevalent arguments for and against the 'principles' of revenue allocation so far suggested.

4. A Critical Evaluation of Revenue-Allocation Criteria

This section of the paper will examine the pros and cons of the major criteria for allocation put forward by the various committees set up since the forties.

(a) Principle of Derivation

The difficulty of working out in the minutest details the place of material and non-material categories in the assets and liability columns of the national development balance sheet makes it mandatory to view the principle of *derivation* as superficial and therefore of very limited value for revenue allocation under our circumstances.

States which favour the derivation principle accuse other Nigerian states where natural resources are not yet known to be yielding any revenues, of wanting to reap where they did not sow. Such a sentimental approach is very dangerous and capable of destroying the basis of federalism. Some proponents of the derivation principle argue that beside the loss of revenue, states with oil deposits suffer possible displacement of citizens and environmental pollution. The problems posed by the displacement of citizens and by pollution have to be viewed distinctly from the revenue-allocation angle because there are activities other than mineral prospecting which may also cause the displacement of citizens. For example, when certain homesteads have to give way to a highway or a large-scale industrial complex the affected persons, by virtue of being displaced, may become entitled to a share in the profits or the benefits of the activity.

In the early fifties, derivation was based on the export duties from Nigeria's major cash crops at a time when earnings from those crops accounted for more than 70 per cent of Nigeria's foreign-exchange reserves. Now the argument centres mostly on the country's oilfields and the mining royalties and rents accruing from them. It must be admitted that Nigerian States have been inconsistent in the issue of derivation. They argue for or against the derivation principle depending on their relative position in terms of high revenue-yielding mineral wealth.

The points discount the undue weight attached to derivation. Insisting on derivation will mean discounting other worthy contributions of other states to the entire national wealth. It also gives the false impression, notably in the case of mineral products, that mining or mineral prospecting and production are carried out exclusively in one or two states.

Mineral-rich states have to understand that it is sheer accident of natural location rather than design that mineral deposits are where they are and that there is no positive relationship between the location of mineral deposits and the level of work ethos (in terms of contribution to value added) of the indigenes of the state of mineral derivation. Finally one has to consider the uncertain future with regard to the possible locations of new natural and probably more revenue-yielding resources in other states. No one ever imagined many years ago that Britain would one day discover oil in the North Sea and become an oil-producing nation.

The problems of resettlement and pollution arising from mineral prospecting are better solved as special emergency national problems under the aegis of a national 'package policy of the federal authorities'. Such policy must be divorced from the revenue-allocation formula of the country. Resettlement, pollution treatment and assistance during natural disasters can be provided for either in the constitution or a Decree or Act of Parliament.

Furthermore, the question of monetary compensation for land acquired for the purpose of mineral prospecting should also be part of the package deal for citizens in those areas. One has to observe that there have been instances in Nigeria, where citizens or groups of them in various states have donated large parcels of land for various national projects without any special claim for a part of the national revenue as compensation.

(b) Principle of Origin of Taxes and Duties

Taxes here include both direct and indirect taxes while duties include import duties, excise duties and export duties other than those from produce from land. Taxes, import duties and fees which are based on commodities or services directly consumed by the inhabitants of individual states should go to the states concerned. These include:

   (i) personal income tax,[7]
   (ii) sales and purchase tax (except on produce from land),
   (iii) entertainment tax,
   (iv) cattle tax,
   (v) football pools tax,
   (vi) other betting taxes,
   (vii) motor vehicle tax, and
   (viii) driving licence fees.

The following should go to the distributable pool account:

   (i) import duties on such items as tobacco and beverages (beer, wine and spirits, etc),
   (ii) import duties on motor spirit and fuel, and
   (iii) import duties on other items of personal consumption nature.

While the first group of taxes, duties and fees should go to the state of consumption, the second group of import duties should go to the distributable pools account for *equal* distribution to the states. The items in the second group are better channelled through the distributable pools account because of the difficulty in the determination of the final place of consumption.

All excise duties, export duties other than those on produce from land, import duties other than those classified above (such as import duties on machinery and equipment), companies income tax and capital gains tax should go to the distributable pools account and allocated equally to the states. Because of what is often referred to as the 'Federal Presence', some states have more industries and other federally sponsored facilities. Such favoured states would gain very much to the disadvantages of others if they should also reap the benefits of both the companies income tax and the capital gains tax. The disparity in the density of industries in the states is the direct consequence of the inability of successive federal authorities to locate industries equitably in all the states in order to realise the nationally accepted but hardly practised principle of even development (that is, reasonable dispersal of industries in the states). It is also clear that in states where there have been clusters of major industrial activities, such developments are often accompanied by large-scale social infrastructures by the Federal Government.

To buttress the contention of unevenly dispersed industries one has to refer to a 1973 study of the spatial distribution of the manufacturing industry in Nigeria covering the period 1965-9 conducted by the Centre of African Studies of the IFO — Institute for Economic Research, Munich (West Germany) in conjunction with the Nigerian Institute of Social and Economic Research (NISER), Ibadan.[8] The study used the following variables:

(i) value added,
(ii) numbers of employed per 100 inhabitants or per km^2,
(iii) salaries and wages, and
(iv) output level.

The study revealed the concentration of industrial activity in a limited number of locations in the country. Greater Lagos is by far the most important industrial location in Nigeria. Lagos accounted for 38 per cent of the industrial activity before the civil war. The respective shares of the cities of Kano, Kaduna, Port Harcourt, Ibadan and the Sapele area lay between 6 per cent and 10 per cent, that of Aba about 4 per cent. These seven most important locations alone accounted for approximately 80 per cent of the industrial activity in 1961.[9]

The shares of Zaria, Jos, the cement factories in Nkalagu and Ewekoro, Enugu and Abeokuta ranged between 1 per cent and 3 per cent. The industrial importance of the cement factories in Nkalaga or Ewekoro was higher than that of the industrial enterprises in the towns of Enugu and Abeokuta, as well as the locations Umuahia, Maiduguri, Onitsha, Ilorin or Benin, with their respective shares ranging between 0.5 per cent and 1 per cent. The 18 locations listed above accounted for about 95 per cent of the country's industrial activity in 1965. The remaining 55 locations studied were only of local importance; frequently only one enterprise existed in each location. The enterprises concerned were largely sawmills, palm-oil mills or cotton mills located in small or rural towns.

In 1969 the share of Greater Lagos in the industrial activity of the country rose from 38 per cent to 50 per cent. The level of industrialisation observed in Kaduna was 14 per cent and Kano 11 per cent which were followed by Ibadan with 6 per cent and Sapele 4.5 per cent. Zaria, Jos and Ewekoro ranged between 1 per cent and 3 per cent while the locations Gusau, Ilorin, Abeokuta, Maiduguri, Bacita and Sokoto had shares between 0.5 per cent and 1 per cent. In 1969 these 14 industrial locations accounted for 96 per cent of the industrial activity; the remaining 4 per cent was shared by 44 locations.[10]

If left unchecked, there would be a greater intensification of the process of spatial industrial concentration in the agglomeration areas of Lagos, Ibadan, Kaduna, Zaria and Kano with consequences deterimental to the continued stability of the Nigerian experiment in federalism.

It is therefore clearly inconsistent with the notion of federalism and altogether unfair to the majority of the states which have not benefited adequately from Federal Government patronage that the few industrially favoured states should at the same time consume greater portions of the revenue which results from such investments, either directly through capital gains taxes or indirectly through motor vehicle licence fees and driving licence fees of the employees of such industries or companies in their areas of jurisdiction.

Therefore, until such a time that the federally sponsored industries and allied economic and social activities and amenities are fairly dispersed and investment capital from Nigeria's financial institutions reasonably spread, certain duties and taxes as specified above should be channelled to the distributable pools account.

(c) Principles of Need and Special Geographical Peculiarities

This principle will engender greater confusion and political instability if given a definite place in the allocation scheme. The needs of human beings and their communities are almost limitless. The principle of need hardly presents a reasonable solution to the problem because need is *a priori* immeasurable. If the case of special geographical peculiarities were to apply, every state in Nigeria would have geographical impediments to illustrate that it had a greater need for revenue than the rest of the states. National policies such as the development of river basins (which cut across states) throughout this country are certainly praiseworthy actions aimed at improving the physical areas of depressed states and of providing job opportunities and irrigation facilities. Broad-based problems which require Federal Government's broad-based policy actions should not be linked to the revenue-allocation formula. Among the broad-based problems are drought, erosion and the reconstruction of the war-ravaged areas.

(d) The Principle of Population

In Nigeria population is a major criterion (with the criterion of equality of states) for revenue sharing among the states, especially that portion of national revenue which goes to the distributable pools account.

The criterion of population for revenue-sharing purposes appears to be the greatest single cause of bitter partisan political bickerings in Nigeria. The criterion of population for revenue-allocation purposes should be reviewed because of its explosive and controversial nature.

The criterion wrongly assumes that a well-populated state is, of necessity, poor and is therefore entitled to a greater share of the national wealth. One can also argue on the contrary that a well-populated state depletes a greater portion of natural resources urgently needed by a developing economy like Nigeria's for investment in education and capital formation and should not be awarded more revenue than the less populous state.

Large populations can also have positive effects on savings/investment, on productivity and on consumption. From this point of view one could argue that the higher the population of a state the less the revenue that state should receive from the central government.

The use of absolute numbers of population in each state as the basis for revenue allocation without relating it to the available factor proportions of that state as well as the resources made available to that state by the Federal Government will be scientifically wrong.

Furthermore, national revenue allocated on the basis of population may not necessarily mean that the revenue so received will be actually expended for the benefit of all the people within the state in question. Experience has proved that it is hardly the case in Nigeria. Money allocated on the basis of population has been known to have been spent for the benefit of the few ruling and wealthy classes.

The disputed Nigerian population census is another point which puts the criterion of population to question. Awolowo has rightly observed that it will aggravate provocation if the disputed Nigerian population census is used as the basis for revenue allocation.[11]

In my view, as long as Nigeria uses population as a basis for revenue allocation, the threat of manipulations of census figures will haunt this land and political instability will remain our only lasting legacy to posterity.

Finally, I strongly believe that the continued use of population as a basis for sharing revenue will help to make both the people and governments of Nigeria take the question of population explosion very lightly. This would lead to a situation in which the urgent need for a sound national population policy would be unusually difficult to realise, partly owing to our religious sensitivities but mainly because the states, in their enthusiasm to outbid one another for more population-based revenue would, at least through inaction, render any national population policy inoperative.

In view therefore of these overwhelming negative arguments, the rationality and political wisdom of adopting population as a basis for revenue allocation is questionable. The criterion should be entirely scrapped for revenue-sharing purposes in this country. If population is to be taken into account it should be from an entirely different angle. A detailed *per capita* assets and liabilities study which would embrace every known factor/resource in each state should be made in order to find out which state has the highest *per capita* resource and which has the least. On that criterion revenue could be allocated to the states. It will then be possible to show the position of each state on the scale. But with time, such an exercise is bound to generate much political heat. Any principle which will use population figures in one way or the other should thus not be encouraged.

(e) The Technical Committee's Criteria

Aboyade's Committee has been commended and criticised. Those that commend the Committee's recommendations believe that it has succeeded in de-emphasising politics in revenue allocation. Those that criticise them believe that the committee's recommendations are not quantifiable, and that they have created more problems than they were supposed to solve.

In a sharp reaction to the recommendations of the Technical Committee on Revenue Allocation, a prominent Nigerian economist, Pius

Okigbo, described the report as 'distinguished by its elegance but perhaps dominated by the pursuit of novelty rather than political intuition'.[12]

Okigbo criticised the Committee's dismissal of nearly all of the known criteria. His comments may be summarised as follows:

1. Revenue allocation exercises are only marginally economic but principally a matter of political compromise.

2. In consideration of the CDC's recommended division of powers and functions between Federal, State and Local governments, a division which tends to assign greater developmental responsibilities to the states and local governments, the share of revenue recommended for these two lower tiers of government will be insufficient for their obligations.[13]

3. While it is true that the use of raw unweighted population data cannot be defended except on special grounds, certain needs still depend on population. Examples are primary schools, hospitals and household water requirements.

4. The Technical Committee scorned the principle of derivation yet certain revenues such as land tax, personal income tax and local government property tax which are derived locally are recommended.

5. No one who believes in development planning can dismiss *need* as an omnibus and immeasurable criterion.

6. The principle of *even development* is discarded by the Technical Committee but at the same time 'access to development opportunities' is proposed, and

7. *Equality of states* is neglected even though the equality of states is a political reality and fiscal policy falls dangerously in the politico-economic arena.

In his own contribution to the debate Ugoh suggested the use of two criteria — population and equality of states on a 70:30 percentage weighting.[14]

5. Conclusion

A majority of Nigerian opinions appear to agree that the new criteria for revenue allocation recommended by the Aboyade Committee do not lend themselves to serious use. They are too complex and full of loopholes and inaccuracies.[15] On the other hand, Okigbo has not seriously demolished the arguments against the use of raw unweighted population data, the principle of need as well as the principle of derivation of land resource for revenue sharing in the socio-political environment of Nigeria.

Assuming two states have equal population figures, the state with an overwhelming majority of its population in the high-income group (top government functionaries, private enterprise executives, rich businessmen, professionals, etc.) is likely to collect more revenue (in the form of taxes) for the provision of basic facilities such as water supply, hospitals, roads, etc., than the other state with a predominantly rural and poor population. The population criterion is as complex and full of loopholes as the new criteria of the Technical Committee which Okigbo and others have criticised.

The principle of derivation should be de-emphasised. Revenue accruing to the nation from the sub-soil (on-shore and off-shore) as well as export duties on produce from land should be paid into the distributable pools account and shared equally among the states on the basis of *equality of states*.

A new revenue allocation formula for Nigeria has not been found. The Constituent Assembly has transferred the decision to the President and to the National Assembly which will begin operations on 1 October 1979. It is hoped that whatever formula that may be found will take the rural areas (Local Government areas) into very strong consideration. A new revenue-sharing formula should make adequate funds available for rural economic and social transformation so that rural people may have an easier life, enjoyed by many urban people today.

Notes

1. *Reports of the Constitution Drafting Committee*, vol. II (Lagos), p. 132.
2. The Report was serialised in the *Daily Times* (Lagos), 5-10, 12 and 14-16 June 1978.
3. For a similar critique of the system of the so-called 'ex-gratia donations' to arbitrarily selected community councils by the ex-administrator of the former East Central State of Nigeria, Mr Ukpabi Asika, see Emmanuel J. Nwosu, 'Toward Integrated Approach to Rural Development in Imo and Anambra States of Nigeria', in *International Review of Administration Sciences*, no. 4 (Brussels, 1976), p. 280.
4. In the United States of America, efforts are also made to use a national revenue-sharing formula 'which would take into account each state's willingness to tax itself' (see Leonard Opperman, 'Aid for the States: Is Revenue Sharing the Answer?' in *The Review of Politics*, vol. 30, no. 1 (University of Notre Dame, Indiana, 1968) p. 45. Also, Adedotun Phillips has indicated that Nigeria's revenue-allocation system has all along lacked an incentive device, for encouraging and

stimulating states' internal tax effort; (A.O. Phillips, 'Reforming Nigeria's Revenue Allocation System' in *Nigerian Journal of Public Affairs*, vol. VI, no. 1 (1976), p. 83.

5. The special grants' account is for the rehabilitation of polluted oil-producing areas, national emergencies, disasters and general ecological degradation. In accepting the recommendations, the Federal Military Government lumped the 3% for the special grants' account with the Federal Government's share and designated the 3% share as a contingency fund.

6. The Federal Military Government accepted the report of the Technical Committee and directed the relevant Federal ministries to take action toward the implementation of the recommendations. See *Government Views on the Report of the Technical Committee on Revenue Allocation* (Federal Ministry of Information, Lagos, 1978).

7. The exception is provided by Decree No. 51 of 1972, whereby the tax paid by the armed forces personnel, external affairs officers and pensioners overseas all go 100% to the distributable pools account.

8. L.H. Schatzl, *Industrialisation in Nigeria: A Spatial Analysis* (Weltforum Verlag, Munich, 1973).

9. In 1965 these seven locations accounted for 77% of the numbers employed, 82% of wages/salaries, 79% of the gross output and 82% of gross value added.

10. Schatzl, *Industrialisation in Nigeria*, pp. 69-70.

11. Obafemi Awolowo, *The Strategy and Tactics of the Peoples' Republic of Nigeria* (Macmillan (Nigeria), 1970), p. 78.

12. Pius Okigbo, 'The Big Debate on Revenue Allocation', in *New Nigerian* (Kaduna), 6 June 1978, pp. 5, 6, 9, 14, 15 and 17.

13. He emphatically states: 'My own sympathies are clearly on the side of those who want to increase the allocation to the states', ibid., p. 6.

14. S.U. Ugoh, 'Report of the Technical Committee on Revenue Allocation: An Appraisal', *Daily Times* (Lagos), 23 and 24 June 1978.

15. For a detailed comment on the new criteria suggested by Abayode's Committee, see Okigbo, 'The Big Debate'.

12 BUDGETARY GOALS AND CONSTRAINTS IN NIGERIA

J.K. Onoh

1. Introduction

The budget is an annual comprehensive report of the state of the nation's economy. It reviews old economic and social problems and anticipates new ones. It surveys the future prospects of the economy and translates problems into goals or objectives. Monetary and fiscal policy instruments, direct economic intervention measures and institutional changes are then chosen and trimmed to match the desired objectives so that a country's internal and external equilibrium may be restored.

In a relatively fully employed economy which possesses all the attributes of the trade cycle such as expansion, boom, recession and depression, it is easier to analyse the economy and to appraise the consequences of budgetary provisions. A relatively fully employed economy is endowed with developed money and capital markets, the bedrock upon which the success of monetary policies squarely depends. It provides more reliable statistics relating to powerful economic indicators such as agricultural output, industrial output, employment level, investments, profits, market interest rates and balance of payment statistics. Monetary and fiscal policies, economic intervention measures and measures relating to institutional changes can only be properly applied to achieve the desired effects and to influence the programmed objectives if reliable vital statistics for policy analyses are available.

In an economy characterised by unemployment, which is not the consequence of recession or depression and which is highly import dependent, that is, with high import/GNP ratio, monetary policies have limited application because of the absence of a developed financial market, the action centre of monetary policies. Fiscal policies have also a limited application in the Keynesian sense because the Nigerian economy is not a relatively fully employed one which gradually lapsed into depression. There is therefore a limit to fiscal policy application in Nigeria. Deficit expenditure, for example, will not draw back idle resources into production as would be the case in a depressed economy. The policy of deficit expenditure has to be carefully weighed because it

194

can trigger off a dangerous inflationary pressure. Besides the limitations in terms of scope and choice of instruments in a non-classical economy such as Nigeria's, the danger is real that the available instruments may be so fractured, improperly or untimely applied that they achieve very little goals or even produce counter results.

Apart from the above situations which are endogenous to Nigeria there are exogenous factors emanating from other economies with which Nigeria has economic and trade relations which distort the effects of policy instruments. A good example of exogenously militating factors are the world monetary crisis and the world-wide inflationary pressure. The former has thrown the entire world monetary system out of equilibrium making external reserve management obviously difficult especially for the developing countries. It has destroyed the system of adjustable pegs reached at Bretton Woods in 1944. It has burst the wider exchange-rate band established by the Smithsonian Agreement in 1971 and sent two major world reserves, trading and intervention currencies, the dollar and sterling, floating at the world-exchange market. The dollar also lost its gold convertibility in the same year. The loss was a great set-back to the international monetary system. The exchange rates of these two major currencies have been cascading in terms of other world currencies. In fact their unique reserve, trading and intervention qualities have been very much impaired. Unfortunately Nigeria is forced to hold most of her external reserves in the asset portfolios of the dollar and the sterling countries because stronger currencies, like the German mark, are not used as a reserve currency. The West German authorities will only permit Nigeria to hold a small proportion of her foreign reserves in Deutschmark assets.

As the dollar and the sterling currencies continue to float and their rates continue to cascade, Nigeria's external reserves denominated in those currencies continue to erode in value. The real purchasing power of Nigeria's external reserves continue to fall making normal imports very difficult in terms of quantity and quality. The world-wide inflationary pressure accentuates the import problems and helps to worsen the country's overall balance of payments. The world monetary crisis and the world-wide inflationary pressure slow down developmental programmes and make the avowed policy of industrialisation, full employment and social change difficult to achieve.

2. Identification of Economic and Social Problems

Past Nigerian budgets have attempted to identify some of the economic and social problems of the country. Other problems have also been deduced by critics and analysts of the Nigerian economy. The following problems have so far been identified:

(a) low-growth rate of the economy;

(b) a very expensive and large defence-oriented army with zero-productive capacity in peace time;

(c) high inflationary pressure arising from:

> (i) low crude-oil production and the lack of automaticity of OPEC oil price adjustment to world inflationary prices,
>
> (ii) low agricultural output,
>
> (iii) high level of money supply arising from excessive military expenditure, government expenditure on projects with no direct capacity effect such as the FESTAC, World Scout Jamboree, West African Games and to an extent the Trade Fair Complex, and
>
> (iv) excessive deficit expenditure of Federal and State governments;

(d) a fall in government revenue as a result of diminishing oil revenue;

(e) housing shortage; and

(f) foreign exchange earning and reserve management problems.

The above problems have been the targets of budgetary policy measures over the years.

3. Budgetary Policy Objectives

Identified economic and social problems must be translated into a set of objectives or goals and matched with the appropriate policy instruments for achieving the stated objectives. If the objectives are achieved the economic and social problems would have been eliminated or reasonably reduced. The budgetary policy objectives derive from the national policy objectives of Nigeria as contained in the *Third National Development Plan 1975-80*, vol. 1.[1] The broad long-term national objectives are as follows:

(a) increase in *per capita* income,
(b) more even distribution of income,
(c) reduction in the level of unemployment,
(d) increase in the supply of high level manpower,
(e) diversification of the economy,
(f) balanced development, and
(g) indigenisation of economic activity.

The main policy objectives which Nigerian budgets have stressed are the following:

(a) efficient utilisation of limited resources through the re-ordering of government priorities,
(b) reduced government expenditure,
(c) re-engagement of the traditional resource base neglected because of the rich oil sector,
(d) fight against inflationary pressure,
(e) income redistribution,
(f) self-sufficiency in food through agricultural production,
(g) greater incentives to local industries, and
(h) an increase in the export of traditional produce in order to influence the balance of payments position and release pressure on the dwindling external reserve level.

The budgetary policy objectives are directly interpreted from the identified economic and social problems. However, the objectives must in turn be backed up by appropriate policy instruments. This is where the real problem lies. Under monetary policy there are no less than ten instruments of monetary and credit control ranging from variation in the percentage or structure of liquidity ratio, cash reserve ratio, interest rate restructuring, open-market operations, credit measures of various shades, stabilisation securities, special approval for loans etc. In the arena of fiscal policy there is equally a variety of policy instruments. But most of these policy instruments are nonstarters for an economy such as Nigeria's and do not therefore make any meaningful economic-social impacts. Some are simply blunt and unresponsive. The set of monetary and fiscal policy instruments available to an economy like Nigeria's are limited both in scope and choice. Nigerian authorities have been forced to engage some of them in their classical forms, others in fractured forms and some in redesigned forms. A good example of a redesigned instrument is the credit guidelines embodied in the monetary policy circulars of the Nigerian Central Bank. The fact is that there is a scarcity of effective policy instruments. Consequently the limited instruments have been unable to influence the desired objectives for neutralising the identified problems. Hence those problems continue to perpetuate themselves year in year out.

4. Instruments of Budgetary Policy

Nigeria is a mixed enterprise economy where the public and the private sectors play clearly defined roles. The overall aim of the government is to influence the economy to grow at a faster rate in order that the growing unemployed labour force may be absorbed in gainful occupations. Through gainful employment more output (income) will be generated, and the average standard of living and the social conditions of Nigerians will thereby be raised.

To achieve budgetary policy objectives economic activities of both the public and private sectors are orchestrated through the application of a variety of policy instruments. The broad instruments are the following:

(a) fiscal policy instruments;
(b) monetary and credit policy instruments;
(c) instruments of direct control; and
(d) changes in institutional arrangements.

These broad instruments and their sub-divisions of instruments have been coded for the purpose of this study and specified below:

1. Instruments of Fiscal Policies   (Code)

   Balances   A

   Balances at the beginning of fiscal year   A1
   Overall balance (deficit/surplus)   A2

   Government expenditure   B

   Agricultural production   B1
   Manufacturing and quarrying   B2
   Transport and communication   B3
   Education   B4

	(Code)
Health	B5
General administration	B6
Defence and internal security	B7
Subsidy and capital transfer to firms	B8
Transfer payments to households	B9
Government purchase of goods and services	B10
Payment of wages and salaries	B11
Transfer payments to foreigners	B12
Loan on-lent to states	B13

Government revenue	C
Personal income tax (direct tax)	C1
Company tax (direct tax)	C2
Petroleum-profit tax (direct tax)	C3
Capital gains, casino and airport taxes (direct tax)	C4
Import duties (indirect tax)	C5
Export duties (indirect tax)	C6
Excise duties (indirect tax)	C7
Property tax	C8
Inheritance tax	C9
Transfer payments from abroad	C10
Interest and repayments	C11
Mining royalties, rents and fees	C12
Earnings of corporations	C13
Fines and fees	C14

2. Instruments of monetary and credit controls (Code)

Government borrowings and lendings	D
Credit to foreigners	D1
Credit to households and firms	D2
Credit from foreigners	D3
Credit from households and firms	D4

Management of public debt	E
Open-market operation (sale of government securities)	E1
Open-market operation (repurchase of government securities)	E2

	(Code)
Instrument of interest policy	F
Minimum rediscount rate (bank rate)	F1
Fixing of ceiling rate	F2
Low- and high-lending rates for production and consumption activities respectively	F3

Instrument of direction and credit creation control	G
Credit guidelines (in favour of production sector)	G1
Credit ceiling	G2
Liquidity ratio variation	G3
Special deposits by commercial banks	G4
Cash reserve ratio	G5
Stabilisation securities	G6
Special central bank approval for certain loans	G7
Moral suasion	G8

Instrument for controlling lendings and borrowings of non-banking financial institutions	H
Control of borrowing of corporation and nationalised industries	H1
Control of new issues of corporation and firms	H2
Control of hire purchase	H3
Control of other financial institutions (e.g., merchant banks, insurance and investment banks)	H4

Instruments of exchange rate control	K
Revaluation	K1
Devaluation	K2
Currency Float	K3

	(Code)
3. Instruments of Direct Control	
Control of Balance of Payments	L
Control of private imports	L1
Control of government imports	L2
Control of private exports	L3
Exchange control	L4
Deferred payment system for imports	L5

	(Code)
Price control	**M**
Price control of goods and services	M1
Rent control	M2
Control of dividends	M3
Control of wages and salaries	M4

4. Changes in institutional arrangements

Institutional changes through changes in instruments	**N**
Changes in transfer payments to households	N1
Changes in subsidies to firms and farmers	N2
Changes in tax system	N3
Changes in credit system	N4
Changes in direct control	N5
Increase in the proportion of loans and advances to indigenous enterprises	N6
Pioneer industry tax concession	N7

Institutional changes through the production sphere	**O**
Agricultural land reforms	O1
Indigenisation of the economy	O2
Creation of national institutions (e.g., banks)	O3
Changes in government participation in the economy	O4
Changes in market structure (competition)	O5
Special agricultural credit scheme	O6

By varying an instrument or a combination of instruments certain positive or negative effects may be generated in the economy which may influence the objectives. Some of the instruments are capable of achieving significant positive effects while the effects of some may be insignificant. Others may not have immediate direct effects but are indirectly capable of positive or negative influences on the set-out objectives in the long run, depending on the upward or downward variation of the instruments and also on the degree of variations. Some of the instruments may run counter to the objectives if applied, some may be unresponsive. A good example is the interest rate in a developing economy. The effects the variety of instruments may have on the economic objectives will generally depend on the level of development the economy had attained in terms of structural changes, level of employment, the degree of dependence, the ratio of imports to GNP, etc. A

sharp and effective instrument with respect to an advanced economy
may be less use when applied to a developing economy which is still on
the verge of economic take off.

5. Budgetary Constraints

A number of factors constrain the realisation of policy objectives and
they differ from economy to economy. It is not possible, however, to
discuss all the constraining factors in this chapter. Discussion of budgetary constraints will therefore be limited to the major ones affecting
the Nigerian budgetary system. These constraints may have relative
validity in other countries of the same economic structure, political
and economic systems and of the same level of development.

(a) Constraint Arising from the Choice of Instruments

A developing economy such as Nigeria's is confronted with a variety of
instruments not designed for a developing economy but originally con-
ceived for an advanced economy which suffers from cyclical fluctuations. In Table 12.1, an attempt has been made to tabulate the set of
objectives of the Nigerian budgetary system and the possible instruments which are likely to influence the objectives positively or nega-
tively. The degree of effectiveness of the instruments can only be
viewed in relative terms. However, one can state generally that the relative size of the instruments in terms of the envisaged policy results,
the appropriate choice and combination of groups of instruments and
their timely applications will determine their relative effects on the
economy and on the objectives.

The fewer the objectives the greater the chances of their realisation
because the complex problem of choosing and combining multiple-
policy instruments becomes greatly reduced. If there are few policy
instruments they are easier to manoeuvre than when there are many. In
a developing economy, however, where there are numerous objectives
to be realised policy makers strive to combine a series of instruments to
achieve a number of objectives at the same time. Under the circumstances some of the instruments intended to achieve a specific objective or
objectives may run counter to one or more of the other objectives pursued by the authorities. A good example of an objective which may
activate a countervailing instrument is defence and internal security
expenditure. National defence and security objective counters anti-
inflationary objectives. The former expands money supply while the

Table 12.1: Degree of Effectiveness of Instruments in Relation to Objectives

Objectives (Codes)	Directly positive and significant instruments (Codes)	Directly positive but insignificant instruments (Codes)	Indirectly influencing positive (negative instruments) (Codes)	Instruments militating against objectives (Codes)
(a)	B1, B13^a, F3^b, G1, O1, O6	B9, B11, D2	B3, C6, L1, L3^c, L4, L5, N2, N4, N6	M1
(b)	B2, B8, B10, G1, L1, N6	B10, D2, L2	B3, C2, C4, C5, C7, F3, G2, H4, L4, L5, N2, M4, O5	H1, H2, M1, M3
(c)	B2, B8, B13^d, D2, G1, N6		B3, B9, B10, C2, C4, C5, F3, H2, H4, L1, L2, N2, N4, O2	K1, M1, M3
(d)	B8, C5, L1, N7	L2, N6	B10, C2, D2, F3, G1, L4, L5, N2, N3, N4, O2	M1
(e)		D3, D4, E1, G1	F1, H4, M3, M4, N3, N4	H2
(f)	B1, B2, B8, G1, M1, M4	B10, F1, L1, L2	B4, B11, L4, L5, N2, N4, O2, O4	H2
(g)	B1, B2, B10, M1	B9, B11, N1, O6	D2, M4, O1, O5	L1, L2, L4, L5
(h)	B1, B2, B10, E1, G2-G7, M1, M2, M4	A1, A2, F3	C2-C4, G8, H1, H4, N1, N4	C3, L1, L2, L4, L5
(i)	B9, B11, C1, C2, C8, C9	F3, G1	M1, M2, N3	C5, C6
(j)	C5, H3, L1, L4, L5		N1, N3	
(k)	B1, B2, C10, L1, L2, L4, L5	C12, K2^e	A1, A2, B4, B6, B7, N1, N2	B12, C6, D1, D3
(l)	H1, L2, O4		N2, O2, O5	B8, B13, D1, D2
(m)	B1, B2, B4	B5, B8, B11		M4

Notes: ^{a} If a part of the loan to states is invested in agricultural production.
^{b} If the minimum-lending rate favours agricultural loans.
^{c} If Nigerian food exports are banned.
^{d} If a part of the loan is used for the opening up of new industries.
^{e} Not useful for developing economies with mainly exportable commodities which are demand and price inelastic in the international market.

latter is intended to contract money supply. In Nigeria, for example, the recurrent and capital expenditure for defence and internal security constitutes a sizeable proportion of the budget (see Tables 12.2 and 12.3). Expenditure of that nature has no productive capacity effect in the economy. It only enhances liquidity, increases aggregate demand for goods and services and fans the flames of inflation which other policy instruments are intended to counter. In order to minimise the countervailing effects of policy instruments a developing economy has to rank and limit her short-term budgetary objectives so that a better combination of instruments with minimum countervailing effects on objectives may be achieved.

(b) Constraint Arising from Deficit Budgeting

The Federal and the State Governments' deficits continue to increase year by year as shown in Table 12.4. Between 1970 and 1977, State Governments consistently incurred deficits. In 1977 the deficit of all the states amounted to a little over 50 per cent of their total expenditure. The Federal Government, on the other side, incurred deficits between 1970 and 1977, with the exception of a minor surplus in 1971 and 1973 and a major surplus in 1974 and 1977.

The Federal Government and the State Governments incurred deficits between 1970 and 1977 with the exception of 1974. The surplus of 1974 may be explained by the monetisation of oil revenue by the Federal Government and the increase in world oil prices in that year. Table 12.4 speaks for itself. The consequence of the overall deficit is felt in the economy in a number of ways. The Federal Government has to borrow from the Central Bank as well as from the public to bridge the deficit gap. This implies competing with the private sector in the open market for funds. Most projects started by the Federal and State Governments have not been realised because of the inadequacy of their funds. Contractors who have not been paid for a job completed refuse to take up further contracts with the Government with the consequence that most projects which are of economic importance or quasi-economic importance are grounded. Where the Federal Government succeeds in borrowing from the Central Bank as statutorily allowed such funds have their inflationary impacts on the economy because the money borrowed from the Central Bank has no direct relationship to productivity. Unlike the revenue from taxes Government borrowings from the Central Bank implies additional injection of money stock in the economy.

Table 12.2: Federal Government Current Expenditure (Jan.-Dec.) in Nm

Function	1969 Amt	1969 %	1970 Amt	1970 %	1971 Amt	1971 %	1972 Amt	1972 %	1973 Amt	1973 %	1974 Amt	1974 %	1975 Amt	1975 %	1976 Amt	1976 %	1977 Amt	1977 %
1. Administration	225.6	47.3	578.8	56.2	370.2	32.9	498.3	35.3	454.3	37.4	555.4	20.5	1,040.4	22.3	1010.2	18.5	1,055.4	16.6
General Administration																		
Defence and internal security																		
2. Economic services	22.2	4.6	24.2	2.4	45.0	4.0	46.2	3.3	52.4	4.3	74.4	2.7	131.8	2.8	141.8	2.6	191.7	3.1
Agriculture	4.8	1.0	4.4	0.4	6.6	0.6	12.4	0.9	13.4	1.1	24.6	1.0	38.8	0.8	18.5	0.3	42.0	0.7
Construction	11.8	2.5	13.2	1.3	24.0	2.1	20.8	1.5	22.0	1.8	30.8	1.0	55.3	1.2	73.7	1.4	73.0	1.2
Transport & comm.	3.8	0.8	4.0	0.4	8.6	0.8	7.4	0.5	9.8	0.8	9.9	0.4	20.0	0.4	27.3	0.5	27.1	0.4
Other econ. services	1.8	0.3	2.6	0.3	5.8	0.5	5.6	0.4	7.2	0.6	9.1	0.3	17.7	0.4	22.3	0.4	49.6	0.8
3. Social and community services	12.0	2.5	16.6	1.6	30.3	2.7	29.4	2.1	31.1	2.6	94.9	3.5	287.5	6.0	634.6	11.6	368.5	5.9
Education	3.6	0.7	3.2	0.3	6.8	0.6	7.3	0.5	10.4	0.9	62.5	2.3	218.9	4.6	522.0	9.6	248.4	4.0
Health	7.2	1.5	12.0	1.2	21.4	1.9	19.9	1.4	18.3	1.5	29.1	1.1	62.4	1.3	83.5	1.5	85.1	1.4
Other social and comm. services	1.2	0.3	1.4	0.1	2.6	0.2	2.2	0.2	2.4	0.2	3.3	0.1	6.2	0.1	29.1	0.5	35.0	0.5
4. Transfers	217.4	45.6	409.6	39.8	678.4	60.4	838.4	59.4	675.3	55.7	1,986.2	73.3	3,265.4	68.9	3,673.0	67.3	4,652.5	74.4
Public debt servicing:																		
a) Internal	25.6	5.3	31.0	3.0	92.2	8.2	67.7	4.8	62.4	5.1	104.4	3.9	155.2	3.3	311.4	5.7	155.3	2.5
b) External	46.0	9.6	99.6	9.7	43.2	3.9	26.2	1.9	30.8	2.6	29.1	1.1	32.7	0.7	30.4	0.6	36.3	0.6
Statutory appropriation to states	138.2	29.0	267.6	26.0	496.0	44.2	331.0	23.4	307.3	25.3	643.0	23.7	1,039.9	21.9	1,142.8	20.9	1,572.5	25.1
Non-statutory appr. to states	*	*	*	*	*	*	*	*	11.8	1.0	0.5	—	9.1	0.2	502.2	9.2	424.4	6.8
Pensions and gratuities	7.6	1.7	8.2	0.8	17.0	1.5	13.5	1.0	13.4	1.1	15.4	1.1	23.3	0.5	42.0	0.8	30.1	0.5
Develop. fund	—	—	3.2	0.3	15.0	2.7	400.0	28.3	249.6	20.6	1,193.8	44.0	2,005.2	42.3	1,644.2	30.1	2,433.9	38.9
Total	477.2	100.0	1,028.2	100.0	1,124.4	100.0	1,412.4	100.0	1,213.1	100.0	2,710.9	100.0	4,740.1	100.0	5,459.6	100.0	6,253.1	100.0

Note: * Less than N0.2 million.
Source: Central Bank of Nigeria, *Annual Report and Statement of Accounts* of various years.

Table 12.3: Federal Government Capital Expenditure (Jan.-Dec.) in Nm

Function	1969		1970		1971		1972[b]		1973		1974		1975		1976		1977	
	Amt	%	Amt	%	Amt	%	Amt	%	Amt	%	Amt	%	Amt	%	Amt	%	Amt	%
1. Administration	55.6	49.6	140.4	71.9	47.8	40.5	108.8	24.1	133.8	23.7	268.3	17.3	747.8	21.3	795.4	18.8	1,013.4	18.6
General administration													393.7	11.2	376.1	8.9	518.8	9.5
Defence and internal security													354.1	10.1	419.3	9.9	494.6	9.1
2. Economic services	22.4	19.9	31.0	15.9	32.6	27.6	132.9	29.5	249.5	44.1	466.1	30.1	1,314.7	37.4	2,231.4	52.6	3,124.6	57.4
Agriculture	2.4	2.1	4.8	2.5	5.4	4.6	20.7	4.6	35.4	6.2	87.4	5.6	211.2	6.0	129.2	3.0	113.7	2.1
Manufacture and Quarrying[a]	3.8	3.4	5.0	2.6	—	—	2.8	0.6	—	—	—	—	—	—	574.4	13.6	959.6	17.6
Transport and comm.	10.6	9.4	19.2	9.8	23.8	20.1	90.9	20.1	122.0	21.6	254.9	16.5	710.8	20.2	1,277.2	30.1	1,758.7	32.3
Other econ. services	5.6	5.0	2.0	1.0	3.4	2.9	18.5	4.1	92.1	16.3	123.8	8.0	392.7	11.2	250.6	5.9	292.6	5.4
3. Social and comm. services	1.6	1.4	2.8	1.4	5.2	4.4	42.0	9.3	40.4	7.1	358.1	23.1	927.4	26.3	899.7	21.2	824.9	15.2
Education	1.6	1.4	2.8	1.4	1.6	1.4	21.3	4.7	16.3	2.9	134.4	8.7	631.1	17.9	529.2	12.5	255.8	4.7
Health	*		*		2.6	2.2	6.8	1.5	16.6	2.9	14.2	0.9	20.4	0.9	56.8	1.3	38.7	0.7
Other social and comm. services	*		—		1.0	0.8	13.9	3.1	7.5	1.5	209.5	13.5	275.9	7.8	313.7	7.4	530.4	9.8
4. Transfers	32.6	29.1	21.2	10.8	32.4	27.5	167.6	37.5	142.0	25.1	456.9	29.5	528.3	15.0	315.4	7.4	479.4	8.8
Financial obligations	2.0	1.9	0.4	0.2	11.6	9.9	12.2	2.7	11.4	2.0	131.0	8.5	217.8	6.2	114.8	2.7	41.7	0.8
Loan on-rent to states'	30.4	27.0	20.8	10.6	20.8	17.6	155.4	34.4	130.6	23.1	325.9	21.0	310.5	8.8	200.6	4.7	437.7	8.0
reconstruction	0.2	0.4	—		—		—		—		—		—		—		—	
Total	112.2	100.0	195.4	100.0	118.0	100.0	451.3	100.0	565.7	100.0	1,549.4	100.0	3,518.2	100.0	4,241.9	100.0	5,442.3	100.0

Notes: [a] Until 1974 the figures reflected expenditure for construction.
[b] 1969-71 reflect January to September only.

Source: Central Bank of Nigeria, *Annual Report and Statement of Accounts* of various years.

Table 12.4: Revenue and Expenditures of Federal and State Governments (Nm)

Items	1970	1971	1972	1973	1974	1975	1976	1977
1. Current revenue of all states	313.3	372.0	489.8	510.3	837.9	1,830.4	2,154.9	2,729.3
2. Current revenue of Federal Government	633.2	1,169.0	1,404.8	1,695.3	4,537.0	5,514.7	6,765.9	8,042.4
Total	946.5	1,541.0	1,894.6	2,205.6	5,374.9	7,345.1	8,920.8	10,771.7
1. Expenditure of all states	557.2	642.4	862.4	1,056.5	1,579.6	3,363.2	4,838.7	6,681.5
2. Expenditure of Federal Government	1,127.0	997.4	1,463.6	1,529.2	2,740.6	5,942.6	7,856.7	8,823.8
Total	1,684.2	1,639.8	2,326.0	2,585.7	4,320.2	9,305.8	12,695.4	15,505.3
1. Overall deficit/surplus (all states)	−244.0	−270.4	−372.6	−546.2	−741.7	−1,228.9	−2,683.8	−3,952.2
2. Overall deficit/surplus (Federal Government)	−493.7	171.6	− 58.8	166.1	1,796.4	− 427.9	−1,090.8	1,709.7
Total	737.7	− 98.8	− 431.4	380.1	1,054.7	−1,656.8	−3,774.6	−2,242.5

Sources: Central Bank of Nigeria, *Annual Report and Statement of Accounts* of various years and State governments' *Approved Estimates*

Table 12.5: States' Revenue/Expenditure and Federal Transfers (Nm)

Items	1970/71	1971/72	1972/73	1973/74	1974/75	1975/76	1976/77	1977/78
1. Current revenue of all states	313.0	372.0	489.8	510.3	837.9	1,830.4	2,154.9	2,729.3
2. Independent revenue of states	82.6	120.2	140.6	200.9	246.9	777.0	797.0	923.1
3. Transfers to states from Federal Government	230.4	251.8	349.2	309.4	591.0	1,053.4	1,361.8	1,806.3
4. 2. as % of 1.	26.4	32.3	28.7	39.4	29.4	40.4	36.9	33.8
5. 3. as % of 1.	73.6	67.7	71.3	60.6	70.6	59.6	63.1	66.2
6. Total expenditure of states:	557.2	642.4	862.4	1,056.5	1,579.6	3,363.2	4,838.7	6,681.5
(a) current expenditure	(314.0)	(354.4)	(436.2)	(566.3)	(697.6)	(1,706.4)	(2,127.1)	(2,691.1)
(b) capital expenditure	(243.2)	(288.0)	(426.2)	(490.2)	(882.2)	(1,656.8)	(2,711.6)	(3,990.4)
7. Overall surplus/deficit of states	−244.0	−270.4	−372.6	−546.2	−741.7	−1,228.9	−2,683.8	−3,952.2

Sources: Central Bank of Nigeria, *Annual Report and Statement of Accounts* of various years and Federal and State governments' *Approved Estimates*.

Deficit budgeting has a distortionary effect on a developing economy such as Nigeria's because deficit expenditure can not be classically applied with the same effects as was the case during the depression. In an economy which had attained full employment of resources before lapsing into depression it is possible to use deficit expenditure to draw back idle resources into economic use. This may not apply satisfactorily in a developing economy. On the contrary it causes inflation and shifts business from productive activities to speculatory activities which only enhance the inflationary pressure. Extreme care has to be taken in the determination of the size of the deficit in the budgetary system of developing economies.

(c) Constraint Arising from Delay in the Disbursement of Statutory Allocations

This is a major constraint in the effective execution of state projects. As Table 12.5 suggests State Governments depend to a large extent on the Federal Government for most of their funds. Over 50 per cent of the State Governments' revenue is derived from Federal Government sources. The low tax yields in the various states make it extremely difficult for the states to be dependent on themselves for the greater proportion of their revenue. The Federal Government has to provide the balance to enable the states carry out their recurrent and capital expenditure. The statutory allocations which the Federal Government provides the states are at times not released for several months because of bureaucratic bottlenecks. Consequently the State governments find themselves in an embarrassing situation of not being able to carry out their normal development functions. By the time the statutory grants are released or partly released by the Federal Government the fiscal year may have run into its third quarter. Local governments are themselves constrained from carrying out their functions as their statutory allocations from the State governments are also delayed. The State and Local governments are then compelled to rush their programmes which under the circumstances are either half-way abandoned or are poorly and badly executed. The delay in the release of statutory allocations to the states is a major constraint for the 19 states which make up the Federal Republic of Nigeria and whose activities go a long way to determine the overall economic and social performance of the Nigerian economy.

The non-statutory grants which the Federal Government awards the states are discriminatory because there are no clearly defined criteria for awarding non-statutory grants. The Federal authorities apply their discretion in such awards and in most cases the most deserving states do not benefit adequately from non-statutory grants.

(d) Constraint Arising from the Pattern of Federal Government Expenditure

This is a major constraint because it runs counter to the concept of even and balanced development which has been greatly stressed. There is no law restricting the expenditure of Federal revenue; the Federal authorities reserve the right to apply the revenue in any State or States of their choice which may not necessarily be the State in greater need for funds. Consequently it has not been possible to achieve even development. There is a tendency for Federal authorities to concentrate Federal projects in specific areas without any consideration for other areas. The Federal Government is the biggest spender in the economy. Federal projects have significant impact on the overall employment level of the economy and in particular in those areas where they are sited. Major projects normally have forward and backward linkage effects, they obviously have employment and income effects which some areas do not benefit from. If the constraint on the path of balanced development is not removed and if the Federal expenditure and allocation of projects should continue unchecked a situation of dual economy may result which is normally characterised by societal tensions. Egalitarianism can only be achieved where projects are located in a balanced manner in an integrated economic system.

Besides the unbalanced siting of Federal projects the pattern of Federal Government budgets for recurrent and capital expenditure until 1975 reveals some neglect in the areas of economic, social and community services. Tables 12.2 and 12.3 provide data of Federal Government expenditures in the various units which are of national interest.

(e) Revenue Constraint

The major source of revenue of the country is indirect taxes, because of the difficulty in the assessment and collection of direct tax from taxable adults and firms. It has not been possible to evolve an appropriate machinery for the assessment and collection of taxes. The inefficiency of tax officials and to some extent, the corruption of some of them, make it extremely difficult for adequate revenue to be realised through direct taxes. The burden of direct tax falls squarely on the salaried group of workers while the rich businessmen and contractors continue to evade tax. Because of the indirect nature of the tax both the rich and the poor bear the brunt irrespective of their income levels. This defeats the objective of income redistribution. The heavy indirect taxes continue to widen the gap between the rich and the poor, contrary to the objective of bridging the income gap.

(f) Constraint in the Production Sphere

It is only a production-oriented economy that can satisfy the labour force's yearnings for greater income and greater employment. It has not been possible in Nigeria's case to achieve accelerated production activities capable of employing the growing population in gainful occupations. In the agricultural sphere output has fallen and has continued to fall. Policy instruments have not succeeded in generating greater agricultural output. The exodus of people from the rural areas to urban centres in search of better paying jobs has worsened the problem of agricultural production and aggravated the problems of unemployment and urban social problems. A decline in agricultural and industrial outputs does not augur well for an economy striving towards full employment of resources. Imports of food, goods and services continue to increase year by year. A number of policy measures have been taken to reverse the trend but no significant results have been achieved.

(g) Reserve Management Constraint

Reserve management has been a major constraint since 1974 when the country had an external reserve capacity which could support about 25 months of imports. Unfortunately for Nigeria the world-wide inflation, the floating of the reserve currencies such as the dollar and the pound sterling in which Nigeria keeps her reserve assets had repercussions on the real value of the Nigerian external reserves. For a decade Nigeria has been confronted with the problem of reserve management, that is, the problem of investing or keeping the external reserves in relatively safe assets. But it has not been possible to find such safe assets which cannot be readily theatened by inflationary pressure or by the consequence of the floating dollar and sterling currencies. As already stated, the relatively safe assets such as the Deutschmark cannot be held as reserve assets. Nigeria has had no other option than to continue to hold a greater portion of her reserves in the dollar and pound sterling assets which are very sensitive to world inflationary impacts and to the present world monetary crisis.

Another constraint is that Nigeria has no long-term reserve policy. Nigeria's reserve policy is highly short. There is no long-term reserve target around which monetary policies can be planned. Instead Nigerian authorities allow the external reserve level to accidentally realise itself. Monetary, fiscal, economic and institutional measures are then taken to stop the declining reserve level and to hold the dwindling reserve position in check. Until a long-term reserve policy is evolved and the proper instruments designed to achieve a long-term reserve target are designed, reserve management will continue to constitute a problem to the Nigerian monetary authorities.

6. A Review of the Effects of Budgetary Measures

Budgetary measures are aimed at increasing home productivity especially in the agricultural and manufacturing industries, at reducing inflationary pressure and at improving the external reserve level.

Reduced government expenditure is expected to reduce the growing level of money supply, a major source of inflationary pressure. Price control measures are to assist in the fight against inflation. The permissible rate of expansion of banks' total loans and advances has been reduced from 40 per cent to 30 per cent in order to slow down bank credit money – another source of increased money supply and money-velocity. Import prohibition is to alleviate the adverse balance of payments position and to release pressure on the dwindling reserve level.

In order to assess the effectiveness of past budgetary measures in terms of the intended objectives one should study some of Nigeria's economic indicators as compiled by the Central Bank of Nigeria. There are several economic indicators in an economy but some of them are regarded as major indicators. Their movements are closely watched. They reveal how far policy measures have succeeded.

Table 12.6: Some of Nigeria's Economic Indicators

Items	1975	1976	1977	1978
Consumer price index (rural)	(100)	123.3	136.3	158.8*
Consumer price index (urban)	(100)	124.3	141.3	170.5*
Index of industrial production	125.7	143.3	134.9	134.1*
Bank credit (Nm)				
To government	−1,281.5	199.5	2,094.4	2,965.3[a]
To private sector	488.6	2,617.3	3,514.4	4,136.3[a]
Money supply (N'000)	2,044.059	3,292.996	4,794.413	4,763.008[a]
Foreign exchange reserve (Nm)	3,702.7	3,482.5	3,037.0[b]	1,334.3[a]
Food imports (Nm)	298.8	441.7	499.1[b]	na.

Notes: *June figure 1978.
[a] August 1978.
[b] Food import till August 1977. Estimate for the year based on an eight-month average will give a total food import amounting to N748.8 million in 1977. An exponential projection will put the import at about N1 billion in 1978.
Sources: Central Bank of Nigeria, *Annual Report* and *Monthly Reports*.

Price index, for example, is a measure of rising or falling prices. Table 12.6 reveals that prices are still rising as shown by both the rural and urban consumer indices. Consumer-price indices however tell the average price situation. Some prices may be rising and some may be falling. For example, food prices which constitute a part of the general consumer-price index and which are not reflected separately on the table have fallen. The fall in food prices may be attributed to increasing agricultural output as a result of effective government agricultural policy measures. One may also be tempted to interpret the falling food prices as a consequence of increased food imports as revealed in Table 12.6. In 1975 Nigeria imported food amounting to N298.8 million. In 1976 the level rose to N441.7 million. In 1977 the estimated food import was N748.8 million and by exponential projection food imports for 1978 reached the N1 billion estimate. These obviously alarming trends may have necessitated the revolutionary agricultural policies of the preceding year such as the agricultural loans scheme operated by the Central Bank but disbursed by the commercial banks on behalf of the Central Bank and the transfer of agriculture to Schedule III of the Nigerian Enterprises Promotion Decree to encourage foreigners to invest in agriculture. Other incentives of the 1978/9 budget such as the exemption of agricultural plant and machinery from import duty are added incentives to agricultural production. It is too early to evaluate the effect of these measures but it appears that food imports will continue for a long time.

Industrial production has stagnated as shown by the indices of industrial production. Incentives in the area of manufacturing are urgently required by reviewing company taxes and by making raw-material imports easier. Inadequate power supply of the past years may have helped the stagnation.

Money supply had been held reasonably in check and this has obviously slowed down the rate of inflation which in some past years exceeded the 20 points position between two years. Foreign-exchange reserves of Nigeria have not improved. On the contrary they are on the decline. The import prohibition measures have not had the desired effects. There is a feeling that the diminishing foreign-exchange reserve level is the consequence of over-invoicing. The engagement of a Swiss surveillance company to check the prices and quantities of imports to Nigeria is aimed at improving the reserve position. The fear is deep, however, that the measure may boomerang. Imports of machinery and plant required for developmental and industrialisation programmes may be hampered because they may fail to arrive on schedule to harmonise with the phases of the development programme. All these may lead to an inflationary situation which may be very difficult to contain. It may be true that Zambia employs such a surveillance agency to control her imports, but Zambia's volume of trade is small relative to Nigeria's and Zambia trades mainly with Britain which makes control easy. Nigeria on the other hand has widely diversified trade links with many countries and firms.

In order to improve the foreign-exchange position the Nigerian Government incurred in 1978 a Euro-dollar loan totalling N627.4 million which is about 63.1 per cent of all public external debts. In 1979 the Federal Government began to negotiate additional loans.

7. Conclusion

From the above discourse one can say that Nigeria is confronted by a number of problems in terms of policy objectives and in terms of instruments for realising those objectives. In view of the inexperience of our policy makers and policy executors in the manipulation of a complex set of instruments to achieve a multiple set of objectives it may be extremely useful if budgetary policy objectives are kept as limited as possible so that a few, but appropriate, instruments may be effectively applied to realise the limited objectives of the fiscal year. A distinction should therefore be made between short-term policy objectives and long-term policy objectives. Nigeria's policy objectives which are long-term in nature should be taken care of by the long-term development plans. Budgetary policy objectives should be realisable within the twelve calendar months that make up a fiscal year. It is therefore absolutely necessary to differentiate between long-term objectives and short-term objectives in future budgetary exercises.

Notes

1. *Third National Development Plan 1975-80*, vol. 1 (Central Planning Office, Federal Ministry of Economic Development, Lagos), p. 29.

13 SOURCES OF FINANCE FOR NIGERIAN COMPANIES

Obi Mordi

1. Introduction

The method of financing business depends largely on the type of business. The type of ownership of business has always been a convenient criterion of business classification, for instance:

  (i) single (sole) proprietorships;
 (ii) partnerships;
(iii) joint stock companies[1] (private and public);
 (iv) national (state) corporations;
  (v) co-operatives[2].

Literature abounds which discusses exhaustively these types of business including their advantages and disadvantages. This chapter therefore will not belabour the usual arguments. Of major interest will be the aspect of finance sources for the various types of business. There are two methods of financing: the traditional method based on type of ownership and the (economic) developmental approach which emphasises (economic) sectoral pattern of business activity. This chapter will be concerned with the latter. Some businesses are not financed in the form of cash directly but in kind. This will be treated briefly and separately.

Financing national corporations is largely a budgetary affair of the owner-government. Even when the corporations borrow funds externally, the ultimate debtor is the owner-government. The corporations function as appendages of the government under the supervision of the relevant ministry or authority. Though the existence and functioning of national corporations have often become topical issues, it is not so much the issue of knowing the sources of their finance that has aroused public interest, but rather their management and pricing policies. These do not fall within the scope of this chapter, which also will exclude the issue of the state corporations and the co-operatives.

2. Type of Ownership and Sources of Finance

(a) Finance of Single (Sole) Proprietorships

Finance of single proprietorships derives largely from the capital or financial resources of the owner. If the proprietor's capital base is not enough to support the business only three sources are open to him:

(a) finance from friends and relations;
(b) finance from banks;
(c) finance from the Government(s).

Obviously, his ability to attract capital from the creditors depends on the amount of confidence placed in him with respect to repayment. While it is possible for him to attract funds from his friends and relatives sometimes without much rigour and stringency, the banks and the government(s) will usually demand from him clear evidence of profitability and financial viability. Further, while a bank may sometimes not bother itself with the reasonableness of the project from the socioeconomic point of view, the government(s) will not only look into this issue but will also further adjudge the project in terms of the government's priorities with respect to optimal development of the economy. Sole proprietorships are inherently small-scale industries.[3]

Actual government support of sole proprietorships depends on financial and budgetary measures. It is not only the level of budget allocation for small-scale industries that matters, but also the availability and disbursement of funds at the material time. The problem of small-scale industries credit scheme will be discussed later. One can only remark at this stage that a sum of N20m has been earmarked, to use the official jargon, for small-scale industries during the plan period 1975-80.[4]

(b) Finance of Partnerships

Sources of finance for partnerships do not differ in any significant way from the case of sole proprietorships. Other than the fact that a partnership widens the capital base in the sense that there are contributions (in cash and in kind) by more than one person, partnerships and sole proprietorships are largely in the same category with regard to sources of finance.

This is particularly so as partnerships would usually be in the category of small-scale business. Furthermore, there is no limit, as is the case with sole proprietorships, to each and every partner's liabilities to creditors.[5]

(c) Finance of Joint Stock Companies

The traditional sources of finance for public companies are subscription to equities (stocks or shares), borrowing through issue of debentures (bonds), borrowing from banks (and other companies), ploughing back the companies, profits and, in the case of Nigeria, exploiting loopholes in taxation regulations. Emphasis in this section will be on public companies. Private companies, which, strictly speaking, are joint-stock companies, are as yet not predominant in the economy. Like public companies, the liability of a private shareholder is limited; the company is a legal person. Unlike public companies, the shares are not transferable; the number of partners should not be more than 50, and invitation to the public to subscribe to shares is not allowed. Private companies are largely small businesses which, among other socio-economic considerations, provide families or close associates with an economically safe platform to venture into business without the fear of losing more than the share contributions of members.

(i) Equities. The recent indigenisation exercises have helped to increase tremendously the number of public companies and the shareholding habits of Nigerians. This is simply because most companies have, perforce, become 'Nigerian companies', with public issues of equities, and also with 'Nigerian citizens' acquiring the shares. Business indigenisation has added another criterion in discussing the sources of finance to companies in the Nigerian context, namely the criterion of citizenship. It is now meaningful, with regard to politico-economic sensitivities, to distinguish between 'foreign' and 'indigenous' sources of funds.

This distinction should not be confused as such with the distinction between *external* and *internal* sources of funds.[6] The criterion for the latter distinction could be termed that of fund-ownership whereby funds generated within the company are grouped as internal finance while funds generated from outside, say loans, debentures, equities are grouped under external finance. One important feature of the indigenisation exercise is the evidence produced that capital is not only available from the masses, if tapped in appropriate denominations, but also that at least the urban Nigerian masses have become conscious of the importance of equities as a viable avenue for investment. Almost all the share issues were oversubscribed. For instance, the issue of the Nigerian Bottling Company was oversubscribed 3.6 times, while that of R.T. Briscoe (Nigeria) Limited was oversubscribed as much as 6.5 times.[7] In the first half of 1977, in the new-issues market, the nominal value of shares of the twelve companies quoted was N78.5 million. All were over-subscribed.[8]

A misconception on equities and business financing should be pointed out. It is not always the case that share 'floating', as it is sometimes termed, by companies leads to an increase in capital base. In this regard one has to distinguish between 'offers for sale' and 'offers for subscription', even though both lead to an injection of external funds into the issuing company. Whereas offer for subscription would usually lead to increase in the capital base of the company, it is not necessarily the case with offers for sale as this is actually for replacement of capital: the previous shareowners are being bought off by the company.

(ii) Reinvestment of Profit. Reinvestment or ploughing back of profits is an internal source of finance usually considered 'safe', particularly in terms of cost. The availability of profit reserves is itself a function of the dividend policy of a company. In the recent past an interesting controversy did arise as to the particular dividend policy of Nigerian companies in the indigenisation era.[9]

The controversy is beyond the scope of this chapter. One can only repeat the obvious here that the more liberal the dividend policy, the less the availability of retained earnings for re-investment. Table 13.1 presents the capital (issued and paid-up), current earnings (E), retained earnings (RE) and the percentage of retained earnings to current earnings.

The figures in brackets under retained earnings represent the amount of dissavings in order to pay dividends. That is, not only were the whole current earnings used up for dividend payments but also the previously accumulated profits were depleted to the extent of the figures shown in brackets. This applies also to the figures in brackets in the column showing percentage relation of retained earnings to current earnings. The result of subtracting 100 from the figures in brackets shows the extent of depletion of accumulated reserves, over and above the depletion of current earnings, in percentage of current earnings. On the aggregate, for the 13 companies, the amount of depletion of both current and old earnings (profit reserves) by some companies in 1970 and 1972 far outweigh the profits retained by the rest of the companies. Hence in 1970 and 1972, N1.5 million and approximately N6 million respectively were dissaved.[10]

(iii) Loan Financing. There are various forms of borrowing by business firms such as bills of exchange, trade debts, intercompany debts, bank loans, overdrafts, etc. These forms of loans are usually short-term.

Table 13.1: Capital and Retained Earnings (1969-72) in 13 Selected Companies (N'000)

	1969				1970				1971				1972			
	Cap.	E	RE	%	Cap.	E	RE	%	Cap.	E	RE	%	Cap.	E	RE	%
Bata Nigeria Ltd	800	434	274	63.1	800	814	404	49.6	1,200	979	179	18.3	1,300	808	(512)	(163.4)
Nigerian Breweries Ltd	4,000	2,475	475	19.2	4,000	1,286	(714)	155.5	4,000	3,483	1,083	31.1	4,000	3,011	(389)	(109.7)
Lever Brothers Nigeria Ltd	2,400	1,003	283	28.2	3,400	1,528	428	28.0	3,400	1,994	114	5.7	3,400	2,712	132	4.9
P. Z. & Co. (Nigeria) Ltd	1477.2	321	321	100.0	1477.2	385	200	51.9	1477.2	412	(79)	119.2	1477.2	460	(426)	(192.6)
The Metal Box Co. Nigeria Ltd	1,800	450	225	50.0	1,800	204	(21)	110.3	2,160	389	(214)	155.0	2,160	489	219	44.8
R.T. Briscoe (Nigeria) Ltd	400	146	106	72.6	400	252	152	60.3	400	578	418	72.3	400	1,164	124	10.6
Berger Paints (Nigeria) Ltd	437.5	106	106	100.0	437.5	112	3	2.7	437.5	234	15	6.4	863.7	304	(144)	(147.4)
Nigerian Bottling Co. Nigeria Ltd	524	158	53	33.5	141.4	247	(820)	(432.0)	1,414	520	273	52.5	1,600	955	475	49.0
Vono Products Ltd	500	186	86	46.2	500	284	184	64.8	500	418	118	28.2	500	458	208	45.4
Blackwood Hodge Nigeria Ltd	100	104	4	3.8	100	165	37	22.4	100	651	69	10.6	440	906	526	58.0
Daily Times of Nigeria Ltd	1269.4	183	69	37.7	1513.8	428	265	61.9	1513.8	482	278	57.7	1513.8	546	243	44.5
Costain (W.A.) Ltd	799.2	21	(111)	(628.6)	799.2	156	(108)	(169.2)	799.2	424	160	37.7	799.2	739	(300)	(140.6)
CFAO (Nigeria) Ltd	4,000	1,115	955	83.8	4,000	1,462	362	24.8	5,200	2,541	1,701	66.9	5,200	1,142	202	17.7
Total		6,702	2,805	41.8		7,323	(1521)	20.8		13105	3,314	25.3		14694	(5964)	40.6

Source: Uzoaga and Alozieuwa, 'Dividend Policy in an Era of Indigenization', Tables III and VII, pp. 470 and 473. Percentages are the present author's computations.

Of particular interest, considering the attention it commands, is long-term financing. Before discussing issues of long-term financing, a few comments on short-term financing may be necessary.[11]

Business financing through bills of exchange is on a very small scale; the business community rather avails itself of overdraft facilities and book-debts generally. In particular, the Central Bank of Nigeria does not seem to encourage financing through this medium. The sectoral distribution of loans prescribed by the CBN guidelines for the commercial banks and the merchant banks allows them only a maximum of 2 per cent share, respectively, in their overall loan disbursements.[12]

The commercial banks have often not had a good reputation with the indigenous business community. According to Ebiefie, 'in almost all the countries [which have faced colonial structure of commercial banking] the lesson has been the same i.e. these banks have shied away from providing development oriented funds to enterprises in general and to indigenous entrepreneurs in particular.'[13] Most commercial banks formerly had been foreign owned.

Usually the explanation for this has been based on the self-liquidating loans doctrine and the cliché of commercial banks borrowing short and lending short. To these have been added the view that Nigerian businessmen are 'poor lending risk'. Although an evidence of lack of financial support to indigenous borrowers may be adduced, it is relevant to point out that, besides 'prejudice', a number of objective factors may have contributed to this.

For instance, the general shortcoming of managerial competence does not encourage any belief in the ability of the loan applicant to repay. This problem is often compounded by nonavailability of acceptable security (collateral), although what should be considered acceptable security has often been subject to the whims of unco-operative expatriate bank bosses. Further, not all the commercial banks have the technical expertise to assess business properly. Of course, the better organised a business, the greater its chance of attracting loans.

This seems to be confirmed by Table 13.2 which shows that in the period 1970-2 as much as 18,776 applications by indigenous sole proprietors and partners accounted for only 24 per cent of loan disbursements, whereas 50 per cent was granted to only 3,208 indigenous incorporated companies. The commercial banks have painful experience of occasional loan defaults.[14]

Despite this, it was evident that commercial banks cannot be relied upon to provide finance for development which requires long-term funding. In order to cope with developmental requirements a number of long-term finance arrangements have been introduced and periodically modified. This leads to development financing, the criteria for which go beyond that of type of business ownership. Development financing will be looked into later. Before that, two features of fund generation will be described. They are finance in kind and finance through exploitation of loopholes in tax regulations.

Table 13.2: Expatriate Commercial Bank Loans to Indigenous Borrowers (1970-72)

Year	Individuals		Sole Proprietors		Companies		Total	
	No. of Borrowers	Amount N'000	No. of Borrowers	Amount N'000	No. of Borrowers	Amount N'000	No. of Borrowers	Amount N'000
1970	17,598 (77%)	21,057 (28%)	4,292 (19%)	18,292 (25%)	1,010 (4%)	35,082 (47%)	22,900	74,431
1971	20,938 (73%)	34,538 (27%)	6,229 (22%)	33,037 (26%)	1,469 (5%)	61,799 (48%)	28,636	129,374
1972	31,091 (75%)	45,084 (24%)	8,245 (20%)	41,904 (23%)	2,049 (5%)	96,830 (53%)	41,385	183,818
Total	69,627 (75%)	100.679 (26%)	18,766 (20%)	93,233 (24%)	4,528 (5%)	193,711 (50%)	92,921	387,623

Source: Ebiefie, 'The Performance, Scope and Problems of Commercial Banks' (computed from Table 2, Loans to Indigenous Borrows (Expatriate Banks), p. 12). The percentages, in brackets, are based on respective row totals.

(iv) Financing in Kind. The possibility of financing in kind is not limited to any specific type of business organisation even though it is now being discussed, out of convenience, under joint-stock companies. For instance, in sole proprietorships or partnerships capital can be contributed in kind. Some aspects of business transactions are classified as finance in kind although certain forms of cash payments may be involved.[15] This is because sometimes the need for equipment may outstrip the existing level of financial resources. The firm would thus consider it expedient to hire the equipment. Even if a firm is sufficiently liquid to purchase equipment it may well be more rational to hire it if its use is only temporary.

Transactions of this nature usually involve goods that are durable, like plant and machinery. A number of schemes make such financing in kind possible. Examples are hire-purchase agreements, rental or hire agreements, sale and lease-back schemes. These forms of finance are external. Statistical information on these are not readily available.[16]

(v) Tax Regulations and Business Finance. A taxpayer's efforts to reduce his tax burden by exploiting loopholes within any existing taxation laws in the country is generally accepted as legitimate. One effective way the Nigerian firms have avoided commensurate tax payments is through keeping inadequate records or no records at all. It is convenient to distinguish, from this chapter's point of view, two types of exploitations — *tax evasion* and *tax diminution.*

(a) Tax evasion. Tax evasion is a dishonest attempt at concealing taxable income from the tax authority either by way of book manipulations or by keeping one's existence secret. Even some companies, with elaborate letterheads, turn out to be non-existent!

Tax evasion is not specific to any particular type of business, though some may be more prone to it than others. The institution of private companies seems to create an exploitative forum for tax evasion. Membership of such companies is open to husband, wife and children. Minors, in certain cases, are exempt from tax payments.[17] Thus minors could be injected in one form or the other into the business and taxable income siphoned through them away from tax authorities. Some proprietorships are acquired in the name of minors.

According to Amaizu, 'as our economy becomes more and more sophisticated and as our businessmen become more and more aware of avenues of cheating within the framework of the law, more private companies will be incorporated in the future'.[18]

(b) Tax diminution. Tax diminution, unlike tax evasion, is an honest attempt by a self-reporting taxable person at not showing more taxable income than required by existing laws. This is achieved through availing oneself of certain authorised claims or concessions. Such claims, in the Nigerian context, include, for instance, tax holiday for pioneer industries, N6,000 tax-free profit for all incorporated businesses and capital allowances.

The tax burden is reduced only when the taxable person knows the specific tax concessions and claims them. Such concessions may arise when economic development is being regulated through fiscal measures. A few examples, based on the Companies Income Tax Act, 1961, would suffice.[19]

The Companies Income Tax Act allows a company to deduct from profits before computing taxable income, 'any sum payable by way of interest on any money borrowed and employed as capital in acquiring profits'. This concession is also granted when a loan is used on revenue account (advertisement charges, staff wages etc.), provided the expenditure is wholly for the payee's business. The interest payable is deductible from profits before computing taxable income. If the deductible interest exceeds the current profits, the resulting loss can be carried forward and set against future profits.

Capital allowances are granted for loan money used in acquiring 'qualifying assets'. Qualifying assets are categorised and capital allowances granted accordingly, as indicated in Table 13.3.

Table 13.3 Assets and Capital Allowances

Assets	Initial Allowance	Annual Allowance
	%	%
Building expenditure	5	10
Industrial building expenditure	15	10
Mining expenditure	20	12½
Plant expenditure	20	12½
Plantation expenditure	25	15

As in the case of deductible interest, capital allowances can be carried forward against future profits if the present profits are unable to accommodate the allowance.[20]

Business financing through tax evasion or tax diminution is external, namely, external fund from the Federal Government, and is unauthorised. Building of inflated reserves and delay in tax payments are temporary or short-term external finance too.

3. Development Planning and Business Finance

The only difference, and a fundamental one too, between this approach to discussing business finance and the other approach considered as traditional is the inclusion of some macro-economic criteria, in addition to micro-economic criterion of the individual firm's profitability, in order to attract funds. Five such macro-economic criteria are (a) sectoral distribution, (b) regional distribution, (c) employment generation, (d) local raw materials utilisation and (e) conservation of foreign exchange.

Finance, for qualifying firms, does have the same feature, for example, equity finance and loan finance, as in the previous approach.

However, the sources of these categories of finance differ somewhat. In the case of new firms, there are in fact only two major sources: finance from the Federal Government through the relevant ministries, and finance from the development banks. Since the development banks are financed mainly by the Federal Government it means that the ultimate source of the funds is the Federal Government. The following discussion will focus attention on (a) small-scale industries credit scheme; (b) medium- and large-scale industries finance scheme and (c) Central Bank's credit guidelines.

(a) Small-Scale Industries Credit Scheme

From the Nigerian point of view an industry is considered small scale if its capital outlay is not above N60,000 and its employment level not beyond 50 workers.[21] Small-scale industries are, organisationally speaking, of two basic types: the non-factory and the factory type. Self-employed craftsmen who apply traditional means of production in their home with little or no machine equipment belong to non-factory type. These do not qualify for the financial support discussed presently.

Of interest are the factory-type small-scale industries. The ministry directly responsible for the small-scale credit scheme is the Ministry of Trade. Although small-scale industries issue has attracted much publicity in the country the actual financial support provided for them and their performance have left a lot to be desired.

Table 13.4 provides data on loan applications and approval in the former East Central State of Nigeria, as at August 1973.[22] As can be observed from Table 13.4, only about 1.1 per cent of the total amount applied for was approved and only about 4.1 per cent of all the applications were considered. Further, no fund was provided in the areas of raw-materials production and manufacturing (miscellaneous). Yet these are areas that need a great deal of support.

In the 1975-80 *Third National Development Plan* the sum of N20m was voted for the small-scale industries credit but so far only about N6m has been granted in the two budget years 1975/6 and 1976/7. In the current year no appreciable effort has been made by the Federal Government to approve small-scale loans; there seems to be a problem of budget allocation and release of funds.

It might be pertinent to observe that officialdom may be showing signs of disenchantment and weariness already with a small-scale finance programme that has been plagued by wide-scale repayment default.[23]

(b) Medium- and Large-Scale Industries Finance Scheme

(i) General comment. Economic development to provide broad-based industrial and commercial infrastructure dictates the creation of banks that can cope with the requisite funding, usually medium and long-term. The finance houses that perform this function have come to be known as development banks.

Nigeria has a number of such banks, catering, as the names imply, for different types of industrial/commercial sectors: for instance, the Nigerian Agricultural Bank (NAB), the Nigerian Bank of Commerce and Industry, the Nigerian Industrial Development Bank (NIDB) and the Federal Mortgage Bank.[24]

Other than the fact of different sectoral emphasis their operational patterns are largely similar. Even in certain situations they could work in concert to support a venture. For instance, the NAB and the NIDB could jointly support an agro-based industry.

(ii) Business Finance and Sectoral Distribution: the Role of Central Bank. (a) Controlling Flow of Funds to Business Sectoral Distribution. The Nigerian business field has featured mainly commercial activities. This derives from the early development of the Nigerian businessman as an appendage, in the name of 'factor', of colonial commercial houses, distributing and supplying commodities. The imbalance in economic development became pronounced after independence, with the industrial (manufacturing) sector virtually undeveloped.

In order to encourage industrial growth and diversification the Central Bank of Nigeria issues directives periodically to the commercial banks and the merchant banks, guiding their loan activities. The aim is to channel funds more to industrial activities than to commercial activities in order to achieve some level of complementarity in sectoral development. The directives are being constantly reviewed.

The current directives for the commercial banks (Schedule I) and the merchant banks (Schedule II) are provided in Tables 13.5 and 13.6.

Observation of the two schedules shows, among other things, that manufacturing has a preponderant share, and that the merchant banks have a greater role to play in supplying funds (60 per cent) to firms under 'production', than the commercial banks (48 per cent). Divergencies between prescribed and actual figures may be due to, among other things, time dimension: half-year figures instead of annual figures.

Further, according to the directives, the distribution of merchant banks' assets portfolio should be as follows:

Table 13.4: Data on Loan Applications and Approval as at August 1973 — East Central State

Serial No. (1)	Sector (Industries) (2)	No. of loan applications (3)	Total amount of loan applications (4)	No. of approved applications (5)	Total amount of loans approved (6)	Loans approved ratio (%) (7) Amount (6/4)	Application (5/3)
1.	Food Processing	625	9,121,760	22	143,500	15.7	3.5
	a) Rice milling	156	1,848,000	6	37,500	20.3	3.8
	b) Garri processing	188	2,654,260	1	8,000	0.3	0.5
	c) Bakery and confectionery	242	4,054,100	15	98,000	24.2	6.2
	d) Others	39	565,400	—	—	0.0	0.0
2.	Furniture and cabinet construction	99	2,993,700	3	30,000	10.0	3.0
3.	Building materials industry (including bricks and tile-making)	101	2,915,060	6	38,000	13.0	5.9
4.	Textile/garment/tailoring	184	3,585,780	21	53,500	14.9	11.4
5.	Raw materials production and processing including mining	15	688,000	—	—	0.0	0.0
6.	Manufacturing miscellaneous	205	4,603,760	—	—	0.0	0.0
7.	Engineering works (mechanical)	129	2,849,200	10	71,440	25.1	7.7
8.	Engineering works (electrical)	93	1,499,600	4	9,930	0.7	4.3
9.	Leather goods industry	58	1,150,900	4	25,800	2.2	6.9
10.	Printing and book production	200	3,976,900	—	—	0.0	0.0
	Total	1,709	33,384,660	70	372,170	1.1	4.1

Source: O. Mordi; 'Small-Scale Industries and Economic Development', pp. 17 and 18.

Table 13.5: Prescribed Composition of Banks' Loans and Advances to Various Sectors/Sub-Sectors of the Economy in 1976 and 1977/78 Fiscal Years — Schedule I — Commercial Banks

A. Preferred sectors/sub-sectors[a]	Percentage Share of loans and advances	
	Prescribed	Actual[b]
(i) Production	48.0	48.4
Agriculture	6.0	3.4
Mining	2.0	1.3
Manufacturing	30.0	28.6
Construction	10.0	15.1
Residential building	(5.0)	
Other	(5.0)	
(ii) Services	10.0	8.0
Public utilities	2.0	1.2
Transportation and communications	8.0	6.8
Total A.	58.0	56.4
B. Less-preferred sectors/sub-sectors[a]		
(iii) General Commerce	30.0	28.6
Exports	6.0	4.7
Imports	10.0	11.9
Domestic trade	12.0	10.4
Bills discounted	2.0	1.6
(iv) Others	12.0	15.0
Credit and financial institutions	3.0	2.9
Government	2.0	1.6
Personal and professional	4.0	5.9
Miscellaneous	3.0	4.6
Total B.	42.0	43.6
Total A. and B.	100.0	100.0

Notes: [a] 'Preferred' and 'less-preferred' are substituted for 'productive' and 'less-productive' formerly used in the designation of sectors A and B.

[b] 'Actual' refers to 1976 (average: January-June).

Table 13.6: Schedule II — Merchant Banks

A. Preferred sectors/sub-sectors	Percentage Share of loans and advances	
	Prescribed	Actual[a]
(i) Production	60.0	54.9
Agriculture	6.0	0.8
Mining	2.0	2.3
Manufacturing	36.0	33.4
Construction		19.3
Residential building	(5.0)	
Others	(11.0)	
(ii) Services	10.0	4.2
Transport and communication	8.0	4.2
Public utilities	2.0	—
Total A.	70.0	59.1
B. Less-preferred sectors/sub-sectors		
(iii) General commerce	23.0	29.1
Exports	5.0	0.3
Imports	11.0	22.8
Domestic trade	5.0	1.6
Bills discounted	2.0	4.4
(iv) Others	7.0	11.8
Credit and financial institutions	3.0	6.5
Government	2.0	2.3
Miscellaneous	2.0	3.0
Total B.	30.0	40.8
Total A. and B.	100.0	100.0

Notes: [a] Actual refers to 1976 (January-June).

a) A minimum of 50 per cent of total loans and advances shall be of medium- and long-term nature with maturities of not less than 3 years.
b) A maximum of 10 per cent of loans and advances shall be of short-term nature maturing within 12 months.
c) A maximum of 15 per cent of total assets shall be in equipment leasing business.
d) A minimum of 30 per cent of total funds raised from other banks shall be in liquid assets.[25]

(b) Encouraging Flow of Funds to Local Farmers. Local farmers are in fact the agricultural counterpart of industrial sole proprietors and partners. Unfortunately no attention has been seriously focused on them as it has on their industrial counterparts, in the issue of business financing. Even the much heralded Operation Feed the Nation (OFN) has not created any appreciable impact, despite the millions of naira expenditure, on the actual farmers in the farm lands — somehow the funds have managed to elude them!

Any programme of support for small businesses must take into consideration the issue of funding and organising both the small firms and the small farms, if they qualify. To this end, it seems that the Agricultural Credit Guarantee Scheme Fund Decree 1977 is an attempt at providing funds directly to farmers and corporate institutions. The present level of funding is N100m. The scheme, which is to be executed through guaranteeing loans to qualifying farmers by the Central Bank (Agricultural Finance Division), would function effectively only through the commercial banks. The commercial banks provide a wider network of subsidiaries and branches relatively close enough to local farmers.

4. Conclusion

The main sources of business finance in Nigeria have been discussed, but some sources, in so far as they involve fraudulent exercises, may remain unknown; more and better control devices may minimise the practice. Some sources are publicly self-evident. Established institutions such as the development banks for instance are relatively easy to identify.

Between the two extremes are a range of sources, intracompany finance ('parent company' abroad financing or being financed by a subsidiary), intercompany finance, suppliers' credit and certain forms of finance generated within the firm.

Information on the above-mentioned sources as well as on other ancillary issues are usually observed under the guise of 'business conservatism'. Sometimes, in the Nigerian context, business conservatism becomes a euphemism for managerial incompetence in keeping poor or no records at all. This becomes evident when surveys are conducted.

The Central Bank attempts to study and monitor, among other things, business financing through business surveys. The first but unpublished survey of 1977 which restricted itself to the Lagos metropolitan area is a remarkable effort, even if the response did not generate reliable information. A second survey is planned, hopefully to cover the country. Perhaps, improved business practice and seminars would provide the basis for greater response and co-operation in studying business management and finance.

Notes

1. In the USA joint-stock companies are called 'corporations'. To avoid confusion, this paper will not use the American terminology. Further, to ensure familiarity with the Nigerian environment the term 'national (or State) corporations' has been used in preference to 'Nationalised industries', a terminology more popular in traditional literature. 'Corporations' would include national (State) boards and authorities.
2. And other similar organisations.
3. 'The main objectives of the Government programme for the development of small-scale industries are the creation of employment opportunities, mobilisation of local resources, mitigation of rural-urban migration, and more even distribution of industrial enterprises in different parts of the country. These will be achieved through suitable incentives designed to give complementary assistance in financial, management and technical aspects of the business. The main vehicles for administering incentives are the Industrial Development Centres and the States Small-Scale Industries Credit Schemes.' Federal Republic of Nigeria, *Third National Development Plan, 1975-80*, vol. I, p. 155.
4. Ibid., p. 164.
5. The only exception is the case of 'limited partners'. Under the Limited Partnership Act, 1907, the limited partners, unlike the general partners, are liable only to the extent of their contributions to business. From the point of view of Nigerian business mentality, it is hardly possible to find a 'union', that is, a joint ventureship of 'limited' and 'general' partners. They will find it difficult to function. The need for 'limit' to liabilities without the business necessarily going 'public' has been contained in the Nigerian Companies Act, 1958. Chapter 37, Section 128 makes provision for 'limited Private Companies'. In this case, the maximum number of partners is 50.
6. This latter distinction was used by Adeyemo in his paper; see M.A. Adeyemo, 'Business Finance', in *Management in Nigeria*, vol. 4, no. 4 (November-December 1968), p. 129.
7. Unfortunately, there has not been any statistical compilation of this to pro-

vide not only statistical details but also overview of all company experiences.

8. Central Bank of Nigeria, *Developments in the Nigerian Economy During the First Half of 1977*, p. 29. The twelve companies include SCOA, BEWAC.

9. See for instance W.O. Uzoaga and J.U. Alozieuwa, 'Dividend Policy in an Era of Indigenization', *Nigerian Journal of Economic and Social Studies*, vol. 16, no. 3,(November 1974), p. 461; and E. Inanga, A. Soyode and W.O. Uzoaga, 'Dividend Policy in an Era of Indigenization: Comments' ibid, vol. 17, no. 2 (July 1975), p. 133.

10. This, according to Uzoaga, appears to be a 'raid' by expatriate firms on their reserves for fear of indigenisation. Further, 'the raid was too obvious to escape public regulation'. In fact the Government has regulated that no more than one-third of current earnings be distributed as dividends!

11. The importance of the various types of short-term finance cannot be doubted; attention is focused here however on bills of exchange and commercial bank financing generally.

12. Central Bank of Nigeria, 'Developments in the Nigerian Economy During the First Half of 1977, (mimeo), pp. 12 and 13.

13. E.O. Ebiefie, 'The Performance, Scope and Problems of Commercial Banks in Nigeria as a Source of Financing Indigenous Business', in *Financial Institutions and the Business Community* (Economic Development Institute, University of Nigeria, Enugu Campus, 17 December 1973), p. 5.

14. The increasing rate of default in repayment of commercial bank short-term loans has produced, according to Obih, 'unscheduled long-term borrowers'. See C.K.N. Obih, 'Financing Indigenization: The Role of Commercial Banks', in *Financial Institutions and the Business Community*, p. 24.

15. Adeyemo, *Management in Nigeria*, p. 136.

16. Efforts are being made currently to systematically obtain information from firms on sources of business finance.

17. For instance, Section 11(a) Finance Law of the former East Central State (now Anambra/Imo States) exempts an individual up to the age of 16 years from tax payment on that part of his income arising from his personal effort.

18. P.I. Amaizu, 'Tax Evasion, The Law and Solution', in *Seminar on Tax Collection in The East Central State of Nigeria – Report of Proceedings* (Economic Development Institute, UNEC, 1973), p. 94.

19. A fuller discussion is contained in C. Njokanma, 'Financial Institutions and the Business Community: The Income Tax Perspective', in ibid.

20. Allowances like these and other tax concessions continue to change. See A.C. Ezejelue, 'Process of Evolution of Direct Taxation in Nigeria', unpublished mimeo., 1977. Department of Accountancy, University of Nigeria, Enugu Campus.

21. Obi Mordi, 'Small-scale Industry and Economic Development', paper presented at the seminar on Owner-Manager Industries in the Nigerian Indigenization Era, The Institute of Management and Technology, Enugu, March 1974.

22. By 1973 the issue of small-scale industries had become very topical in the country.

23. So far no official and reliable statistics have been published on defaulters, though officials continue to mention this impasse.

24. The Federal Mortgage Bank operates solely in the economic area of housing financing: residential and commercial.

25. Central Bank of Nigeria, 'Developments in the Nigerian Economy During the First Half of 1977', pp. 12-14.

14 HOUSING SCHEME FINANCING IN NIGERIA

A.C. Ezejelue and Moses Bakpa

1. Introduction

One of the major problems concerning home ownership is the problem of finance. Only a few people in a society can afford to finance their own homes alone, without recourse to financial institutions. In the past people saved a part of their income over a long period to build a house of their own. Today it is difficult to save enough to build a house because of the inflationary costs of building materials, which in Nigeria are in the three digit inflationary zone.

Recently, the Federal and State governments have shown much interest in urban housing programmes. Measures have been announced to stimulate the activity of private estate developers. The Mortgage Bank was set up to grant credit to all mortgage institutions for transmission to individual borrowers. Commercial and merchant banks have been requested to extend 5 per cent of their loanable funds to residential buildings. Also, insurance companies have been requested to invest up to 25 per cent of their life funds in real estate.

In order to liberalise land acquisition for residential housing, the Federal Government required all State governments to acquire large tracts of land near major towns — as recommended by the Anti-Inflation Task Force in 1975 — lay them out and lease them to individuals and institutions for allocation to their staff for building owner-occupied houses.

Most people, who wish to build homes, now turn to surplus economic units for loan. Such economic units are the commercial banks, the mortgage banks, etc.

2. Sources of Housing Finance

In Nigeria there are diverse sources for housing financing. They include the following:

(a) Savings and loan
(b) Lagos State Development and Properties Corporation (LSDPC)

231

(c) Commercial banks
(d) Insurance companies
(e) Staff-housing programme for government officials
(f) Company housing scheme
(g) Nigeria Building Society (NBS)
(h) Federal Mortgage Bank of Nigeria (FMBN)

(a) Savings and Loan

Nearly every state in Nigeria has a housing corporation or a housing development authority and every housing corporation has a savings and loan department. The savings and loan department of each housing development authority or corporation constitutes the first line of housing finance. Prospective house owners save with the savings and loan department of the housing corporation. When 20 per cent of the estimated cost of the building has been saved the corporation provides the saver with the additional funds and helps in the acquisition of the house. Houses so acquired are mortgaged to the savings and loan department, which specifies and administers the terms of repayment. Alternatively, the applicant is allowed to invest an equivalent of 20 per cent of the cost in the physical construction of the building. The savings and loan department assesses the amount so invested and provides the balance in the form of long-term loan. The contributions of savings and loan to housing has not been very significant because of limited funds. Government financial assistance, if any, is very insignificant, hence the small impact in housing development.

(b) Lagos State Development and Properties Corporation (LSDPC)

The Lagos Executive Development Board (LEDB) together with the Ikeja Area Planning Authority, and the Epe Town Planning Authority were established in 1972 by an edict. The three later fused into what is now called the Lagos State Development and Properties Corporation.

The Lagos Executive Development Board did not engage in mortgage financing until 1973. Rather it was only concerned with the following:

(a) outright sale of its own built-up houses. Buyers of those houses were financed by the Nigeria Building Society.
(b) rehousing of persons displaced in central Lagos. The cost of this scheme was mainly borne by the Federal Government; and
(c) housing scheme for low-income group in Lagos, the Federal

Government provided a grant of N1m.

In 1973 an investment department was created to carry out mortgage financing. The corporation initially allocated 100 units of completed houses to the department on loan basis as a part of its working capital. In addition it gave 7 per cent of any of its newly completed houses to the department.

The above arrangement in effect shows that the corporation is mainly concerned with outright sale of buildings. The few houses on mortgage basis are to be sold as follows:

(a) 20 per cent of cost as down payment;
(b) balance of 80 per cent to be repaid over a period not exceeding 25 years; and
(c) an interest of 7.5 per cent per annum.

Only those who operate savings and loan accounts with the corporation are accommodated by the mortgage arrangement. There are many applicants but the corporation can only accommodate a small percentage of eligible applicants.

The Lagos State Development and Properties Corporation only gives loans for the purchase of houses which the corporation builds. The corporation has the responsibility to plan and develop estates only. The corporation has a long-term plan to provide loans to people to acquire houses outside the estates.

Requirements similar to those of the NBS are to be met before an applicant can be accommodated by the mortgage scheme. They include the following:

(a) proof of income;
(b) payment of tax; and
(c) down payment of personal contribution.

A good number of the 19 states of the federation operate housing development corporations which operate in ways similar to those of the Nigeria Building Society (now the Mortgage Bank) and the Lagos State Development and Properties Corporation.

The following institutions are responsible for housing development in Nigeria:

(a) NNDC Properties Limited

(b) Lagos State Development and Properties Corporation
(c) Ibile Properties Limited
(d) Bendel Development and Housing Authority
(e) Nigerian Housing Authority
(f) Wemabod Estates Limited
(g) Oyo State Housing Corporation
(h) Ogun State Housing Corporation
(i) Ondo State Housing Corporation
(j) Imo State Housing Corporation
(k) Federal Mortgage Bank.

(c) Commercial Banks

Commercial banks constitute also an important source of finance for home ownership. The Central Bank's credit guideline makes it mandatory for the commercial banks to provide a certain percentage of their credit for estate developments. The percentage credit provision of estates may be varied by the Central Bank from time to time depending on housing needs.

Table 14.1 shows how commercial banks channelled their funds in the period 1971-5. It is not possible to ascertain what percentage was actually devoted to housing as the loans for real estate and constructions are lumped up together. The allocation for loans and advances to real estate and construction increased from 7.1 per unit of aggregate bank loans and advances in 1971 to 13.1 per unit in 1978 and dropped to 10 per cent in 1976 and 1977. Like other housing-scheme finance companies, commercial banks lend at a time a proportion of the total cost of a building in order to minimise losses should the borrower default, which is the practice in most parts of the world as well as in Nigeria. As Dyer observed, 'it is simply courting danger to agree to advance the maximum sum on a building project'.[1]

The question of whether security is to be demanded or not is left to the banker. Generally the determinant factors include the amount involved, the background of the customer and his ability to repay. Before an application is considered in the first instance the banker will want to know, among other things, whether the building plan had been approved and whether the applicant has good title to building land.

(d) Insurance Companies

Insurance companies have to invest their funds in order to meet future obligations to their policy-holders. The funds are widely placed with other financial institutions. Large sums of money are placed on the deposit accounts of commercial banks, invested in various government securities or are applied for home-ownership financing. Insurance policy-holders, especially life policy-holders, benefit immensely from building loans. Such houses are accepted by insurance companies as mortgages in addition to security provided by the policies. Usually not more than 80 per cent of the actual value of houses are financed by insurance companies.

Table 14.1: Loans and Advances Classified by Purpose (Per Cent)

Category of Borrower	1971	1972	1973	1974	1975	1976	1977
A: Productive sectors/sub-sectors							
(i) Production	37.4	38.0	38.3	43.6	44.2	48.0	48.0
Agriculture, forestry and fishing	2.3	2.3	3.1	3.1	2.5	6.0	6.0
Mining and quarrying	2.4	2.0	1.6	1.2	1.5	2.0	2.0
Manufacturing	25.6	25.8	24.0	28.4	27.3	30.0	30.0
Real estate and construction	7.1	7.9	9.6	10.9	13.1	10.0	10.0
(ii) Services	6.4	7.6	8.1	7.5	7.5	10.0	10.0
Public utilities	0.4	0.8	0.4	0.8	1.2	2.0	2.0
Transportation and communication	6.0	6.8	7.7	6.7	6.3	8.0	8.0
Total A.	43.8	45.6	46.4	51.1	51.7	58.0	58.0
B. Less productive sectors/ sub-sectors							
(iii) General commerce	41.1	36.8	34.4	30.0	30.4	30.0	30.0
Export	13.1	11.7	10.1	8.2	6.1	6.0	6.0
Import	13.9	11.4	9.4	8.5	12.2	10.0	10.0
Domestic trade	11.9	12.5	13.4	11.4	10.4	12.0	12.0
Bills discounted	2.2	1.2	1.5	1.9	1.8	2.0	2.0
(iv) Others	15.1	17.6	19.2	18.9	17.9	12.0	12.0
Credit and financial institutions	1.4	2.2	1.6	1.9	2.5	3.0	3.0
Governments	0.9	1.3	2.1	2.4	3.4	2.0	2.0
Personal and professional	6.9	8.2	7.6	6.5	6.0	4.0	4.0
Miscellaneous	5.9	5.9	7.9	8.1	6.0	3.0	3.0
Total B.	56.2	54.4	53.6	48.9	48.3	42.0	42.0
Total A. and B.	100.0	100.0	100.0	100.0	100.0	100.0	100.0

Source: Central Bank of Nigeria, *Annual Report and State of Accounts* of various years.

As Table 14.2 suggests, mortgage loan on real estate rose from an insignificant 2.9 per cent in 1971 to 12.2 per cent in 1975. This reveals a phenomenal contribution to real-estate development by insurance companies. The average for the five-year period is 7.4 per cent. Recently, assurance companies have been requested by the Federal Government to invest up to 25 per cent of their life funds in real estate.

Table 14.2: The Life Fund/Mortgage Loan by Insurance Companies

Year	Life Fund	Mortgage loan on real estate		Loan to policy-holder	
	N	N	%	N	%
1971	25,132,718	738,358	2.9	2,305,436	9.2
1972	31,409,084	973,864	3.1	2,351,070	7.5
1973	44,938,035	2,118,103	4.7	3,419,181	7.6
1974	55,511,168	5,128,854	9.2	3,203,060	5.8
1975	70,481,443	8,591,959	12.2	4,057,766	5.8
	237,472,448	17,551,138	7.4	15,336,513	6.5

Source: Returns of insurance companies of various years.

(e) Staff-Housing Programme for Government Officials

Senior officers in most government ministries, corporations and agencies are assisted by the Government in the financing of home ownership. This scheme has not been extended to the low-income group. Government or corporations guarantee housing loans for their senior civil servants who may wish to apply to the Mortgage Bank for housing loans.

(f) Company-Housing Scheme

Some large companies provide housing loans to their senior staff. The gesture has a two-pronged objective — as an incentive and as an investment. The scheme is laudable but like housing loans for government officials only few individuals are privileged as the scheme does not extend to junior workers.

(g) The Nigeria Building Society

The Nigeria Building Society, popularly known as the NBS, has been converted to the Federal Mortgage Bank. Of all the housing-development organisations the Nigeria Building Society was the only one that operated nationwide and contributed most to housing development in the country through home financing.

(i) Developments in Net Mortgage Assets and Advances of NBS. Table 14.3 shows the developments in the net mortgage assets and profit (loss) of the NBS. The encouraging trend reveals the strides made by the NBS towards housing development. Table 14.4 reveals recent advances which have increased phenomenally.

The NBS advances rose from a little over N2,000 in 1957, the year of establishment, to about N13m in 1975, while the cumulative advances stood at over N32m in the same year. The NBS also provided funds for those who wished to purchase homes built by the states' various housing corporations. In the 1975 financial year, the society processed 1,012 applications compared with 845 applications in the 1974 financial year. Insurance companies provided some of the funds required by the NBS to augment NBS shareholders' own funds.

Table 14.3 Net Mortgage Assets/Profit (Loss) of NBS

Year ended 31 December	Net mortgage assets N	Profit (Loss) before tax N
1957	2,302	(15,156)
1958	227,592	(16,390)
1959	1,007,634	22,486
1960	2,943,516	117,034
1961	4,927,160	206,946
1962	6,108,004	233,178
1963	6,682,364	136,076
1964	6,811,278	217,642
1965	7,362,512	253,526
1966	7,953,076	206,256
1967	8,232,704	207,256
1968	8,178,086	198,216
1969	8,562,556	219,516
1970	9,182,236	44,752
1971	11,343,200	519,972
1972	13,302,006	605,786
1973	14,787,685	607,508
1974	20,823,414	972,104
1975	32,466,545	1,066,025

Source: Nigeria Building Society, *Report and Accounts, 1975*, p. 13.

Table 14.4: Recent Advances of NBS

Year ended 31 December	Advances during the year N
1971	not available
1972	3,033,316
1973	2,557,010
1974	7,407,598
1975	12,972,770

Source: Nigeria Building Society, *Report and Accounts* of various years.

(ii) Mortgage Policy of the NBS. Every Nigerian of the age of 21 and above was entitled to an NBS loan for any of the following purposes:

(a) to buy a home;
(b) to build a home;
(c) to repair and renovate an existing home;
(d) to redeem an existing account with other house financiers; and
(e) to purchase a building plot of good title.

To be entitled to a loan certain basic requirements had to be met:

(a) Land. An applicant in the first instance must have a plot of land on which he proposes to build his house. The land could be freehold or leasehold but it is imperative that the applicant should have a good title to it.

(b) Building Plan. The building plan must be approved by the public authority responsible for this. The approved plan must be submitted along with the loan application. Essentially only loans for residential buildings were granted.

(c) Types of Buildings. The type of building is usually residential with all its ancillaries.

(d) Proof of Income. A satisfactory evidence of applicant's income must be submitted. Pay-slips are sufficient evidence and where these are not available a written confirmation by a senior officer is tendered.

(e) Payment of Income Tax. All applicants must have paid their income taxes for the two years immediately preceding the application date. Tax receipts or other evidence were expected to back the claim.

(f) Personal Contribution. The applicant was required to show proof of his contribution to the project. Applicant's contribution was set at between 10-20 per cent of the project cost. Such contribution was considered a proof of willingness to be committed to the project. The contribution was deposited with the savings and loan department. Alternatively the contribution could be made in the form of a partly built-up house.

(g) Rate of Interest. The Nigeria Building Society charge a rate of interest of 3 per cent per annum, worked out on a discount basis. Formerly rates as high as 8 and 6 per cent were charged, but when the Federal Government intervened, the rate was reduced to encourage home ownership.

Table 14.5 shows the monthly mortgage redemption at the annual interest rate of 3 per cent.

Table 14.5 Monthly Mortgage Redemption — Naira and Kobo Currency at Annual Interest Rate of 3 per cent

Advances N	5 Years	10 Years	15 Years	20 Years	25 Years
10,000	181.96	97.69	69.81	56.01	47.86
15,000	272.90	146.54	104.71	84.02	71.79
20,000	363.92	195.38	139.81	112.03	95.71
30,000	545.89	293.06	209.42	168.08	143.57
40,000	727.85	390.77	279.22	224.05	191.42
45,000	818.60	439.60	314.13	252.10	215.36
50,000	909.39	488.46	349.03	280.06	239.28
55,000	1,000.33	537.31	383.93	308.07	263.21
60,000	1,091.77	586.15	418.84	336.07	287.14
65,000	1,182	635.00	453.74	364.08	311.07
70,000	1,273.73	683.84	488.65	392.08	335.00

Source: Nigeria Building Society, *Mortgage Policy*, p. 3

(h) The Federal Mortgage Bank of Nigeria (FMBN)

A decree promulgated by the Federal Government in January 1977, converted the Nigeria Building Society (NBS) into the Federal Mortgage Bank. The assets and liabilities of the Nigeria Building Society were also transferred to the Mortgage Bank.

The FMBN started with a capital of N20m for its services. This was divided into N100 denomination per share. The amount was certainly inadequate for Nigerian housing needs. The sum of N150m share capital budgeted in the Third National Plan for the purpose of housing finance of the NBS is now under the management of the FMBN and is spread out as shown in Table 14.6.

Table 14.6 Spread Out Share Capital of the Federal Mortgage Bank

Year	Amount (Nm)
1975-6	15
1976-7	22
1977-8	30
1978-9	37
1979-80	45
	151

Source: Federal Ministry of Economic Development, *Third National Development Plan 1975-80*, p. 379.

In April 1977, the Mortgage Bank went into operation with a spread-out share capital of N150m. The Bank among other things is expected to augment the sum through the mobilisation of savings from the public. Such savings are to be invested in projects involving the financing of houses and the production of building materials.

The activities of the Bank include the following:

(i) mobilisation of savings from the public;

(ii) investment of such savings in manufacturing and/or production firms;

(iii) granting long-term credit facilities to indigenes who want to build or buy houses; and

(iv) to aid mortgage institutions so that they can grant comparative facilities to indigenes.

The Mortgage Bank also has the power to accept long-term deposits from mortgage institutions, trust funds, post offices and from private individuals.

For the purposes of financing housing scheme, the FMBN has developed the following savings plans; target savings, term savings and popular savings.

(i) Target Savings Plan. The FMBN's four-year target savings plan is designed, among other things, to help those whose personal target in life is to build a house. It simply involves depositing a regular monthly fixed amount, as much as the depositor can afford, but subject to a minimum of N5 per month, for four years. The target savings account is opened with the first month's deposit in any of the FMBN's branches; the monthly payments can be made by cash personally, or by postal order or cheque which can be mailed, or through a banker's order or through the depositor's employer. The target savings account earns 5.5 per cent assured interest per annum as shown in Table 14.7.

Table 14.7: Target Savings Interest Rates at 5.5 Per Cent Per Annum

Monthly deposit N	Cumulative deposit in 4 years N	Accrued tax-free interest N
5	240	27
10	480	55
60	2,880	332
100	4,800	554

Source: Target Savings Interest Rates, 'Get the Facts' (FMBN, November 1978).

Both the savings and the accrued interest are kept safe and secure for the depositor without any charge.

The advantages of the target savings plan to depositors include:

(a) the security and safety of savings in a bank owned and backed by the Federal Government;

(b) a high rate of tax-free interest (that is, 5.5 per cent per annum);

(c) it affords an easy and convenient method of saving; and

(d) it carries a big payoff in four years to enable the depositor to meet his housing target.

In view of the high interest rate on this account, no withdrawals are made during the four-year target period. Any premature withdrawal, however, results in a substantial loss of interest as a penalty. At the end of the four-year period, the depositor obtains his savings and the accrued interest by exercising any of the following options:

(a) have an FMBN popular savings account opened for the balance in the target account;

(b) have FMBN term savings certificates issued; or

(c) have a cheque for the entire amount in the account mailed to the depositor directly.

(ii) Term Savings Plan. One of the aims of this plan is to assist those persons who have a three- or a five-year goal to buy or build a house. The five-year term savings account paying 6 per cent tax-free interest per annum in compound interest is FMBN's highest yielding savings plan. The three-year term savings plan earns 5.5 per cent tax-free interest per annum in compound interest.

The minimum monthly deposit under this plan is N200. More could be deposited, but only in multiples of N100. Withdrawal on this account is possible after maturity. This account, which has benefits similar to those of the target savings account, is also very simple to open and operate.

At the three-or five-year maturity, the depositor may elect one of the following:

(a) to convert the three-year account into a five-year plan and become eligible for 6 per cent compound interest at the new maturity date two years later;

(b) to open a new three- or five-year account at the prevailing interest rates;

(c) to transfer the investment to an FMBN popular savings account; or

(d) to withdraw both the capital invested and all accrued interest.

(iii) Popular Savings Plan. This plan, *inter alia*, encourages saving towards the cost of a house. It carries all the advantages of the other two plans as regards convenience, ease, security, interest etc. Unlike the other plans, the deposit is always available for withdrawal up to N500 in any month without notice subject to maintaining the required minimum balance of N15. Larger withdrawals and closure of account are permissible with only one month's notice. The minimum deposit to open this account is N15, and thereafter, the depositor pays in any amount he can from time to time.

This account attracts an interest rate of 5 per cent per annum. This means that every N100 left in this account for one full year grows to N105.00 and for four full years grows to N121.55.

3. Conclusion

The importance of housing in Nigeria today, especially in the urban areas, is so crucial that government, at all levels, attaches high priority to it. The Federal Government has a policy of allocating funds and other resources for housing development in conjunction with the efforts of the state governments and private employers. More specifically, the Federal Government has recently decided to sell its 1,000 housing units in the satellite town of Lagos to public officers on an owner-occupier basis. This policy is now pursued in other towns by both the Federal and the State Governments.

Besides, it is now required that every firm or organisation with at least 500 employees should introduce a housing scheme and/or a housing loan scheme for its employees. Also with effect from 1976-7 fiscal year an enhanced capital allowance on housing estates was introduced ₃o as to encourage and give assistance to any companies, groups of companies or organisations that are prepared to put up housing estates under given conditions. As an added incentive, Government has volunteered to provide the infrastructural facilities of the housing estates. The Land Use Decree of 1978 was promulgated with a view to making land acquisition for housing and other purposes very favourable.

One other area which requires government attention in order to further facilitate housing programmes is in the approval of building plans. The inability of the town planning office to approve building plans quickly, even when they meet the required specifications, contributes to the delay in starting off housing schemes in many Nigerian towns. Table 14.8 illustrates building activities in a Nigerian sample town, Owerri. This table shows that not all plans submitted have been approved for various years.

Table 14.8: Building Activities in Owerri

Year	Plans submitted Permanent structures	Temporary structures	Total	Plans approved	Structures built and officially controlled
1970	56	372	428	39	—
1971	231	116	347	113	6
1972	275	78	353	201	39
1973	274	61	335	169	42
1974	293	20	313	170	44
1975	578	11	589	206	52
1976	711	64	775	204	11

Source: Fingerhuth and Partners, *Imo State Capital Owerri*, p. 113.

With the intensification of government's efforts on housing schemes, it is hoped that the various housing financing institutions will be further encouraged into intensifying their own efforts in the same direction.

Note

1. L.S. Dyer, *A Practical Approach to Bank Lending* (The Institute of Bankers, London, 1974), p. 74.

Part Four:

OTHER FINANCIAL INSTITUTIONS

15 NOTES ON THE NIGERIAN INDUSTRIAL DEVELOPMENT BANK LIMITED (NIDB)

M.I. Chidozie

1. Introduction

Although institutional arrangements for the provision of long-term industrial finance are not new, development banks as a catalyst for industrial development are by and large a post-Second World War phenomenon. The French Credit Mobilier of 1852, the Japanese Industrial Bank of 1902 and the industrial banks of Germany have to be sharply distinguished from the development banks which were established in the post-war years in the developing countries of the world. The last few decades have witnessed the determination of the less developed countries to accelerate the pace of economic development. This determination manifests itself in the strong accent on industrialisation policies. But enthusiasm to develop rapidly through industrialisation is one thing and the realities of the constraints to develop at a faster pace is another. Rapid industrialisation has been impeded in most countries by the lack or by the inadequacy of various infrastructure for industrial development such as industrial capital, a dynamic capital market and the shortage of technical know-how.

2. The Establishment of the Bank and its Capital

The Nigerian Industrial Development Bank Limited was established on 22 January 1964 by reconstituting the Investment Company of Nigeria Limited (ICON) which was incorporated in Nigeria in 1959 as an industrial development finance company.[1] At its inception, it had an authorised capital of N10m. The authorised capital was made up of N4m in ordinary shares and N500,000 in non-voting preference shares. Ordinary shares worth N2.04 million or 51 per cent of the bank's voting capital was classified as 'A' ordinary shares and reserved for Nigerian subscribers and international organisations such as the International Finance Corporation, an affiliate of the World Bank (IBRD) of which Nigeria is a member. The remainder of the voting capital was classified as 'B' ordinary shares and could be subscribed to by any interested investor whether Nigerian or foreign. The issued capital has since been converted into stock.[2]

The establishment of NIDB was the result of a successful negotiation between the representatives of ICON and a steering committee composed of prominent Nigerians. The government of Nigeria which played a very active role in encouraging its formation supported the bank by making available to it the sum of N4m long-term interest-free loan subordinated to the equity.[3] This loan together with its paid-up capital raised NIDB's total initial resources to N8.50 million.

NIDB has powers to borrow up to three times the issued share capital, reserves and subordinated borrowings of the company. The law establishing the NIDB imposes a borrowing limit on the company which may only be exceeded if authorised to do so. The borrowing limits were fixed at N26.4 million and N30 million in 1968 and 1971 respectively. The World Bank also provided a loan of $6 million (N4,286,000) for the financing of the foreign-exchange component of its investments. By 31 December 1975 the financial resources of NIDB stood at N87 million — N11 million in equity and N76 million in loans borrowed from home and abroad.[4]

3. General Policies and Scope of Activities

The bank provides medium- and long-term loans to enterprises in Nigeria which are privately owned and managed. NIDB finances both the public and the private sectors. The public sector is financed in the hope that the shares purchased by government will eventually be sold to private interest. It sometimes makes equity investments. Financial assistance is available to limited liability companies registered in Nigeria especially if such companies are either wholly Nigerian owned or where Nigerians control a substantial percentage of the equity investment.[5]

The scope of its lending or equity participation is presently limited to manufacturing, non-petroleum mining activities and all aspects of tourism including the financing of hotels of international standard. Service industries are generally excluded from loan accommodation except where there is prospect of manufacturing in the short term. Proposals for subordinate loans could be for a new project or for an expansion. Agriculture, trade and transport are outside its financing sphere.

4. Principles Governing the Bank's Financial Participation or Assistance

To attract the bank's financial assistance, a project must be viable and it must inspire confidence. Any potential proposal must possess the following requisites:

(a) the project must be economically desirable, contribute to the raising of the living standard of Nigerians, provide employment and conserve foreign exchange;

(b) it must be technically feasible – this means that the technical process involved should be capable of being carried out in a Nigerian environment;

(c) it must be commercially profitable – the venture must be capable of making profit, taking into account the cost of production;

(d) the cost of the project must be comparatively reasonable and must include provision for contingencies and working capital;

(e) the quality of management of the project must be sound;

(f) the project must be in line with the overall government development programme;

(g) the size of investment must at least be considerable – minimum loan investment is N20,000 and the maximum which could exceed N5m will depend on a number of criteria, including total project cost and debt/equity ratio – NIDB equity investment does not normally exceed one-fifth or 20 per cent of the paid-up capital;[6] and

(h) the interest rate charges must be flexible from time to time to reflect NIDB's cost of borrowing. It is payable half-yearly on 1 January and 1 July and computed on the balance on the client's account.

In the case of the underwriting of shares or debentures, the bank debits charges and commissions against the company in question. The appropriate time for the payment of the charges and commissions are normally stipulated. Where the prospectus provides for the payment of brokerage fees to banks and brokers, the bank's stockbroking subsidiary (ICON Securities Ltd) must be paid the brokerage fees at the rate which other banks and brokers charge.

Where the bank grants loans, the standard ranges of interest and other charges were previously determined by the NIDB board but the fixing of interest rates as from 1978 is the prerogative of the Central Bank. At the time the NIDB board fixed the interest charges, it considered the rates charged by banks and financial institutions and also the risk involved. The bank collects commitment charges at a nominal rate from the date the loan agreement becomes effective. It is 0.5 per cent of the undisbursed part of loan payable six months from the date of acceptance of the offer. Loans are given for periods ranging from five years to 15 years. A period of moratorium on capital repayment is permitted. The period of moratorium is normally two years from the estimated date of completing the project. For amortisation, the minimum term is five years and the maximum 15 years. The debts repayment range is therefore between seven and 17 years.[7] It must however be noted that during the period of grace, the interest must be paid. Non-repayment of loan and interest attracts charges which are determined according to the degree of deviation.

All actual legal or other charges incurred in the examination of title to property and document preparations are recoverable from the applicant irrespective of the eventual outcome of the project.

5. Security for the Loans

All loans must be secured. The form of security is determined as circumstances demand. The following are normally acceptable: legal mortgages of fixed assets — normally the first legal mortgage is on the fixed assets of the project and a second charge on the floating assets. For the purpose of overdrafts from commercial banks for working capital, NIDB allows the following:

(i) second charge on the floating assets;[8]
(ii) guarantees given by reputable banks or parent company;
(iii) pledges of government securities;
(iv) stocks quoted on the Stock Exchange; and
(v) valuable personal property.

All these are acceptable. The value of the security pledged should at least be 1.5 times the proposed NIDB loan investment.

6. The Bank's Contributions to National Economy

NIDB was founded to fill the obvious gap in the country's financial system. Its function is basically the provision of medium- and essentially long-term finance for industries. Through this and through its efficient supervisory machinery, it puts the industries so financed on a firm footing.

In the year of its establishment, it made N2.8m sanctions and 24 per cent of the sum went to Nigerian controlled companies. By 1970, in spite of the civil commotion, the annual sanctions had risen to N6.4m and 73 per cent of the sum went to Nigerian controlled companies. In 1977 the Federal Government directed the bank to issue from then on not less than 80 per cent of its sanctions to indigenously controlled companies. The bank has adhered to the directive. In 1974 about 94.7 per cent of the sanctioned loan of N18.8m went to indigenously controlled business.[9]

Table 15.1: Bank's Sanctions (1974-77)

	Sanctions for the year	Cumulative total sanctions	Yearly amount in Nm	Cumulative total in Nm amount
1974	22	–	18.8	
1975	40	264	59.8	133.3
1976[a]	28	292	51.4	184.7
1977[b]	26	318	73.9	258.6

Notes:

[a] Obtained by subtracting the cumulative total of 1975 from that of 1976 as published in *Business Times*, Lagos, 7 February 1978, p. 13.

[b] See publication of E. Heart, Assistant Controller, Public Relation Unit of NIDB in *Business Times*, Lagos, 7 February 1978, p. 13.

Source: *NIDB Bulletin*, vol. 2, no. 1 (June 1976), p. 19.

Table 15.1 shows the performances of the bank in the last four years. The yearly sanctions in monetary terms increased from N18.8m in 1974 to N59.8m in 1975, an increase of about 218.085 per cent. There was a decline in the trend in 1976 when only N51.4m was sanctioned, an increase of 173.4 per cent with 1974 as the base year. In 1977 sanctioned loans rose to a total of N73.9m, an increase of 293.08 per cent.

Table 15.2: Percentage Increase in Loan Sanctions (Base Year, 1974)

1975	–	81.%
1976	–	27.27%
1977	–	18.18%

The loan sanctions were either for new projects or for the expansion

Table 15.3: Some of the NIDB Sanctions in Each State

Company	State	Project	Equity N	NIDB Participation Loan N	Total N
Katsina Oil Mills Ltd	North Central	Food and beverages	–	700,000	700,000
Piramo Oil Mills Ltd	North Eastern	Food and beverages	–	600,000	600,000
Nigerian All Etr. Ltd	Lagos	Metal	160,000	560,000	720,000
Aba Hotel Ltd	East Central	Hotel and tourism	–	800,000	800,000
Prospect Textile Mills Ltd	Kwara	Textile	–	500,000	500,000
Nigagrob Ceramics Ltd	Western State	Ceramic	180,000	1,100,000	1,280,000
Edo Textile Mills Ltd	Mid West	Textile	–	600,000	600,000
Kano Dyeing Mills Ltd	Kano	Textile	–	430,000	430,000
Calabar Veneer & Plywood Ltd	South East	Wood	39,600	248,612	288,212
Cross River Mills Ltd	South East	Wood	26,286	138,100	164,386
Amakiri Furniture Co. Ltd	Rivers	Furniture	–	50,000	50,000
Plateau Concessions Ltd	BenuePlateau	Mining	–	40,000	40,000
Sokotan Ltd	North West	Leather	–	160,000	160,000
Total			405,886	5,926,712	6,332,598

Source: B.U. Ekanem, 'The Role of the NIDB in Industrial Financing and Its Critics' (NIDB, Aba, 1973), p. 24.

Table 15.4: Sub-Sectoral Distribution of NIDB Sanctions in 1976 (in N'000)

Sub-Sector	No. of projects	Cost of Product			NIDB Participation		
		Equity	Loan	Total	Equity	Loan	Total
Textiles	—	—	—	—	—	—	—
Food and beverages	5	77,440.0	169,780.0	247,220.0	2,500.0 (3.2)[a]	18,350.0 (10.8)	20,850.0 (8.4)
Metal products	4	2,427.0	6,492.6	8,919.6	200.0 (8.2)	2,500.0 (38.5)	2,700.0 (30.3)
Wood products	1	240.0	578.3	758.3	—	250.0 (48.2)	250.0 (33.0)
Chemical and chemical products	7	39,000.0	100,954.6	139,954.6	1,730.0 (4.4)	16,998.0 (16.8)	18,728.0 (13.4)
Leather and leather products	—	—	—	—	—	—	—
Paper and paper products	1	80.0	183.0	263.0	—	125.0 (68.3)	125.0 (47.5)
Hotel and tourism	1	370.0	752.0	1,222.0	—	650.0 (86.4)	650.0 (57.9)
Others	9	8,515.6	22,949.6	31,465.2	1,450.0 (17.0)	6,630.0 (28.9)	8,080.0 (25.7)
Total	28	128,072.6	301,630.1	429,702.7	5,880.0	45,503.0	51,383.0 (12.0)

Notes:
[a] Figures in brackets were originally computed by Obi Mordi and indicate percentages of NIDB participation based on respective cost items.
Source: NIDB, *Annual Report and Accounts*, 1976, p. 28.

of existing ones and they embraced a variety of sectors from food and
beverage manufactures, textiles, hotels and tourism, metal and chemical
industries. In 1975, 23 out of the 40 sanctions made were for new projects and 17 for the expansion of old projects. Out of the total amount
sanctioned, 21.9 per cent went to textiles, 37 per cent went to food
and beverages, 19 per cent to hotels and tourism and the rest to chemical and metal industries.[10]

As at 31 December 1977 the total sanctions cumulatively stood at
N258.6, and the total number of projects at 318. Altogether, N25.7m
was in equity while the remaining N234.9 was given as subordinate
loans.[11]

7. Conclusion

The magnitude of the bank's contributions to economic development
of the Nigerian economy requires no emphasis. The projects sponsored
by NIDB offer job opportunities to many Nigerians thereby helping to
alleviate the unemployment problem.

Apart from enhancing employment opportunities, these projects will
increase output and by so doing help to conserve the country's foreign
exchange and provide a base for acquiring technological know-how.

Notes

1. *Nigerian Year Book* (Daily Times Press, Lagos, 1971), p. 259.
2. Ibid., p. 259.
3. Ibid., p. 261.
4. *NIDB Bulletin*, vol. 2 (January-June 1976), p. 19.
5. NIDB *General Policies* (NIDB Limited, Lagos), p. 3.
6. Ibid., p. 4.
7. Ibid., p. 5.
8. *Nigerian Year Book*, p. 266.
9. Adamu Ciroma, 'Toast Speech' in *NIDB Bulletin*, vol. 2, no. 1 Lagos 1976,
p. 9.
10. Public Relation Department, NIDB 'Highlights of NIDB Annual Report
1975' in *NIDB Bulletin*, vol. 2, no. 1, p. 19.
11. E. Hearts: 'NIDB Achievements' in *Business Times*, Daily Times of Nigeria
Limited, Lagos, 7 February, 1978, p. 13.

16 NOTES ON THE NIGERIAN AGRICULTURAL BANK

C.C. Nweze

1. Introduction

In Nigeria, agriculture is as important as petroleum which now domi-nates the entire economy, but it has suffered some neglect since petro-leum became a major contributor to the economy. Most of the problems encountered by this sector of the economy can be attributed to inadequate investment in agricultural development and to wrong development priority. After political independence in 1960 the Federal Government of Nigeria realised the need to promote economic development but the initial efforts were mainly concentrated topsidedly for over ten years in assisting small- and large-scale industries by the establishment of various types of industrial banks and in the development of the stock market. It was only in 1973 that the Nigerian Agricultural Bank was established to assist agricultural activities.

Under the first National Development Plan, 1962-68, out of the public-sector expenditure estimates of N1,353 million, only N183.8 million or 13.8 per cent was allocated to agriculture which employs more than 70 per cent of the country's labour force. This notwithstanding, it is lamentable that at the end of the plan period only 57 per cent of the amount allocated to agriculture was actually spent.

It was, however, during the Second National Development Plan, 1970-74 that the government seemed to realise, although belatedly, that Nigerian agriculture suffers a general problem of low productivity. Production techniques are poor, there are few intermediate inputs and yields are low. Infrastructural facilities are inadequate and the marketing, storage and credit systems all call for a reform.[1] But the low-income farmers are unlikely to be capable of raising their productivity, improving their production techniques, applying adequate inputs and increasing farm yields substantially without a more adequate provision of finance. Thus the Nigerian Agricultural Bank was set up to provide this much needed finance to farmers in order to increase the quantity and quality of primary products.

The Nigerian Agricultural Bank Limited (NAB) was established in 1973. The initial resources of the bank were an authorised capital of N1m, fully subscribed by the Federal Government. It has its head-

255

quarters at Kaduna in Kaduna State with area offices in some of the states' headquarters.

These area branch offices are the Ibadan office, which caters for Oyo, Ogun, Kwara and Lagos States, the Benin office which serves Bendel and Ondo States, the Sokoto office which serves Niger and Sokoto States, the Enugu office for Anambra, Cross River and Benue States and the Port Harcourt office for Imo and River States. The Bauchi office serves Bauchi, Gongola, Borno and Plateau States, and the Kaduna office serves Kano and Kaduna States.

2. Aims and Objectives

The principal objective of NAB is to provide credit and loans for agricultural development and thereby enhance the level and quality of agricultural production including the following aspects: horticulture, poultry, farming, pig breeding, fisheries, forestry and timber production and the marketing of such products in Nigeria. The bank, however, does not confine itself to these operations alone; it also finances and encourages such agro-based industries as starch, vegetable oil and food canning.

The bank aims at improving rural life and the agricultural economy of the country by increasing income and the purchasing power of the rural population. This is in keeping with the government's policy of rural development in order to stem the unprecedented 'rural exodus' to the few congested urban centres by those in search of either white- or blue-collar jobs, especially since the end of the civil war in 1970.

The rural area is the seat of agricultural production. Over 70 per cent of the population is engaged in primitive farming, which usually results in low yield. It is this poor yield of rural farms coupled with government neglect in the provision of basic amenities in the rural areas that has given rise to the 'mass exodus' of people to the urban centres in search of urban jobs and urban pleasures.

3. Organisational Structure of the NAB

The bank is controlled by a board of directors which is the policy-making body of the bank. The bank employs a general manager who co-ordinates its overall activities and who is responsible to the board of directors. All the area offices have their area managers who co-ordinate the activities of the branch offices and who are responsible to the general manager.

There are three main departments of the bank: the project and consultancy department, the administration and finance department and the operations department, each of which is headed by a departmental manager.

There are two sub-departments which cannot be rightly called separate departments, these are: the legal division and the appraisal and evaluation division.

(a) Project and Consultancy Department

This conducts the feasibility study of a project when the client submits an application with detailed information about it. The study involves visits to the project's site or location and the verification of the information submitted.

The bank sponsors only those projects which are economically and commercially viable. A project will be economically desirable if it shows promise of raising the living standards of the people, providing employment opportunities and is capable of being carried out under existing conditions. Before a project is deemed viable, raw materials, machinery and equipment, essential services, technical and managerial personnel and labour must be available. It will be commercially viable if it is capable of making a satisfactory profit, taking into consideration the costs of production and sales proceeds and the possibility of the surplus or gross profit being able to repay the borrowed funds and interest charges. If the project and consultancy department considers the proposal satisfactory, it makes its recommendation which is passed to the operations department for review and consideration.

(b) Operations Department

This department undertakes its own study of the project in order to ratify the recommendations of the project and consultancy department; it has the power to reject or accept these reports. If the department is convinced that the project is good, it will prepare a report that will be submitted to the board of directors for study and approval.

(c) Administration and Finance Department

After the approval of the project, the finance department sanctions the loan and disburses the fund after certain legal requirements have been satisfied. It keeps accurate records of its expenditure on the project. No disbursement is made until the department is satisfied that all necessary legal documents concerning the project are complete. These documents include a proof of title deeds to the land, the registration of such land according to the Land Registration Act and other documents as may be required by the bank.

NAB usually monitors the progress of any project it finances. This is normally done by periodic visits to the project site by NAB executives and technical staff to obtain a first-hand and visual impression of its progress. The frequency of the visits depends on the circumstances of each case. Visits are usually carried out by the appraisal and evaluation division in conjunction with the administration and finance department. If the project faces any problem the two departments study the problem and make recommendations.

4. Security and Resources

NAB normally requires its clients to provide adequate security cover before it can grant loans to such persons. Such securities include:

(i) first legal mortgages on fixed assets like building and land. The value of the assets must be related to the project being financed by the bank;

(ii) government securities, bonds, shares of reputable companies and other marketable securities; and

(iii) bank and personal guarantees.

The bank, being aware of the difficulties prospective Nigerian clients usually encounter in producing adequate securities, sometimes allow the land on which the project is being undertaken to be mortgaged as collateral security.

5. Nature of Lendings

The bank makes direct and indirect loans. Direct loans are loans directed to individual farmers, co-operatives and governments. Indirect loans are those channelled to farmers and other government units such as the marketing boards through the government. In the latter case government provides the guarantee.

The minimum loan the bank can grant to an individual is N5,000. There is no upper limit but the approval of loans for big projects is sub-

Figure 16.1: Organogram of NAB as at 1 January 1978

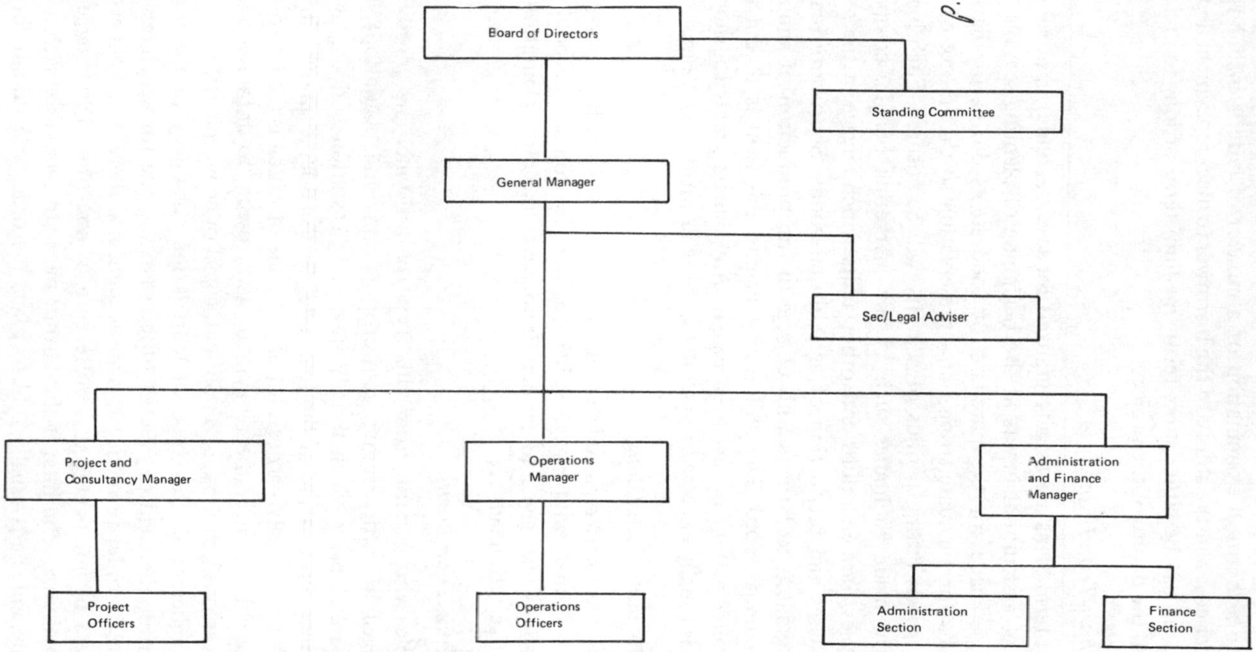

```
                          Board of Directors
                                 |
              +------------------+------------------+
              |                                     |
        Standing Committee                          |
                                                    |
                          General Manager           |
                                 |                  |
              +------------------+------------------+
              |                                     |
                                          Sec/Legal Adviser
              |
    +---------+---------+-------------------+
    |                   |                   |
 Project and      Operations      Administration
 Consultancy       Manager         and Finance
  Manager             |              Manager
    |                 |                 |
 Project        Operations      +-------+-------+
 Officers        Officers       |               |
                          Administration     Finance
                            Section          Section
```

Source: Staff Disposition (Supplied by Enugu Branch Manager)

ject to a thorough examination of a number of criteria including total project cost and the ability of the borrower to meet repayment demands. The loan can be either short term, medium term or long term depending on the nature of the project.

(a) Short-Term Loans

Short-term loans are usually granted for seasonal and occasional purchases of agricultural inputs at the beginning of planting seasons. It can also be made for the purchase of food items during the harvesting periods for adequate storage and preservation so that the provision of such goods during periods of scarcity will be ensured. Such loans are mostly made to bodies such as the marketing boards, co-operative societies, farmers' clubs and other units which engage in the seasonal purchases and production of agricultural goods. Short-term loans are also granted to farmers who engage in the production of annual and semi-annual crops. The philosophy behind this loan is that it will be recovered within or just over a year. Any person granted a short-term loan is usually expected to pay back the loan within two years.

(b) Medium-Term Loans

These are loans repayable within two to five years. It is mostly granted to farmers who engage in livestock production such as poultry and pigs. It is also given to farmers who have root-crop plantations with short gestation periods.

(c) Long-Term Loans

People who benefit from this type of assistance are mostly those engaged in cattle rearing, root-crop farming and plantations such as cocoa and palm which usually have long gestation periods. Owing to the long-term nature of the loan and the usual large amount involved, the loan normally carries a lot of risk, one of which is the borrower not being able to meet the repayment term owing to unforeseen circumstances, such as those of a political, social or economic nature. Another risk inherent in this type of loan is the possibility of the borrower diverting the fund to avenues other than the one for which it was provided. In order to reduce this antecedent risk therefore, NAB evolved a system of not paying the entire sum at one time. Disbursements are normally made in bits. If the farmer needs to purchase machinery and equipment, he is usually told to place the order and submit the bill to the bank which pays for and clears the goods when they arrive at the harbour for onward transfer to the farmer, or the bank can order, pay for and deliver the plant or equipment to him. If the farmer needs some buildings constructed on the farm, the bank instructs him to award the contract and the contractor's bills will be settled by the bank in accordance with the terms of the contract. Long-term loans are normally granted for a period of five to 15 years.

Before NAB concludes any long-term loan agreement, apart from the securities which are usually demanded as outlined above, the following are expected from the recipients of NAB loans:

(a) every loan recipient must keep accurate accounts of his or her business activities. A comprehensive statement of affairs which could be audited, if need be, must be kept;

(b) the progress report of the farm must be made periodically and sent according to the requirements of the company.

The rate of interest chargeable on loans depends among other things on the risk content of the project under consideration and takes into account the prevailing interest rate structure in the capital market and the practice of the commercial banks and other financial institutions. The Central Bank of Nigeria regulates the interest rates of all agricultural and allied loans.

6. Achievements

Since the establishment of the bank in 1973, it has been putting in every effort within the limits of its powers and resources to see that its objectives are achieved.

In order to revitalise the palm-produce sector which has been on the decline, and which since 1972 has virtually disappeared from the list of export commodities, various loans and grants have been given to the various state governments and companies since 1974. For instance the Nigerian Agricultural Bank approved a loan of N10.6m to the Oil Palm Industry Company for the establishment of two oil-palm estates in Bendel State. The bank also granted the Cowan Oil Palm Estate the sum of N3m to embark on an eight-year oil-palm replanting programme.

For the 1975/6 fiscal year, the bank budgeted about N46m as loans for the development of 50 agricultural projects throughout the Federation.[2] The states which benefited from the scheme were Sokoto, Kaduna, Kano, Kwara, Bendel, Cross River and Rivers.

The bank has financed a catalogue of projects since it was established and these are in all areas of the Federation. They include a starch mill in Ihiala, poultry farms in Ngwo and Awka, a crop project in Gboko and a cattle project in Oyo State, timber industry in Oyo, a poultry project in Kano, an oil-palm project in Bendel State and a fishing project in Rivers State.[3]

7. Conclusion

The activities of the Nigerian Agricultural Bank have been quite impressive and commendable. There is no doubt that if the bank maintains the pace, the rate of agricultural development, which has been lagging behind the annual rate of population growth (one of the main causes of the present inflation in the country), will level up and even overtake population growth in the near future.

Notes

1. Federal Republic of Nigeria, *Second National Development Plan, 1970-74*, p. 104.
2. See 'NAB News', *Nigerian Business Digest*, no. 37 (May 1975), p. 5.
3. Oral communication from the NAB's Enugu branch manager.

17 NIGERIAN INSURANCE COMPANIES AND FINANCIAL INTERMEDIATION

T.O. Ugha and O.A. Onwuteaka

1. Introduction

Insurance companies mobilise savings originating with individuals and business firms. Both life and casualty or non-life insurance companies raise their funds by selling their services to the public.

Life insurance companies mobilise savings by selling protection against the loss of income from actuarially premature death or retirement. In the first instance payments are made to the deceased's living beneficiaries who relied on his income during his lifetime and in the second to the insured himself. Besides pure risk protection most insurance services involve some savings.

Insurance companies offer additional savings opportunities in the form of annuity or endowment policies. Premiums charged to policies are related both to the amount of risk protection purchased and the amount of savings or the present value of the guaranteed future income. Because their sources of funds are primarily long term and their outflows highly predictable actuarially life insurance companies can invest primarily in long-term assets.

Casualty or non-life insurance companies on the other hand sell protection against the loss of property resulting from accident, fire, theft, negligence and other predictable reasons. The companies sell secondary securities in the form of premiums whose prices are related to the actuarial probability of the occurrence of the event triggering the loss. Until insured losses are realised, the casualty companies invest the funds in primary securities. Because the probability of events resulting in property loss is more difficult to calculate than the probability of human death, the payment patterns of casualty insurance companies are more uncertain than those from life insurance companies and casualty companies invest more heavily in short-term highly marketable securities.[1]

The sources of funds held by insurance companies for the payment of losses are the paid-in capital, paid-in surplus, earned surplus, premiums paid in advance of services performed and income from the prudent investment of these funds. Of all these sources the one that

263

really provides investable funds is the premiums. The paid-up capital for instance is normally deposited with the Central Bank of Nigeria as stipulated by the Insurance Decree 1976. Profits are either distributed as dividends to shareholders or ploughed back into the business.

2. Investment Outlets

Investment deals with the process of adjustment, from the actual stock of capital to the desired stock. In other words, any act which results in an increase in the stock of capital whether it is in the form of real asset or financial asset is considered an investment.[2]

When an insurance company talks about its investment, what strikes the mind is the ploughing or involvement of its surplus funds in investment in financial assets. The purpose of investment is to put its available fund to use or lend it to others in the hope of earning a return or dividend or interest. With this objective in mind, any security exchanged for the investment must be good enough to ensure the safety or non-depletions of the capital invested. The question which may arise is that if insurance companies desire to cue up their investment portfolios only against sound securities and such securities are not forthcoming, must they not invest? Good management demands that insurance companies invest their funds in accordance with the dictates of the liabilities lying against such funds. For this reason insurance funds are divided into two broad classes namely life funds and non-life funds. Life funds are the premium accruals from life policies. The claims and maturities arising from life policies are calculable in time and size. Non-life business is essentially short term, and is available to unexpected heavy losses without any control on their frequency. It will therefore be foolhardy investing long with such funds. Usually non-life funds must aim at liquidity, which means that stock acquired with non-life funds must be easily convertible into cash.

Generally, a wide range of investment outlets are open for the willing insurer in a developing economy in spite of the limitations held out by such an economy. The outlets include the following:

(i) Cash Deposit. This is cash deposited in registered banks either in the form of time deposits or fixed deposits. The deposits earn interest but the size of interest earned depends on the type of account operated. A fixed deposit attracts a higher interest rate than a time-deposit account.

(ii) Government Securities. In developing countries, there is always a ready market for government securities. The demand is motivated by such factors as safety and liquidity which the securities represent and offer. Government securities are the 90-day treasury bills, the one- or two-year treasury certificates (Nigerian war-time fund-raising instrument) and ten–twenty-year development stocks. All these bear fixed interest rates and are guaranteed by the governments issuing them and are redeemable by the Central Bank.

(iii) Mortgage and Debentures. Investments here are usually long term. It is an area where the insurers should feel free to invest because they are in a very good position to study the local conditions affecting both the property and the security offered by such a property mortgaged. They offer a good pit for life funds since the investments are medium to long term. The interest rates are also high and attractive.

(iv) Real Estate. Investment in real estate is another investment outlet but is fraught with problems. Before the Land Use Decree 1978 was promulgated which entrusted all lands to the government, lands were communally owned or were in dispute. In the circumstances it was difficult for insurance companies to acquire land for real estate development. With the new Land Use Decree 1978 it is now easier for the insurance companies to develop real estates with their life funds as building, industrial or agricultural lands can now be easily acquired by applying for occupancy to the State or Local Government. Real estate involves the development of property which may be leasehold or freehold.

(v) Equity. This involves long-term investment with life funds. Equity investment is highly risky and could lead to a loss if adequate care is not taken to ensure that the shares bought are those of sound and reliable companies in order to minimise risks. Foreign insurance companies were restricted from investing in equity. The fear was that foreign companies may ultimately control a number of industries and the Nigerian economy eventually. The Indigenisation Decree has made it mandatory that Nigerians control the equity holdings of a majority of incorporated companies including insurance companies, so the fear of foreign control of the economy through insurance equity investment has been overcome. All insurance companies can now invest in equity but within the stipulations of the Insurance Decree 1976.

(vi) Policy Loan. This is granted by insurance companies to life policy-holders based on surrender values of such policies. In other words, the policy is used as collateral for the loan and the amount of loan remains within the surrender value of the policy.

3. Investment Pattern of a Nigerian Insurance Company

The Universal Insurance Company is a typical Nigerian insurance company. It is owned by the Imo and Anambra State Governments.

During the year which ended on 31 December 1976 it made a total cash investment of approximately N1,054,357. At the end of the year it recorded an encouraging investment income of N163,582 being accruals from sundry investment outlets. This income represents 15.5 per cent of the company's total investments. But a great part of the income was realised from a particular source — *real estates*.

Investment for the Year ended 31 December 1976

1. Land and buildings	N251,241
2. Secured loans	32,450
3. Unsecured loans	69,009
4. Quoted investments book value	651,657
5. Unquoted investments	50,000
Total investments	N1,054,357

(i) Real Estate. The company has acquired and developed land at Lagos and Enugu. The sum of N251,241 was in fact invested in the building of houses in these two towns. Some of the houses in Enugu are occupied by the company's senior staff who pay a token monthly rent only. None of the Lagos houses is occupied by a member of the company's staff and each attracts a substantial amount of rent. It is in fact from this form of investment that the company realised a large part of the quoted investment income. The company has plans to increase its investments in real estate but this plan appears to be frustrated by some problems.

The biggest problem the company is encountering is that of acquiring good title to land. In many parts of Nigeria, before the Land Use Decree 1978, acquisition of land for development purposes met stiff opposition. In most cases the land-owners saw the move as exploitation. It is generally believed that compensations which the government or its agency is willing to pay for land acquisition is considerably lower than that obtained in the open market. But there are extreme cases where even after an agreement had been reached on adequate compensations a second party suddenly emerges claiming title to the land. The reconciliation or litigation between rival owners normally takes a long time during which capital is tied up.

Other problems are of a technical nature. When land has been acquired, there has always been the problem of developing it. The contractors very often are unable to execute the job within an agreed time, because of lack of building materials. When materials are available the costs may be too exhorbitant for the project to be economical. Even though real estate may be a profitable venture for insurance companies legal limitations restrict them from investing all their funds in real estate. The Insurance Decree 1976 limits investments in real property to 10 per cent of non-life funds and 25 per cent of life funds. In view of the housing shortage in the country and the greater yields in this area of investment there should be greater relaxation of the regulations restricting insurance companies from investment in real property. The experiments made by the Universal Insurance Company in the area of real property should encourage the relaxation of restrictions.

(ii) Secured Loan. These are mainly policy loans which are limited to 90 per cent of the surrender values of life policies. The amount of secured loan granted so far has been relatively small because many policy-holders are ignorant about the existence of such loan facilities. For the year ended 31 December 1976 the secured loan of the Universal Insurance Company amounted to N32,450 and attracted interest. The budget speech of the 1978/9 fiscal year streamlined the interest rate of insurance banks for loans with that of commercial banks.

(iii) Unsecured Loan. For the year ended 31 December 1976, loans amounted to N69,009. These were mainly loans given to members of staff for the development of real property, other than for the purchase of personal vehicles. Unsecured loans also attract interest.

(iv) Quoted Investments. For the year under review, the company invested the sum of N651,657 in the purchase of shares in other companies. This amount represents the book value of the investment. The market value of the investment is, however, N660,850 which involves a hidden profit or appreciation amounting to N9,193. Here again is another outlet that contributes appreciably to the investment income

of the company. The yields are, however, limited by the dividend policies of the individual company in whose shares the Universal Insurance
Company has invested. Government directives on the payment of dividends is another stumbling block. At present it is set at 33.3 per cent.

(v) Unquoted Investment. N50,000 worth of unquoted investments
financed two subsidiary companies — the Ridgeway Investment Company and the Premier Brokers and Agencies. The Ridgeway Company is
a real property development company and engages the services of
experts. Premier Brokers solicits for insurance business on behalf of the
Universal Insurance Company and other interested insurance companies
and makes its revenue through this medium.

4. Growth of Insurance Premium Income in Nigeria

The insurance industry in Nigeria, over the past two decades, has witnessed tremendous expansion. The number of companies and the size
and speed of their branch networks can be used as rough indicators of
their growth. It is obvious that the industry's expansion rate has been
very rapid. The number of insurance companies rose from 35 in 1960
to 77 by the end of 1976.

The growth of the industry has made itself manifest in the parallel
growth of its net premium income.[3] Premium income, being the most
important source of insurance funds, can be used to give a picture of
the growth of insurance funds and invariably their sources in Nigeria.

A breakdown of the net premium income of insurance companies
into various types of policies will give a rough picture of the primary
sources of these funds. Thus the figures for marine insurance will give
an idea of how much is contributed by importers and exporters, the
figure for motor insurance will give an idea of what proportion comes
from motorists and that will also apply to the other classes of the business.

Applying this breakdown the picture that emerges with respect to
the growth of premium income of insurance companies in Nigeria is
given in Table 17.1.

From Table 17.1 it is observed that the net premium of the insurance industry rose from N7m in 1960 to approximately N52m in 1974,
an increase of 643 per cent over the period. Out of this, non-life business moved from about N6.4m in 1960 to N32.4m in 1974, while life
business moved from N0.6m in 1960 to N19.6m over the same period.

Thus non-life business increased from 407.5 per cent as against a more massive increase of 3,092 per cent recorded by life insurance business.

Table 17.1: The Growth of Premium Income by Type of Insurance Business (Nm)

Type	1960	1963	1965	1970	1972	1974
Fire	0.878	2.084	2.662	1.464	2.749	3.895
Marine	0.166	0.490	0.470	0.920	1.684	2.372
Motor	4.422	5.398	7.272	5.667	13.708	19.256
Workmen's compensation	0.276	0.566	0.566	0.646	1.543	1.846
Miscellaneous	0.640	1.262	1.262	0.643	1.776	3.106
Accident				0.911	1.520	1.911
Total Non-Life	6.382	9.800	12.586	10.251	22.980	32.386
Total Life	0.614	2.526	5.138	4.705	8.060	19.601
Grand Total	6.996	12.326	17.724	14.956	31.040	51.987

Source: A. Oyejide and A. Soyode, 'Some Features of the Insurance Industry', *Nigerian Journal of Business Management*, vol. 1, no. 4, (September/October, 1977)

This growth in the net premium income of the insurance industry especially the life net premium shows that more funds are continually being placed at the disposal of the insurance companies. The rapid growth of the life insurance business can be attributed to the following factors:

(i) growth in personal income;
(ii) literacy level; and
(iii) appropriate tax policies.

The rapid growth of the Nigerian economy over the last 15 years — fuelled in particular by the oil boom — is an accepted fact.[4] To the extent that an increasing number of literate income earners have emerged and to the extent that their incomes have rapidly increased, so has the life business expanded. Government tax policy gives a strong and positive encouragement to this growth. An individual is allowed to write-off as much as N2,000 of his annual income as a tax deductible element if he has life insurance up to that amount. This is a strong inducement of which more and more people are taking advantage and it probably lies at the heart of the massive growth of the life insurance business. With the rise in total premium income to N160m[5] in 1975 and with the growing rate of life funds it is bound to constitute a greater proportion of the industry's premium income in the nearest future.

The above analysis of the relative growth of the life insurance net premium fund has been necessitated because of the peculiar nature of these funds. For practical purposes these funds belong to the policy-holders and are being held by the insurance companies which stand in the position of trustee.[6] Good management requires that these funds be prudently invested. Because of their long liability implications life funds form most of the investable funds of insurance companies.

5. Insurance Companies and Financial Intermediation

Financial intermediation is a system whereby an economic unit creates and issues financial claims against itself, using its proceeds to acquire and hold financial claims against others. The economic unit can be said to intermediate between the sources of funds that flow to it and the ultimate users of these funds.[7]

Put simply financial intermediaries can be seen as institutions or economic units that intermediate between surplus economic units and deficit economic units. They mobilise the savings from the surplus units and make the savings available to those units that have need for these funds either for investment purposes or otherwise.

Financial intermediaries are usually classified into bank and non-bank financial intermediaries. The main difference between banks and non-banks as financial intermediaries is that banks offer the public a liability instrument that is extensively accepted and used as a medium of exchange, with changes in ownership affected through the clearing system, while non-bank financial intermediaries offer the public liability instruments that are not so used but that have other attractive characteristics. Insurance companies belong to the latter class alongside building societies, trust companies, pension funds, credit unions, consumer loan and finance companies etc.

The significant role of insurance companies as financial intermediaries arises from the fact that the industry serves as an effective vehicle for the mobilisation of national resources by encouraging individuals to save and thereby make available the long-term contractual savings for investment.

The important role insurance companies play in the field of saving mobilisation cannot be overemphasised. Everyone knows that it is not easy to cultivate the savings habit, hence the government encourages people to save through government-approved institutions such as commercial banks, savings banks, building societies and insurance companies.

Savings through insurance policies however have some obvious advantages over other schemes. Apart from the basic life protection by which an immediate estate is created for the benefit of the assured's dependents, savings cultivate thrift in the individual. Tax reliefs, which are allowed on life-insurance premiums are an inducement to cultivate the habit of saving which governments encourage as savers indirectly contribute towards the growth of their national economies.[9]

The insurance companies now have mobilised much capital that did not exist before in any institutional framework. It is customary and indeed part of government legislation in developing countries for life insurance companies to invest a substantial portion of their reserves in long-term government bonds. In Nigeria, for example, life insurance companies must invest a minimum of 25 per cent in Nigerian government securities, and this normally takes the form of investments in development stocks and other securities specified under the Government and Other Securities (Local Trustees Powers) Act and the Trustees Investment Act 1962.

The impact of insurance companies in the provision of capital in Nigeria can be more fully appreciated by an analysis of their asset distribution, shown in Table 17.2.

The role of insurance companies in the provision of capital is of much greater importance than portrayed by Table 17.2. In Nigeria life policies and non-life policy covers have been of particular importance in making finance available indirectly from banks and other financial institutions. For instance the use of life policies as collateral for loans and advances and the enhanced value of real estate and other mortgaged properties covered by general insurance (and thus their greater acceptability as collateral) have been the major solution so far to the chronic problem of inadequate security for bank advances in Nigeria.[10]

Financial institutions have long recognised the futility of their negotiations without adequate insurance protection. No bank manager will issue a letter of credit without ensuring that the goods will be covered by insurance. Insurance companies facilitate the granting of loans by banks to their customers, as financial intermediaries they influence liquidity by lending also on mortgage.

Non-bank financial intermediaries generally have been associated with offsetting tendencies in monetary management. Simply stated this situation would arise where tight money policy, for instance, may be offset by generous credit policy of these institutions. In the case of Nigeria, however, the impact of the insurance industry on monetary policy appears not to be offsetting; aware of the consequences of uncontrolled lendings, the Nigerian budgetary policy of 1978/9 put the lending rate of insurance companies at par with those of commercial banks.

Table 17.2: Distribution of Assets of Insurance Companies in Nigeria 1969-71

Assets	Total 1969	Funds 1971	Gen. 1969	Funds 1971	Life Funds 1969	Life Funds 1971
1. Cash	23.3	24.6	24.5	24.7	23.2	24.5
2. Bills of exchange	5.9	1.9	4.0	0.5	7.2	3.2
3. Interests and dividends and rents	1.1	1.4	0.4	0.8	1.6	1.9
4. Government securities	16.6	19.0	12.3	12.8	19.8	24.9
5. Securities of semi-government bodies	0.3	0.5	0.6	0.8	0.1	0.1
6. Other bonds and stocks	15.9	13.6	21.6	14.4	11.9	12.9
7. Loans to policy-holders	5.3	4.5	1.4	0.2	8.1	8.7
8. Other loans	6.5	5.2	1.7	2.3	9.9	7.9
9. Mortgage loans on real estate	2.0	1.3	1.6	0.7	2.3	1.9
10. Outstanding premiums	5.9	5.3	2.5	6.5	8.3	4.2
11. Other amounts receivable	8.7	11.9	18.3	22.1	2.0	2.2
12. Real estate	4.3	3.5	5.5	2.8	3.4	4.1
13. Equipment, furniture and supplies	1.5	1.6	3.0	2.8	0.4	0.5
14. Other assets	2.7	5.7	3.7	8.5	2.0	3.0
Total	100	100	100	100	100	100
Amount (Nm)	41.0	68.5	17.0	33.5	24.0	38.1
Total capital market assets (4. + 5. + 6.)	32.8	33.1	34.4	28.0	31.6	37.9
Total Loans (7. + 8. + 9.)	13.8	11.0	4.7	3.2	20.3	18.5

Source: Ade T. Ojo, *The Nigerian Financial System* (University of Wales Press, 1976), p. 48.

Table 17.3 shows the ratios between insurance funds and commercial bank deposits for the years 1970-2. The ratio of insurance funds to commercial bank deposits in the period is too insignificant to cause monetary problems.[11]

Table 17.3: Ratio of Insurance Funds to Commercial Bank Deposits
in Nigeria 1970-2

Year (1)	Insurance funds[a] (N'000) (2)	Commercial-bank deposits[b] (N'000) (3)	Ratio (4)
1970	31,289	6,264,276	0.00499
1971	41,038	7,700,606	0.00532
1972	70,517	8,752,104	0.00806

Notes:
[a] Insurance funds included are: life funds, accident, fire, employers' liability, motor, transport, miscellaneous and other classes.

[b] Bank deposits are demand, savings and time deposits.

Source: Mordi, 'Insurance Industry and Financial Intermediation', p. 174.

6. Insurers and the Capital Market

Capital markets generate new equity capital for enterprises that do not have internal resources to maintain an adequate level of equity. Normally a capital market provides insurance companies with viable outlets for their investable funds. In Nigeria the role of the stock exchange and other capital-market institutions in providing suitable investment outlets for insurance funds has not been very satisfactory. An efficient capital market is a market in which prices provide accurate signals for resource allocation, under the assumption that security prices at any time 'fully reflect' all available information.[12] The Nigerian Stock Exchange, which is the cardinal institution in the Nigerian capital market, has not developed appreciably since its inception in 1961. This is evident from the number of stocks quoted on the exchange and the volume of business done on the exchange especially in relation to equity stock. As at March 1978 only 37 ordinary shares and eight industrial loan and preference stocks were listed on the exchange. The rest of the entire 94 securities listed at the exchange were government stocks.

One important function of the exchange should be the reduction of the risk of illiquidity and capital loss on investments in the financial assets traded on it. This can be done by either offsetting these risks against each other or by enabling institutions best fitted to specialise in bearing them. The freedom of investors to express their preferences for certain types of securities is the one that bears directly on the insurance companies. The insurance companies do not exercise the power of choosing from a variety of securities, since very few are listed at the exchange. The attitude of Nigerians in buying stocks to hold also hampers the ability of the stock exchange to function effectively. Insurance companies are therefore left with virtually no appreciable amount of stock to invest their reserves in. In fact the only times these companies have a chance of buying stocks en bloc is when new issues are listed which are usually oversubscribed.

Equity-linked plans which provide some hedge against inflation cannot yet be introduced by insurance companies because of lack of spread of the available securities in the capital market. The task of investing insurance funds is made more difficult because apart from gilt-edged securities guaranteed by government and the few listed stocks, converting other stocks into cash is quite difficult.

Insurance companies in Nigeria can still play a greater role as suppliers of capital funds by increasing their direct lending activities. Loans on policies and collateral loans which at present form an insignificant part of the asset holdings of insurance companies should be considered seriously by them and granted more liberally.

7. Conclusion

Insurance companies have contributed in no small way towards the mobilisation of savings of individuals, which are channelled for investment purposes. With the growth of the Nigerian economy, the insurance companies premium pool continues to grow in consonance with the overall growth of the economy. As these funds grow the insurance companies will come to play an even greater role in the provision of capital funds. When the amount of investments made so far by these insurance companies is considered, their impact as financial intermediaries in Nigeria is appreciated. The role of insurance companies in bridging the gap between surplus and deficit economic units in the economy cannot be overemphasised.

Notes

1. George G. Kenform, *Money, the Financial System and the Economy* (Macnally, Chicago, 1973), p. 54.
2. F.O. Okafor, Lecture notes on 'Investment Analysis', University of Nigeria, Enugu Campus, 1977/8 session.

3. Net premium income is defined as net premium minus reinsurance ceded. This has been used instead of gross premium since we are considering sources of investable funds. Cessions need not be included.

4. For some relevant supporting figures see Central Bank of Nigeria, *Annual Report and Statement of Accounts* (1974) and Federal Republic of Nigeria, *Third National Development Plan, 1975-80*.

5. J.O. Irukwu, 'The Development of Insurance in Nigeria from 1900-1975', WAICA Journal, vol. 1 (1975), p. 13.

6. From a pure legal standpoint this does not hold exactly.

7. Obi Mordi, 'Insurance Industry and Financial Intermediation' in J.O. Irukwu (ed.), *Conference Papers of the Insurance Institute* vol. IV (Caxton Press, Ibadan, 1975), p. 169.

8. E.N. Neufield, *The Financial System of Canada: Its Growth and Development* (Macmillan, Toronto, 1972), p. 20.

9. Moka, 'The role of the Insurance Industry in the Economic Development of a Nation', *The Federal Might* (NICON, Lagos, 1977), p. 4.

10. Ade T. Ojo, *The Nigerian Financial System* (University of Wales Press, 1976), p. 48.

11. The obligation on insurance companies to invest a given percentage of their resources in public debt instruments which are managed by the Central Bank can be dovetailed into desired monetary policy.

12. Eugene F. Fama, 'Efficient Capital Marketing: A Review of Theory and Practice', *Journal of Finance* (May 1970), p. 383.

Part Five

NIGERIA'S EXTERNAL FINANCIAL RELATIONS

18 NOTES ON CONVERTIBILITY AND THE NIGERIAN CURRENCY SYSTEM

A.N. Okoli

1. Introduction

The sterling exchange standard marked the beginning of modern currency exchange in Nigeria. In its narrow sense, the sterling exchange standard implied that the sum total of currencies issued in the overseas territories of the British Commonwealth equalled in effect the total currency circulating within the United Kingdom itself. The only difference was in the physical appearances of the various colonial currencies and sterling. Echoes of such views can be found in the writings of some authors.[1]

Colonial currencies were backed 100 per cent by sterling assets. Such assets consisted mainly of UK government securities. The West African currencies were fully backed by sterling assets throughout the time they constituted legal tender in those colonies.

A currency is fully convertible if it can be freely converted into other currencies by internal and external holders of that currency. Internal convertibility relates to free conversion by the citizens of a country, whereas external convertibility relates to the ability of foreigners to convert a local currency earned through trade or through investment into any foreign currency of their choice without let or hindrance by the local monetary authorities.

The naira is convertible externally because foreigners are allowed under law to repatriate their earnings and other funds. On the other hand, the naira is not fully convertible internally because under the current Nigerian laws Nigerian nationals travelling abroad are allowed an allowance of N500 in foreign exchange and N50 in local denominations. It is illegal to hold foreign exchange or naira over and above that generally allowed to Nigerians travelling abroad except with a special permission from the Central Bank.

2. The West African Currency Board and Convertibility

The West African Currency Board came into existence in 1912. It was similar in structure and operations to those set up in the other British colonies of Central and East Africa and the West Indies. The administration of the board was by and large in the hands of the colonial authorities.

The West African Currency Board like other colonial currency boards was characterised by the rigidity of parity between the local currency and the British pound sterling, 100 per cent sterling assets backing for the local currency, and the automaticity of the systems at the foreign exchange market because of the sterling alignment.[2]

By the 'golden' rule of the exchange standard full convertibility existed between the West African Currency Board pound note and the British pound sterling and there were no restrictions whatsoever on the amount one could convert or reconvert. The convertibility was both external and internal. The issue of units of the domestic currency was directly related to the units of sterling earnings earned through exports to the UK. The tight relationship between local currency and the pound sterling has been one of the major criticisms against the West African Currency Board system which was considered more of a money-changer than an issuing house. The West African currency, which circulated in Nigeria, Gold Coast (Ghana), Sierra Leone and Gambia before independence of those colonies, could only be issued if an equivalent pound sterling had been earned through trade. The policy restricted economic growth in the colonies.[3]

3. The Central Bank of Nigeria and Convertibility

The Central Bank of Nigeria commenced operations in July 1959. One of the functions of the Bank as contained in the Central Bank's Act 1958 is the issue of legal tender notes and coins. Consequently the Bank issued the Nigerian pound notes which replaced those of the West African Currency Board.

Since then, the Central Bank has through its service function changed the currency in circulation in 1968 and in 1973. In 1968 the Central Bank Currency Conversion (Amendment) Decree No. 48 reduced the internal convertibility of the Nigerian pound by making the currency convertible only on the 'Central Bank to Central Bank level', and replaced the existing currency notes with new issues. The 1968 replacement and the denial of convertibility were to make foreign-exchange transactions difficult for the seceding Biafrans who desperately needed foreign exchange for the purchase of arms. In 1973 the replacement was occasioned by the introduction of a decimal currency system.

The point has already been made that the West African Currency Board currency notes related to the pound sterling unit for unit. The Nigerian pound issued when the Central Bank of Nigeria came into operation was also linked to the pound sterling but not in full. In other words, the Nigerian monetary authorities built in fiduciary and non-fiduciary elements into the currency. The Nigerian pound was not completely backed by sterling assets. The flexibility in the new convertibility system created room for monetary management with restraint.

By 1962 the Nigerian pound was defined only in terms of gold following the amended Central Bank Act. One Nigerian pound equalled 2.488 grams of fine gold. The new parity was registered with the International Monetary Fund. Nigeria undertook to defend this rate of conversion in all international transactions involving her currency and other countries' currencies related in gold in accordance with the permissible 2 per cent spread reached in the Bretton Woods accord of 1944.[4]

4. The Nigerian Currency and the Regime of Float

In 1973 the Nigerian currency (naira) was devalued. The devaluation was a consequent of the deteriorating balance of trade of Nigeria. But the immediate causes of the devaluation were the floating of the dollar and the withdrawal of gold backing for the dollar, both in 1971, the floating of the pound sterling in 1973 and the devaluation of the dollar in 1973. There is no fixed exchange rate between the Nigerian currency and any world currency currently. The exchange rate is adjusted by the Nigerian authorities in terms of the ruling foreign-exchange market prices of major world currencies. Although the dollar and the pound sterling are technically no longer reserve currencies since the regime of float, the Nigerian holdings of sterling and dollar assets as well as the assets of stronger currencies like the Deutschmark and Swiss franc determine the relative strength of the naira in the adjustment of the rate of exchange.

In determining the equilibrium rate of exchange, the free-method system cannot be used since Nigeria does not allow her currency to be traded in. The monetary authorities therefore introduced a managed float in which the value of the naira was administratively fixed, depending on the changes in value of a preselected group of currencies.[5]

In fixing the rate of naira, account is taken of the necessity to reduce the rate of imported inflation through exchange-rate policy. This accounts for occasions where the naira rate remained unchanged even when the indication pointed to the upward adjustments.

Other determinants of the rate of exchange in a foreign-exchange market ruled by float are the level of real income and the rate of change of the real income of individual countries; tastes and preferences for domestic versus imported goods in the various countries; relative prices and the rate of change in prices of investments in the various countries.[6] The above factors will in one way or the other increase the income and the propensity to import and export which tells on the exchange-rate parities.

The regime of float compelled the Nigerian monetary authorities to institute a mechanism of managed float for the naira. By this system the exchange rate of the naira is not determined in the same way as the dollar or sterling. The Central Bank chooses a basket of currencies involving Nigeria's major trading partners and through cross-rates computation adjusts the parity of the naira.

Because of the technical problems of credit control and its limited scope in the world financial arena it has become increasingly necessary, in the pursuit of economic goals with a reasonable degree of internal and external stability, to employ other methods to augment, or as an alternative policy matrix, whatever instruments of credit control the Central Bank has at its command. One of these is the control of exchange and exchange transactions.[7]

In 1977 the Nigerian Government promulgated the Foreign Exchange (Anti-Sabotage) Decree. Before then in 1969, the Currency Conversions Decree was promulgated.

One of the aims of these two decrees is to check and if possible eradicate the illegal trading of Nigerian currency across the borders. This check per se connotes the inconvertible nature of the present Nigerian currency. The exchange control act confers on the Central Bank the power to control all movements of the naira into foreign countries and into Nigeria.

When a currency is fully convertible it is demanded of the monetary authorities to ensure that a substantial fraction of the resources handed over to them in return for the currency is held in the form of gold, or foreign exchange easily convertible into gold. Since convertibility is guaranteed, the authorities incur the obligation to exchange currency for gold or some other currency on demand and at any time. It therefore follows that the currency backing cannot be fully employed in some form of long-term investment.[8]

Nigeria in her present stage of economic development and growth cannot bear this burden. The point is, that given the fluctuations of the world prices of primary products which is the backbone of foreign-exchange earnings, she cannot defend a situation of full convertibility. In actual fact, every country would wish her currency were convertible. This is because free convertibility connotes a high level of industrialisation and high economic growth and development.

The problem is that if a developing country like Nigeria were to declare her currency convertible, she will starve herself of the scarce foreign exchange required for priority needs. Since local industries are likely to produce relatively low-quality goods Nigerian nationals would prefer imported goods of higher quality. Invariably the industries will lose the home market and may fold up and such a situation is not desirable in an economy striving for rapid industrialisation and full engagement of its resources.

Notes

1. See for example, Edwin Nevin, *Capital Funds in Underdeveloped Countries* (Macmillan, London 1963), p. 6.
2. 'The West African Currency Board', *Business Times* (Lagos), 14 March 1978, p. 19.
3. This point has been stressed in J.K. Onoh's Lectures on 'Nigerian Monetary and Fiscal Policies', Department of Finance, University of Nigeria, 1976/7 Session.
4. Oral communication from J.K. Onoh.
5. 'Do We Still Need Exchange Control', *Business Times* (Lagos), 22 February 1977, p. 13.
6. John G. Ranlett, *Money and Banking: An Introduction to Analysis and Policy* (John Wiley, New York, 1965), p. 335.
7. M.H. DeCock, *Central Banking*, 4th edn, (Crosby Lockwood Staples, London, 1974), p. 259.
8. Nevin, *Capital Funds*, p. 4.

19 NIGERIA'S BALANCE OF PAYMENTS AND EXTERNAL LIQUIDITY IN THE SEVENTIES

L.O. Mbata

1. Introduction

In the seventies Nigeria's balance of payments accounts were influenced mainly by the 30-month civil war which ended in January 1970, by the revenue from the petroleum industry and by the declining output level of exportable raw materials and cash crops. At the end of the civil war the Nigerian economy was hit by a barrage of problems. The foreign-exchange reserve of the economy was virtually depleted as military hardwares were purchased mostly in cash. The deficit in the balance of trade coupled with the deficits in the Federal and State governments' fiscal budgets brought with them an inflationary repercussion which weakened the base of the economy.

Production in most parts of the country, particularly in the war-torn areas, had come to a halt. There was an unprecedented scarcity of goods and services and the ultimate national goals of rapid economic growth and industrialisation were threatened. Nigerian policy makers were confronted with a number of uneasy options. To reduce imports would heighten the inflationary pressure and to increase imports in order to reduce inflation would magnify and worsen the deficit of the current account and create more balance of payments problems. Non-importation of raw materials would paralyse domestic industrial output as many industries depended to a large extent on imported raw materials which have to be financed with foreign exchange.

Internal monetary measures had proved inadequate as corrective instruments. The banking system was already over-liquid. Commercial banks' liquidity at one time reached a level of 96.2 per cent[1] as against the minimum requirement of 25 per cent. To contend with inflation the authorities had no other alternative than to relax some of the rigid restrictions of the late sixties and to permit imports of certain classified items. The extent of the relaxation depended on the structure of the current account of the balance of payments.

Prior to the Nigerian civil war, trade and foreign exchange transactions with most parts of the world were essentially free;[2] since 1967 exchange control has been in force. During the civil war and till 1974 certain restrictions were imposed on current-account transfers. There was, for example, a mandatory deferred payment period for imports. Non-residents were forbidden to transfer the investment income accruing to them and surcharges were applied to the importation of certain classes of goods while the importation of others was completely banned. Apart from the relaxation of restriction to permit the importation of capital goods, agricultural inputs and other essential goods, import restrictions ruled the balance of payment policies of the seventies.

2. Balance of Payment Analysis

Deficits in Nigeria's balance of payments accounts are manifest in the current account and not in the capital account. Although petroleum transactions recorded increasing positive balances the non-oil commodities depreciated and consequently contributed to the deficits in the current account of the early seventies. Insurance, shipping and other activities under the 'services account' registered negative balances. Policy measures were accordingly directed to correcting the negative factors in the balance of payments. To reduce the high proportion of the cost of services it was made mandatory for all Nigerian importers to insure their goods in Nigeria. Domestic production of goods and services were to be encouraged. Lending rates for loans designated for agricultural and manufacturing activities were reduced and commercial banks were directed to award a large portion of their loanable funds to the productive sectors. Preference was given to indigenous Nigerian entrepreneurs. The measures did have some effects as reflected in the positive increase in the overall balances. From N15.2m in 1969 the overall balance rose to N58.6m and N128.8m in 1970 and 1971 respectively (see Table 19.1). The magnifying effect of petroleum revenue on the balance of payments needs no emphasis.

The non-oil sector made up principally of agricultural commodities has been experiencing deficits which have increased substantially over the years. From a mild deficit of N248.6m in 1969 the non-oil sector scored a deficit of N839.8m in 1971. In 1976 the deficit reached an all-time record level of N5,486.1m.

By 1971 some of the effects of the severe economic and exchange-control measures began to show strongly. The exchange-control measures in particular were unsettling and their repercussions intensified smuggling and other clandestine currency operations which reduced the flow of foreign exchange into official channels. The restrictions on imports had aggravated the inflationary pressure and were becoming cumbersome to administer. In April 1971, many of the import restrictions accordingly were lifted with a few exceptions while some were placed under open general licence.[3] New measures were however lined up for conserving foreign exchange. These new measures included delayed payments of 90 days and 180 days for different categories of goods and reduction of different categories of remittances abroad.[4] The lifting of import restrictions affected the year's balance of payments account adversely while the increased petroleum production of that year favoured the balance of payments account.

At the exchange-rate front, the Central Bank of Nigeria made some adjustments following the suspension of the gold convertibility of the United States dollar on 15 August 1971, and the devaluation of the dollar against gold in December 1971.[5] The first reaction of the Central Bank of Nigeria after 15 August was to run a two-tier exchange-rate system for the Nigerian pound according to whether a transaction was denominated in dollars or in pounds sterling. When eventually the dollar was officially devalued, the Nigerian pound rate was adjusted so that its relationship with the dollar became £N1.00 = US$3.04 instead of the former rate of £N1.00 = US$2.80 — appreciation of 8.57 per cent.[6]

In 1972 the world market prices for agricultural products dropped drastically. The fall in foreign-exchange earning magnified the deficit in the services account of the balance of payments account by 68.8 per cent. The heavy deficit on the non-oil account in 1972 brought down the overall balance in the balance of payments account to N39.6m in spite of the fact that there was a reduction in imports due to accumulated inventories arising from relaxation of restrictions in 1971.

However, 1973 showed signs of improvements in the world market prices for agricultural commodities but domestic demand, a consequence of increased money income, had grown to such a level that the revenue from the non-oil sector could hardly support capital and consumer goods imports. The petroleum industry on the other hand prospered. Posted prices per barrel of crude oil rose from N0.66 a barrel in 1970 to N1.63 a barrel in 1973.[7] There was a huge credit balance of N1,338.8m in the petroleum account resulting in an overall credit balance of N174.4m in the balance of payments.

In the history of Nigeria's balance of payments, 1974 stands out as a special year. The interplay of world political and economic constellations between 1973 and 1974 raised the posted prices of petroleum from its 1973 rate of N1.63 per barrel to an all-time high of N4.83 a barrel.[8] The Nigerian government raised the petroleum-profit tax from 50 per cent to 55 per cent[9] and ordered an increase in oil production

Table 19.1: Balance of Payments of Nigeria, 1969-76 (Summary Statement) (Nm)

Category	1969 Oil	1969 Non-oil	1969 Total	1970 Oil	1970 Non-oil	1970 Total	1971 Oil	1971 Non-oil	1971 Total	1972 Oil	1972 Non-oil	1972 Total
Current Account	+ 140.0	− 248.6	− 108.6	+ 383.6	− 433.6	− 50.0	+ 610.4	− 839.8	− 229.4	+ 612.3	− 940.0	− 327.7
Merchandise trade	+ 236.2	− 69.4	+ 136.8	+ 464.8	− 291.8	+ 173.0	+ 929.8	− 644.8	+ 285.0	+ 1,141.2	− 663.7	+ 477.5
Non-Merchandise trade (i.e., services)	− 96.2	− 200.0	− 296.2	− 81.2	− 186.8	− 268.0	− 319.4	− 196.8	− 516.2	− 528.9	− 257.0	− 785.9
Unrequited transfers (net)	—	+ 20.8	+ 20.8	—	+ 45.0	+ 45.0	—	+ 1.8	+ 1.8	—	+ 14.3	+ 14.3
Capital Account	− 33.4	+ 108.0	+ 80.6	− 130.4	+ 179.6	+ 49.2	− 22.8	+ 316.2	+ 293.4	+ 195.8	+ 73.4	+ 269.2
Balancing Item (errors)	—	—	+ 43.2	—	—	+ 47.4	—	—	+ 54.4	—	—	+ 3.7
Allocation of SDRs	—	—	—	—	+ 12.0	+ 12.0	—	+ 10.4	+ 10.4	—	+ 10.2	+ 10.4
Overall balance	—	—	+ 15.2	—	—	+ 58.6	—	—	+ 128.8	—	—	+ 39.6

Category	1973 Oil	1973 Non-oil	1973 Total	1974 Oil	1974 Non-oil	1974 Total	1975 Oil	1975 Non-oil	1975 Total	1976 Oil	1976 Non-oil	1976 Total
Current Account	+ 1,338.8	− 1,286.1	+ 52.7	+ 5,057.1	− 1,994.6	+ 3,062.5	+ 4,069.0	− 4,026.4	+ 42.6	+ 5,266.2	− 5,486.1	− 219.9
Merchandise trade	+ 1,965.0	− 798.1	+ 1,166.9	+ 5,618.3	− 1,179.0	+ 4,439.3	+ 4,648.3	− 3,161.2	+ 1,487.1	+ 5,826.9	− 4,525.4	+ 1,301.5
Non-merchandise trade (net)	− 626.2	− 452.6	− 1,078.8	− 561.2	− 753.5	− 1,314.7	− 579.3	− 788.4	− 1,367.7	− 560.7	− 871.3	− 1,432.0
Unrequited transfers (net)	—	− 35.4	− 35.4	—	+ 62.1	+ 62.1	—	− 76.8	− 76.8	—	+ 89.4	+ 89.4
Capital Account	+ 64.5	+ 80.3	+ 144.8	+ 135.8	− 141.7	− 5.9	+ 121.4	+ 19.7	+ 141.1	− 42.0	+ 54.5	+ 12.5
Balancing Item (errors)	—	—	+ 23.1	—	—	+ 45.6	—	—	+ 26.2	—	—	+ 34.2
Allocation of SDRs	—	—	—	—	—	—	—	—	—	—	—	—
Overall balance	—	—	+ 174.4	—	—	+ 3,102.2	—	—	+ 157.5	—	—	− 241.6

Note: Surplus (+) Deficit (−)

Sources: Central Bank of Nigeria, *Annual Report and Statement of Accounts* and *Economic and Financial Review* of various years.

by 10 per cent.[10] At the foreign-exchange market, the naira-dollar link was severed leaving the Central Bank to adjust the naira exchange rate based on Nigerian and external indicators. The link tended to suppress the real value of the naira and counteracted the government's anti-inflationary measures. Within four months of freeing the naira (1 April − 18 July), its value appreciated by 6.6 per cent (that is, from N1.00 = $1.52 to N1.00 = $1.62).[11]

The resultant effect of all these changes was an even greater credit balance of N5,057.1m in the petroleum current account of 1974. After deducting the large N1,994.6m deficit of the non-oil sector of the current account the overall current account balance was N3,062.5m and the overall increase in the foreign reserve account was an unprecedented N3,102.2m, that is, N2,900m higher than the 1973 level! The surplus encouraged a mass relaxation of imports restrictions. Excise duties on consumer goods were reduced. Foreign-exchange control was eased in order to increase imports and to curb the raging inflation.

The huge earnings of 1974 were followed by excessive expenditure in the public sector. Spending sprees by the government on non-economic projects was characteristic of 1975 and 1976. The foreign exchange was quickly drained down. By 1975 the balance on current account fell to a paltry N42.6m and the non-oil account suffered an unprecedented deficit of N4,026.4m. The situation was critical but the capital account with a credit balance of N141.1m, increased the balance of payment account to a modest level of N157.5m. The demoralising balance of payments position compelled the Nigerian authorities to reinstate some of the import restrictions which were in force in the pre-oil-boom years.

The spending spree continued in 1976 especially in the public sector. In that year the indomitable oil business fetched the nation the sum of N5,266.2m in terms of claims against foreigners, but the increase in imports for goods and services depressed the overall balance to a deficit of N241.6m.

Without the petroleum industry Nigeria would have suffered serious balance of payments reverses. Net earnings from the petroleum sector rose by 34 per cent in 1972, 44 per cent in 1973 and by 277.7 per cent in 1974. In 1975, production was deliberately reduced by 19.5 per cent in accordance with OPEC arrangements. In 1976 production rose slightly by 4.1 per cent. As Table 19.1 clearly indicates, petroleum is the main foreign-exchange earner for Nigeria and may remain so for some time.

The capital account, which records all sources and uses of funds associated with changes in short- and long-term foreign liabilities and assets (real and financial) of domestic spending units, has been persistently on the credit balance. The persistent credit balances in the Nigerian capital account implies that the aggregate increase of her different claims against foreigners is greater than the aggregate increase of her liabilities in favour of foreigners. This situation has remained so since 1970. The huge investments in foreign securities offer some explanation. The Central Bank of Nigeria, for example, maintained the sums of N3,380m and N3,057m as external reserves in 1975 and 1976 respectively most of which was held in foreign government securities and balances with foreign banks.

Although a developing economy requires a certain amount of foreign-exchange reserves to generate external confidence in the currency and the economy it is not advisable for it to amass reserves beyond the reasonable level required for international co-operation. The currency of a developing country such as Nigeria is most unlikely to be an international trading currency, reserve currency or an intervention currency. Nigeria may not require long-term reserves of the magnitude of 1975 to support her currency against international monetary disturbances resulting from float. Before the emergence of petroleum as the main foreign exchange-earner in the seventies, Nigeria countered the disequilibrium in her balance of payments which arose from seasonal pattern of production and other short-term or transistory disturbances through short-term borrowing, trade credit from trading partners and the use of monetary and fiscal policies.

3. Conclusion

The decline in the country's volume of produced cash crops, the declining demand for them, the poor world market commodity prices and the increasing food imports have affected Nigeria's balance of payments adversely and consequently the country's external liquidity. Given the vast arable land in Nigeria, the beautiful climatic conditions and the age-old traditional heritage of tilling 'mother earth' to feed the peoples, it is highly lamentable that the once proud practice of farming is unconsciously being relegated to the distant past. Despite the huge Federal and State governments' investments in agricultural activities, Nigeria has not been able to produce enough food for the teeming population. Nigeria, which ranked among the world's leading producers and exporters of palm produce, cocoa, cotton seeds, soya beans, ground-nuts, rubber, hides and skins, now budgets millions of naira in foreign exchange each year to import some of these commodities. Some authorities suggest that the growing consumer-goods-oriented industries have attracted away labour from agriculture and created shortages in agricultural commodities production.

Statistics reveal that agricultural production has actually fallen in some cases. The situation is that factors which determine aggregate consumption such as population and the growth in income have increased at a faster rate than the rate of change in agricultural production. Consequently, demand has by far outstripped supply. To improve production an advanced method is required which will raise output if deficits in the non-oil sector of the Nigerian economy are to be halted or reduced at least.

Notes

1. Central Bank of Nigeria, *Annual Reports and Statement Of Accounts for the Year ended 31 December 1970* (Lagos), p. 7.
2. IMF, *Surveys of African Economies* (Washington, DC, 1975), vol. 6, p. 369.
3. Central Bank of Nigeria, *Annual Report and Statement of Accounts for the Year ended 31 December, 1971* (Lagos), p. 11.
4. Ibid., p. 11.
5. Ibid., pp. 12-13.
6. On 1 January 1973, Nigeria introduced a new decimal currency unit, the naira, N1.00 = £N.50.
7. IMF, *Surveys of African Economies*, p. 360.
8. Ibid., p. 361.
9. Ibid.
10. Central Bank of Nigeria, *Annual Report and Statement of Accounts for the Year ended 31 December, 1974* (Lagos), p. 27.
11. IMF, *Surveys of African Economies*, p. 371.

20 DEVELOPMENTS IN NIGERIA'S EXTERNAL ASSETS

S.C. Okafor and O. Unegbu

1. Introduction

All international assets like gold, foreign exchange, approved foreign securities and special drawing rights (SDRs) make up the external assets holdings of a country. By foreign exchange we mean the currencies of other countries, other than that of the holder country, acceptable for the purpose of international trade and transactions. Foreign exchange constitutes an important aspect of international liquidity studies but it forms only a part of a country's total external assets. The term 'external-asset' therefore refers to banking system's and Government's holdings of gold, foreign exchange and probably the special drawing rights.[1]

Thus, in an open economy, the external reserves or foreign assets consist of currencies, IMF gold subscriptions, special drawing rights and other monetisable assets such as short-term bills, medium- and long-term foreign government securities which can be easily monetised or converted into liquid money for use in paying-off or cancelling indebtedness of nations.

All open economies must maintain a reasonable level of external assets to provide insurance against the possibility of international insolvency. The Central Bank is the traditional custodian and manager of external assets. This is necessary because the maintenance of domestic monetary stability (also the responsibility of the Central Bank) is directly related to the maintenance of external monetary stability. Certain expertise is required in the management of the latter to make for an orderly economic development.

Nigeria's foreign-exchange reserves have grown phenomenally in recent times. 'From N438.4m at the end of 1973, it increased to N3540.9m at the end of 1974 and has remained around that level up to the present time.'[2] Looking therefore at the high level of external assets now held by the Nigerian monetary authorities and comparing this level perhaps with the four months' critical import-reserve level first proposed by Robert Triffin in 1960 and generally viewed as the minimum level of reserves expected of an open economy, Nigeria's posi-

291

tion is most encouraging.

In this chapter, attempts will be made to discuss the development of Nigeria's external assets since the colonial era, as well as the developments in the management techniques of the assets.

2. The Era of the West African Currency Board

This was the first financial institution organised in this part of the world and involved four British colonial countries, Nigeria, Gold Coast now Ghana, Sierra Leone and Gambia. Before colonisation, each of the countries had its own medium of exchange. The trans-trading companies became worried about the exchange value of the monies used and brought pressure on Nigerians to accept the British silver coins. Eventually, the British government embarked on the demonetisation of the traditional monies in the West African colonies and enthroned British silver coins.

The drain of British silver forced the British government to set up a committee to investigate the effect on the British economy. The Emott Committee was set up in 1911 to study the desirability of the continued use of British coins in West Africa and to recommend on the possible participation of the colonial governments in the profits arising from the introduction of new currency into West Africa. The result of this exercise was the birth of the West African Currency Board in 1912 charged with the huge responsibility of providing, controlling and maintaining currency to the West African territories, and to specifically accumulate reasonable sterling reserves, as the West African currency maintained 100 per cent backing of the British pound, itself backed by gold.

'During this period, Nigerians had virtually no control over the monetary policy and the monetary management of the currency in circulation in their own area and of the reserves accumulated through foreign trade.'[3]

The sterling-exchange standard was rigidly applied by which sterling assets determined the amount of West African Currency to be issued by the board. Export demand by the British and the production of raw materials by the deprived Nigerians determined the level of external sterling assets held.

During this period also, Nigeria's external assets were held in sterling securities. Colonial monetary policy did not allow for the diversification of external reserves into other vehicle currencies or assets. Reserves were held only in British government securities. The system of reserves and the colonial monetary policies did not encourage the earlier development of the Nigerian money and capital markets and it slowed down the earlier establishment of a central bank.

With the emergence into independence of these colonies – Ghana in 1957, Nigeria in 1960 and with the need for a sound external monetary policy to minimise negative economic influences owing to the interdependence of world economies, the West African Currency and coins died a natural death, ushering in the second era – the era of Central Banking in Nigeria.

3. Developments in Reserve Levels

Established by the Central Bank of Nigeria Act, 1958, the Central Bank of Nigeria started operations on 1 July 1959. It was charged with the functions of:

1. issuing legal tender currency in Nigeria;
2. acting as banker and financial adviser to the Federal Government;
3. maintaining external reserves in order to safeguard the international value of the country's currency; and
4. promoting monetary stability and a sound financial structure in the economy.

On the 31 March 1960, Nigeria's total external reserves stood at £54,714,449 (N109,428,898), made up of £49,880,969 (N99,761,938) in United Kingdom government securities and balances with banks in the United Kingdom and West African Currency Board notes and coins to the value of £4,833,480 (N9,666,960). The presence of the West African Currency Board notes and coins in the external reserves was because the notes were tied to the British pound and convertible 100 per cent, and by the fact that the notes and coins were to continue to be in circulation until completely replaced by the new Nigerian pound. This fact was stated by the then Federal Minister of Finance, Chief F.S. Okotie-Eboh at the opening of the Central Bank building on 1 July 1959, when he said,

While the currency conversion is taking place the West African Currency Board notes and coins with which we have been familiar for many years will continue to circulate and both the Nigerian and

Table 20.1: Return of Assets and Liabilities as at the Close of Business on 31 August 1976 (Central Bank of Nigeria)

Liabilities	N	N	Assets	N	N
Capital Subscribed And Paid up		3,000,000	Gold		15,772,926
General Reserve		16,884,159	Convertible Currencies:		
			Foreign Government Securities and Balances with Foreign Banks		3,361,825,149
			IMF Gold Tranche		24,256,954
Currency in Circulation		1,298,042,341	Special Drawing Rights		43,949,602
			Total External Reserve		3,445,804,631
Deposits:					
Federal and States Governments	854,317,847		Federal Government Securities		245,539,428
Bankers	1,588,722,199		Other Securities		76,812,906
Other	175,769,368	2,618,809,414	Rediscounts and Advances		234,234,969
Other Liabilities		240,294,529	Other Assets		174,638,782
		N4,177,030,443			N4,177,030,443

Source: Central Bank of Nigeria's publication.

the Board's currency will be legal tender. When sufficient of the new notes and coins are in circulation the legal tender status will be withdrawn from the Currency Board's notes and coins.

Table 20.2: Level of External Reserves

Year Ended	Total external reserves (Nm)
1960	343.3
1961	305.5
1962	250.6
1963	192.4
1964	193.5
1965	197.2
1966	184.6
1967	102.2
1968	105.3
1969	114.5
1970	180.4
1971	302.7
1972	273.3
1973	438.4
1974	3540.9
1975	3702.7
1976	3082.6
1977	2765.4

Sources: S.B. Falegan, 'Management of Nigeria's External Reserves'. Lecture delivered to AIESEC National Conference, University of Nigeria, Nsukka, 20 December 1976, p. 37; and Central Bank of Nigeria, *Economic and Financial Review*, December 1977, p. 49.

At the end of the year 1960, the external assets rose to N343.3m and all were held 100 per cent in sterling assets. The major source of Nigeria's external assets as from 1960 up to 1972 was mainly the earnings of agricultural products. Little or nothing was earned from invisible trade. The Central Bank of Nigeria has been the manager of all reserves and the sole dealer in foreign exchange. By the Exchange Control Act of 1962, any Nigerian national who earns any foreign money has to deposit same with the Central Bank of Nigeria or its authorised agent notably the commercial banks. When the foreign money is deposited, the Central Bank will in turn issue Nigerian naira or other Central Bank liability to the depositor of the foreign currency and add the foreign currency to Nigeria's foreign-exchange reserves.

Between 1961 and 1969 Nigeria's external assets fell gradually and in some cases rapidly. From 1970 the external reserve level rose. The low reserve levels between 1962 and 1970 may be attributed to a number of factors, declining output of exportable agricultural produce, falling world market prices of exportable commodities and increased imports for manufactured goods. Between 1967 and 1970 the disruption of the economy as a result of the civil war and the purchase of arms certainly helped to reduce the external reserve level. The increase in the reserve levels beginning from 1971 is due to increased oil production and rising oil prices.

4. External Assets Diversification

The Central Bank of Nigeria Act, 1958 as amended in 1962 empowered it to diversify the external assets into gold, bank balances in convertible foreign currencies, bills of exchange, foreign government treasury bills and foreign government guaranteed securities of not more than ten years' maturity and securities of international financial institutions to which Nigeria belonged. All the non-gold assets must be freely convertible into gold on demand.

The problem of managing the reserves at that time was limited to that of keeping adequate reserves to pay for Nigeria's short-term obligation to foreigners. While this problem may not have been as complicated as that presently faced in managing an excess reserves situation, it was nevertheless taxing for a young Central Bank.

The reconstruction and rehabilitation exercises which followed with the end of the Nigerian civil war in 1970 imposed further strain on the thin reserves of the country. Coupled with the conclusion of the Smithsonian Agreement of 1971 in which new parities between the dollar and other leading currencies were set, some currencies were revalued which meant a devaluation of the dollar. Nigeria followed in the devaluation exercise in January 1973 with the objective of adjusting the external value of the Nigerian naira in terms of the dollar. The reasonableness of this exercise has been challeneged in many quarters as 'it seemed to injure the Nigerian economy by increasing the prices of imported goods while reducing the real purchasing power of the Nigerian naira. It led to speculative businesses and harmed capital formation'.[4]

In this phase, Nigeria experienced a situation which she did not anticipate and was thus ill-prepared. The oil industry brought to the Nigerian coffers vast amounts of money in foreign exchange.

From the Triffin's rule-of-thumb guide to the minimum reserve level a country must hold, Nigeria has been holding reserves in excess of what she requires to finance her foreign obligations. The problem of reserve management therefore changed to that of ensuring that the purchasing power of the excess is not eroded by inflation, that losses as a result of currency fluctuations are minimised and that the excess is invested in such a way as to yield interest. Diversification of reserves into interest-yielding stable assets is relevant especially in the present era of international monetary crisis. 'If official reserve-asset preferences of a Central Bank are unstable, any monetary regime can be subjected to rude shocks that could damage confidence in the reserve media.'[5] Thus with the tremor in the world's currency markets, it became difficult for Nigeria to rely on a single currency as the main source of reserve.

The new situation of excess reserves in a world of floating exchange rates and high inflation called for a new strategy. The Central Bank's answer was the diversification of its holdings of external assets by converting weaker assets into the stronger ones. The policy was aimed at reducing the risk of a heavy loss should the exchange rate of a major reserve currency fall drastically.

Earlier on in 1961, Nigeria became a member of the International Monetary Fund acquiring International Monetary Fund gold tranche and United States dollar assets. In that year, Nigeria's external assets stood at N305.5m, N37.8m less than the 1960 level and consisted of 81.1 per cent in sterling assets, 9.3 per cent in gold and IMF gold tranche and 9.6 per cent in US dollar assets. From 1961 up to 1970, Nigeria's external assets consisted of the above assets but in 1971 special drawing rights were added to the reserve list and formed 7.9 per cent of Nigeria's total external reserves.

In 1974 Deutschmark assets and the French franc were added to the reserve list but prior to 1974 Nigeria held most of her assets in sterling because of the Sterling Guarantee Agreement by which the UK government compensated Nigeria for whatever losses she sustained as a result of the eroding value of the sterling. With the abrogation of the agreement by the UK government in 1974 because of the prohibitive cost of defending sterling, Nigeria converted some of her sterling assets into dollar assets. In 1975 Nigeria held the greater proportion of her reserve assets in dollars and some sterling assets were converted into DM assets; Canadian dollars, Japanese yen and Swiss francs joined the reserve list in the same year. By 1976 it became necessary to diversify some US dollar assets because of the cascading rate of the dollar at foreign-exchange markets. Sterling assets dropped from 33.1 per cent to 17 per cent, US dollar assets from 41.8 per cent to 25.1 per cent. The DM assets gained from 12.5 per cent to 23.9 per cent and the Canadian dollar from 3.4 per cent to 13.4 per cent. In the same year the Belgian franc and the Dutch guilder joined the arsenal of reserves. Table 20.3 is a testimony to the developments in reserve diversification which no doubt has been influenced by the current world monetary moods.

As the oil revenue increased attention was diverted away from agricultural produce with the result that the rate of increase in agricultural produce fell very rapidly while the rate of increase in crude-oil production rose sharply. At the end of 1974, Nigeria's external reserves had increased to N3,540.9m. It rose to N3,702.7m in 1975 and at the end of June 1976, the external assets stood at N3,881.7m. As the external-reserve level rose the rate of import increased with it.

At the end of 1974, Nigeria's reserve of N3,540,9m was enough to pay for 24.4 months of imports at the average rate of N144.8m imports a month. At the end of 1975 the reserves had increased to N3,702.7m, while the average monthly import bill rose to N311.1m. The reserves were thus enough to pay for 11.9 months imports.[6]

The rapid increase in Nigeria's external assets has given rise to other problems of an inflationary nature. The Nigerian economy is over-heated, the increase in reserves has led to an over-expansion of the country's monetary base. Heller had rightly observed that

Acquisition of new international reserves will have a direct impact on a nation's money supply by expanding the monetary base. An increase in the international reserves held may also have an indirect impact on the money supply if the monetary authorities feel that the increase in international liquidity has eased their reserve constraint so that more expansionary domestic monetary policies may be pursued. These increases in the monetary aggregates will in turn have an impact on national inflation rates.[7]

For example, in July 1976, money supply in Nigeria stood at N2,627.8m. In January 1977, it rose to N3,310.9m.

5. Conclusion

The policy of diversification of the external assets is good but not adequate for a developing economy like Nigeria. But it is conceivable that

Table 20.3: Components of Nigeria's External Reserves (Per Cent)

	1959	1960	1961	1962	1963	1964	1965	1966	1967	1968	1969	1970	1971	1972	1973	1974	1975	30 Nov. 1976
Gold and IMF Gold tranche	—	—	9.3	9.2	11.0	9.1	8.6	9.9	19.6	18.6	23.9	15.4	7.9	9.6	10.7	1.1	1.2	1.3
SDRs	—	—	—	—	—	—	—	—	—	—	—	—	7.9	13.4	9.5	1.1	1.2	1.6
Sterling assets	—	100	81.1	80.4	81.0	82.0	80.6	72.0	46.1	61.2	66.3	75.4	73.9	54.0	59.1	57.6	33.1	17.0
US$ assets	—	—	9.6	10.4	8.0	8.9	10.8	17.8	20.2	20.2	9.8	9.2	10.3	23.0	20.4	38.8	41.8	25.1
DM assets	—	—	—	—	—	—	—	—	—	—	—	—	—	—	0.3	1.3	12.5	23.9
French franc	—	—	—	—	—	—	—	—	—	—	—	—	—	—	—	0.1	3.9	5.3
Canadian dollar	—	—	—	—	—	—	—	—	—	—	—	—	—	—	—	—	3.4	13.4
Japanese yen	—	—	—	—	—	—	—	—	—	—	—	—	—	—	—	—	2.1	6.6
Swiss franc	—	—	—	—	—	—	—	—	—	—	—	—	—	—	—	—	0.8	1.3
Belgian franc	—	—	—	—	—	—	—	—	—	—	—	—	—	—	—	—	—	3.2
Dutch guilder	—	—	—	—	—	—	—	—	—	—	—	—	—	—	—	—	—	1.3
WAUA	—	—	—	—	—	—	—	—	—	—	—	—	—	—	—	—	—	X

Notes:
X = Negligible
WAUA = West African Unit of Account

Source: Falegan, 'Management of Nigeria's External Reserves', p. 36.

the Central Bank would have preferred to put more of these assets in stronger currencies such as the Deutschmark, the Swiss franc and the Japanese yen which have been appreciating at the foreign-exchange market. But the governments that regulate these currencies are reluctant to allow their currencies to be used as reserve currencies because of the inflationary consequences of 'hot money' on their economy and also the Central Bank is guided by the need to keep the external assets in currencies that could be used in paying for Nigeria's imports.

The diversification effort has proved inadequate. Nigeria continues to suffer huge losses every year because of the cascading dollar and sterling rates at the foreign-exchange market. The exercise of diversification has only scotched the snake but has not killed it.

With the raging world inflation depreciating the real value of Nigeria's external assets and with Nigeria's infrastructures remaining essentially undeveloped, one is bound to query the rationale in keeping such a high level of external reserves. The reserves should be repatriated to support activities which are genuinely productive such as machines, plants, equipment and tools required for home industries, which would pay better dividends in the long run. Tying the reserve to specific projects will not lead to high inflationary pressures. The fear of dangerous inflation arising from the careless utilisation of resources haunts many minds. Such fears may not be properly founded.

Notes

1. Peter B. Kenen, *Reserve-Asset Preference of Central Banks* no. 10 (Princeton University, New Jersey, 1963), p. 4.

2. 'Managing an Excess Reserve Situation', *Business Times*, vol. 2, no. 21 (Lagos), 22 February 1977, p. 15.

3. J.K. Onoh, 'Developments in Nigeria's External Monetary Management and Policy', an unpublished paper presented at the AISEC Annual Conference, 1977, p. 5.

4. J.K. Onoh, 'Is Devaluation an Answer to the Current Monetary Problems of Developing Economies', *Business Administrator*, vol. 7, no. 1 (University of Nigeria, 1973), pp. 66-72.

5. Norman Crump, *The ABC of Foreign Exchange* (Macmillan, New York, 1965), p. 30.

6. 'Managing an Excess Reserve Situation', p. 21.

7. H.R. Heller, 'International Reserves, Money, and Global Inflation', *Finance and Development*, vol. 13, no. 1 (March 1976), p. 28.

21 NIGERIA AND THE INTERNATIONAL MONETARY FUND

J.K. Onoh and A.U. Chijindu

1. Introduction

Gone are the days when a country of the free-enterprise system could formulate economic policies without regard to the economic consequences such policies might have on other countries with which she has trade or financial relations. The world economies of today are joined together in a network of economic activities so that a disequilibrium in one economy can register its negative impacts on the others. The crisis of the dollar and the sterling is a case in point. All economies of the free world have been adversely affected by the floating dollar and sterling. As Salop rightly observed:

> Because of the close-knit fabric of the world financial community, changes originating in any one major financial centre are quickly felt in others. This means that there is in effect a single foreign exchange market and a single securities market.[1]

The pre-war, the war and the post-war years brought with them a number of painful economic and monetary experiences which underscored the necessity of a supranational institution to regulate international financial flows and to ensure that countries did not suffer unduly from the economic indiscretions of others. It was to discharge these functions that the International Monetary Fund (IMF) was founded in 1946.

The formation of the IMF was a victory for the pro-Keynesian ecomists who held the viewpoint that economic activities have to be regulated, as opposed to the classical viewpoint that the correction of a malfunctioning economy should be left to the 'mysterious' invisible hand.

2. The Establishment, Function and Operation of the International Monetary Fund

The International Monetary Fund is an international financial institution established in 1946 (with the International Bank for Reconstruc-

301

tion and Development) in accordance with the agreement reached during the United Nations Conference of July 1944 in Bretton Woods.

The main aim of the Bretton Woods conference was to establish an international monetary system which would incorporate the benefits of the gold standard but without its rigidities. The conference was held at a time when restrictionist trading practices were the order of the day.

Trade restrictions and other monetary malpractices reduced international trade volume and aggravated the problems of international liquidity perpetuated by the shortage of gold. As Hanson observed, the agreement 'condemned the use of multiple exchange rates, the unilateral blocking of accounts, bilateral trading arrangements, and indeed, in principle, all forms of exchange control'.[2]

The major objectives of the Fund, as summarised by Chandler were as follows:[3]

(a) to re-establish a multilateral free-payments system and to reduce other barriers to trade and international financial flows;
(b) to provide financial aid to member countries suffering from fundamental disequilibrium in the balance of payments; and
(c) to provide an orderly foreign-exchange market system for the trading of foreign exchange and for adjusting exchange rates.

As a first step the Fund worked out a programme for a long-term elimination of exchange restrictions and other trade barriers. Some good results have been achieved. A relatively multilateral free-payments system has been in vogue since the latter part of the fifties.

To counter the then common practice of exchange-rate depreciation in the bid to increase exports, and to reduce imports, the Fund's Agreement directed each member country to establish with the Fund an initial exchange rate which would be allowed to fluctuate only within the narrow exchange-rate band of the Fund, and which each member country was duty bound to defend. A deviation from the exchange-rate band would be allowed only with the express permission of the Fund and for the purpose of correcting a fundamental disequilibrium in the balance of payments. The exchange-rate spread within which a currency was allowed to fluctuate was initially established at 2 per cent, that is, an upper and lower limit of 1 per cent respectively. The spread was increased in 1971 by the Smithsonian agreement to 4.5 per cent, that is 2.5 per cent on either side of the established par value.

The Fund's policy was essentially that of relative stable exchange rates by way of a semi-automatic link of individual currencies with gold, without tying down countries to the rigid monetary policies of the gold standard which demanded the contraction or expansion of a currency by a greater outflux or influx of gold respectively. Thus Article 4, Section 1, of the Fund's Articles of Agreement stipulates that the par value of each country's currency shall be expressed in terms of the weight of fine gold — or US dollars.

The Fund sought to achieve the third objective by providing financial aid to member countries suffering from fundamental disequilibrium in the balance of payments through a pool system referred to as the 'sales of currencies' or 'drawings on the Fund'.

The pool was created to enable a country with a temporary balance of payment deficit to purchase foreign currency from the Fund in exchange for its own thereby making available to countries with balance of payment deficits, the funds of those enjoying surpluses, thus increasing international liquidity. To guide this system of borrowing each member country was allotted an amount of drawing rights, dictated by its quota.

According to IMF rules 25 per cent of a country's subscriptions must be paid in gold and 75 per cent in its own currency. A country's level of quota determines its ability to borrow and a borrowing country must maintain the external value of its currency if other countries are to purchase it. Any country which satisfied the quota level was allowed to borrow 25 per cent of its quota in a given year. But since 1956 a country can borrow up to a 100 per cent of its quota and at times up to 200 per cent at the discretion of the IMF. On no account must a country's currency exceed 200 per cent of its quota. The borrowing ceiling must not exceed the maximum subscription of 200 per cent which can be contributed in a country's own currency.

In effect when a country borrows, it does so by purchasing foreign currencies with its own currency stock with the Fund. If a country borrows by purchasing other countries' currencies the Fund's holding of the borrowing country's currency increases thereby reducing its drawing rights. A country's drawing rights are reduced when the IMF currency stock of the borrowing country increases. On the other hand, the drawing rights of a country whose currency is purchased increases. When a member country purchases foreign currencies it can do so by taking a single currency or a basket of currencies such as the dollar, sterling, the yen and the Deutschmark.

To further increase international liquidity, the Fund in 1970 introduced the special drawing rights, sometimes referred to as 'paper gold'. These special drawing rights (SDRs) represent unconditional rights of

ıber countries to draw currencies of other countries, the amount of
ṇts to be allocated to each member being related to the member's
quota of drawing rights under the Fund's constitution.

The issue of the special drawing rights was necessitated 'by the
failure of gold and other forms of international liquidity to keep pace
with the unprecedented rate of expansion of international trade which
has taken place in recent years.'[4] Hence the International Monetary
Fund actually describes the special drawing rights as 'unconditional
reserve assets' created by the Fund to influence the level of world
reserves. Thus the introduction of the special drawing rights defines an
attempt at freeing international transactions from dependence on gold.

The seventies have been a period of international monetary turbu-
lence. The pound sterling and the dollar have fallen out of favour as
world reserve currencies. The semi-automatic link between the dollar
and gold has been severed by the Smithsonian Agreement of 1971; the
Bretton Woods exchange-rate parities have collapsed and major world
trading and intervention currencies have broken through the widened
Smithsonian exchange-rate band as a result of the floating of world
currencies. Every hope is now centred on the SDRs as the future world
monetary reserves.

3. Nigeria's Quota Position in the International Monetary Fund

Nigeria joined the International Monetary Fund on 30 March 1961.[5]
The Federal Ministry of Finance is the fiscal agent to the Fund on
behalf of the Federal Government. However by delegation the Central
Bank of Nigeria meets the Government's obligations to the Fund, and
hence assumes full responsibilities for rights and obligations to the
Fund.

Prior to joining the Fund Nigeria's monetary structure was linked to
the International Monetary Fund to an appreciable degree via sterling
assets.

Special drawing rights formed part of the Central Bank of Nigeria's
external assets as from January 1970.[6] Nigeria's gold tranche position
in the Fund now forms part of the Central Bank's external reserve
assets.[7]

Table 2.1 shows Nigeria's position in the Fund from March 1961 to
1977. The data indicate Nigeria's position in the Fund over the years
and also the extent of the Fund's influence and its activities on Nigeria's
international financial transactions and on the local financial structure.

Table 21.1: Nigeria's Position in the IMF 1961-77 (Nm)

End of year (except otherwise stated)	Total subscription or quota	Gold subscription	Currency subscription	(3) as % of (1)	Net drawings or net fund sale of currency	Reserve position of drawing rights within gold tranche	N Allocation	Net acquisition or holdings net use	Total (7) & (8)	Total as % of allocation	Total of (6) & (9)
	(1)	(2)	(3)	(4)	(5)	(6)	(7)	(8)	(9)	(10)	(11)
1961 March	35.8	3.6	32.2	90.0	–	3.6	–	–	–	–	3.6
1962	35.8	3.6	32.2	90.0	–	3.6	–	–	–	–	3.6
1963	35.8	3.6	32.2	90.0	–	3.6	–	–	–	–	3.6
1964	35.8	3.6	32.2	90.0	–	3.6	–	–	–	–	3.6
1965	35.8	3.6	32.2	90.0	–	3.6	–	–	–	–	3.6
1966	45.0	5.8	39.2	87.1	–	3.6	–	–	–	–	5.8
1967	45.0	5.8	39.2	87.1	–	3.6	–	–	–	–	5.8
1968	71.4	5.9	65.5	91.7	6.6	5.9	–	–	–	–	5.9
1969	71.4	8.1	63.3	88.7	4.4	8.1	–	–	–	–	8.1
1970	96.4	8.1	88.3	90.6	10.6	8.1	12.0	–	12.0	100	20.1
1971	96.4	8.1	88.3	91.6	10.6	8.1	22.3	–	22.3	100	30.4
1972	96.4	9.2	87.2	90.5	9.5	9.2	32.5	–	32.5	100	41.7
1973	107.1	26.2	80.9	75.5	–	26.3	36.1	1.5	36.1	100	62.4
1974	107.1	26.7	80.4	75.1	–	26.8	36.1	8.8	37.6	104.1	64.4
1975	99.2	24.8	74.4	75.0	133.9	158.7	35.5	11.4	42.3	126.0	201.0
1976	98.9	24.7	74.2	75.0	219.8	244.5	33.4	16.0	44.8	130.0	289.3
1977	106.9	35.1	71.8	67.2	234.2	269.3	36.1	16.0	52.1	144.3	321.4

Sources: Central Bank of Nigeria, *Economic And Financial Review*, vol. 9, no. 1 (December 1971), p. 76; and vol. 15, no. 2 (December 1977), pp. 50 and 51.

Nigeria's quota (subscription) in the Fund (as seen from Table 21.1) has increased substantially over the years, recording a steady rise, from N35.8m in 1961 to N107.1m in 1974. The quota however dropped slightly from N103.4m in 1975 to N98.5m in 1976. In 1977 it recovered to N106.9m.

Columns (2) and (3) shows the naira value of Nigeria's subscription in gold and currency. The percentage of Nigeria's subscription in local currency has been changing as suggested by column (4). The figures in columns (3) and (4) suggest an inverse relationship between gold and currency contributions. As gold subscription increases currency subscription falls. Gold subscription has increased from the stagnant N3.6m position between 1961 and 1965 to N5.8m between 1966 and 1968, and from N8.1m to N9.2m between 1969 and 1972. In 1973 Nigeria's gold subscription shot up to an unprecedented level of N26.2m. In 1970 it reached the level of N26.7m and in 1977 it attained the record level of N35.1m.

The increase in gold subscription and the relative decline in the percentage of local currency subscription as shown in column (4) is the consequence of the world monetary crisis. The sterling float and the loss of gold convertibility for the dollar in 1971 as well as the subsequent dollar float affected adversely the external value of the naira. The rise in the price of gold made it a more reliable reserve asset and more suitable for subscription purposes. As Nigeria's SDRs constitute a part of Nigeria's external reserves, her SDRs policy could not be divorced from the external-reserve policy which in the seventies favoured a diversification of dollar and sterling assets into other assets such as gold, in view of the fact that the USA and the UK governments could no longer defend the exchange rates of their currencies in the spirit of Bretton Woods. The percentage of local currency to total subscription has declined since 1966. Between 1961 and 1965 the percentage of currency subscription stood at the 90 per cent bench-mark. It has fluctuated since 1967 as the world's major reserve currencies, the dollar and sterling, began the first phase of their crisis. The United States was faced with balance of payments problems. Sterling had been shaken by the depressed British economy, and speculation about the devaluation of sterling was rife. Sterling was finally devalued in 1968. The monetary tumor in those two reserve assets in which Nigeria held most of her reserves affected the external value of the naira and was largely responsible for the decline in the local currency component of Nigeria's quota with the Fund and the preference for gold in the subscription. The proportion of gold to total subscription has risen significantly from N3.6m in 1961 to N35.1m in 1977.

Nigeria has preferred subscribing in gold because of obvious advant-ages. Gold prices are no longer pegged. The open-market prices for gold are rising. In the circumstances gold will buy more dollars or any other currency than local currency whose value has depreciated because of the shrinking value of sterling and the dollar.

About 86 per cent of Nigeria's reserve position in the Fund consists of lending to the oil facility. As at the end of 1977 the Fund's holding of Nigeria's currency amounted to about 67 per cent of quota. This implies that Nigeria's gold subscription amounted to about 33 per cent of quota; at that level of gold subscription her contribution in gold exceeded the minimum of 25 per cent prescribed by the Fund. Nigeria's position in gold is about 8 per cent into the super-gold tranche. Nigeria is also expected to contribute approximately SDR 220m to the Witteveen Facility.[8] Nigeria's reserve position within gold tranche (column (6)) has increased remarkably from N3.6m in 1961 to N269.3m in 1977. The increase in national income and petro-dollars enhanced Nigeria's ability to purchase gold whose value continues to appreciate in the world gold market.

Column (7) shows that special drawing rights allocation to Nigeria has increased steadily from N12m worth in 1970 to N36.1m in 1977. This is a proof of Nigeria's increasing borrowing capacity from the Fund, since special drawing rights allocation is a function of a member country's total quota gold subscription and other discretions of the Fund.

The fall in the amount of Nigeria's SDRs allocation in 1975 and 1976 is the consequence of the fall in the quota or total subscriptions for those years – which form the basis for SDRs allocation.

Net acquisitions between 1975 and 1977 respectively (column (8)) have increased the percentage of Nigeria's total holdings with the Fund as suggested by column (10).

The increase suggested in column (11) between 1968 and 1977 is the result of the increase in the two components – 'reserve position of SDRs within gold tranche' and 'total SDRs holdings'.

The data in Tables 21.2, 21.3 and 21.4 further highlight Nigeria's increasing impact in the International Monetary Fund. Tables 21.2 and 21.3 show Nigeria's position in the Fund as at 31 May 1977 under various items.

Table 21.4 spotlights Nigeria's reserve position in the Fund from 1971 to 1977. The remarkable rise from a reserve position of SDR 11m in 1971 to SDR 335m in 1977 is a good indicator of the growth Nigeria has recorded in its activities vis-à-vis the Fund.

Table 21.5 shows the exchange rates of the naira in terms of special drawing rights and the dollar from 1970 to 1977. The exchange rates as the table shows have experienced persistent fluctuations through the years especially as a result of the regime of float. These changes in exchange rates indicate how the internal monetary crisis is linked to the international monetary system. An increase in the amounts of SDRs or dollars exchangeable for the naira depicts an increase in the value of the naira vis-à-vis these two international monetary units and vice versa.

(a) Nigeria's Status in the IMF

A country's voting strength in the Fund depends on the size of the country's subscription to the Fund. The rules of the Fund stipulate 250 votes plus an additional vote of one for every $100,000 of the country's quota. Nigeria has a total of 1,600 votes which represents only 0.5079 per cent of the total voting power of the Fund.[9]

As an Article-XIV country Nigeria is exempted from the IMF full obligation. For example, Nigeria's gold subscription with the IMF stood at the 10 per cent level from 1961 to 1965 as against the prescribed minimum of 25 per cent of quota prescribed for the advanced economies. Although the 10 per cent quota was exceeded in 1966 and 1967 it was only in 1968 that Nigeria's gold subscription attained the 25 per cent mark. By 1977 gold subscription reached the 33 per cent mark.

The Fund has a board of governors, executive directors and a managing director. Out of the 20 executive directors, the 'great five', the US, the UK, Germany, France and Japan who have the largest quotas, have permanent seats. The remaining 15 seats constitute members elected from the IMF's 15 constituencies. Nigeria is in an IMF constituency of 16 countries whose total IMF quota is SDR 1,058m as of the end of 1977. Although Nigeria's quota amounts to 34 per cent of the total quota of the constituency, the executive director of the constituency is from Zambia and his alternate director from Botswana. A Nigerian, however, advises the executive director.[10] Representation of a constituency as an executive director is neither based on the strength of the quota in the constituency nor on the expertise of the member countries of the constituency. Representation is on rotational basis. The rotational method has been criticised. It is felt in some quarters that the relative strength of quota which determines voting strength of a country according to the Article of the Fund should also determine representation in a constituency. A country with the largest quota has greater interest to protect.

Table 21.2: Nigeria's Position in the IMF as at 31 May 1977 (Amounts Expressed in Millions of SDRs)

Allocation	Net acquisition or net use	Holdings	Holdings in percent of allocations	Quota	Gold subscription	Currency subscription	Repurchases of currency subscription	Net borrowings under oil facility
45.6	20.2	65.8	144.3%	135	26.3	108.8	7.5	300.0

Source: IMF, *International Financial Statistics*, vol. XXX, no. 7 (July 1977), p. 8.

Table 21.3: Nigeria's Position in the IMF as at 31 May 1977 (Amounts Expressed in Millions of SDRs)

Total drawings to date	Tranche drawings to date	Buffer stock drawings to	Total repayments by repurchase	Total currencies drawn	Net fund sales of currency
19.5	18.0	1.5	19.5	301.5	301.5

Source: IMF, *International Financial Statistics*, p. 10.

Table 21.4: Nigeria's Reserve Position in the IMF from 1971-77 (Amounts expressed in Millions of SDRs)

1971	1972	1973	1974	1975	1976	1977
11	13	33	34	212	334	335

Source: IMF, *International Financial Statistics*, p. 21.

Table 21.5: IMF-established Exchange Rates (1970-77)

	1970	1971	1972	1973	1974	1975	1976	1977
SDRs per naira	1.4000	1.4000	1.4000	1.2600	1.3254	1.3631	1.3645	1.3216
	1.4000	1.5200	1.5200	1.5200	1.6228	1.5957	1.5853	1.5352
US dollars per naira	1.4000	1.5200	1.5200	1.5200	1.6228	1.5957	1.5853	1.5352
	1.4000	1.4043	1.5200	1.5227	1.5904	1.6248	1.5959	1.5353

Source: IMF, *International Financial Statistics*, p. 283.

(b) Nigeria's Borrowing from the IMF

From 1961 to 1967 Nigeria did not draw from the Fund, nor was any net sale of currency by the Fund recorded. The plausible explanation for this could be that Nigeria's volume of international transactions had not been high enough during this period to warrant an operation of the Fund account.

However in 1968 Nigeria made the first withdrawal of SDR 9.3m for the purchase of gold to increase Nigeria's gold quota to 25 per cent. In December 1970 there was another withdrawal of SDR 8.8m to purchase more gold. By 1972 Nigeria's total borrowings in SDR amounted to 19.60m as a result of other drawings totalling SDR 1.5m under the buffer-stock arrangement of 1972. All drawings have been repurchased by Nigeria from petrol money which accrued since 1972, reaching its highest level in 1974.

As a result of the withdrawals to purchase gold Nigeria's local currency subscription increased dramatically between 1968 and 1972. Following the mechanism of the SDR, an increase in Nigeria's currency subscription reduces her borrowing capacity in SDR. However with the repurchase of local currency in 1973 and 1974 as indicated in column (5) of Table 21.1 Nigeria's currency subscription reduced in those years while the gold subscription increased thereby improving Nigeria's borrowing power. Between 1973 and 1977 currency subscription as percentage of total quota dropped below the 90.50 per cent mark of 1970 (see column (4) of Table 21.1). A drop in the percentage of currency to total quota implies an increase in the percentage of gold subscription and an increase in Nigeria's borrowing capacity. Nigeria was able to repurchase her currency as a result of her increased reserve position as suggested by Table 21.2. Table 21.3 summarises Nigeria's position in the IMF as of 31 May 1977.

4. Conclusion

Since its establishment, the International Monetary Fund has continued to grow in strength as an international financial institution. Its growth is connected with the growth in the economic strength and the number of member countries.

As the Fund grows in strength, its effect on the international financial system increases; and by its already outlined functions, the member countries' economic growth is further enhanced. In the same breath, as the number of member countries swells and as they grow in economic strength, they contribute more to the growth of international trade through their contribution to the growth of the Fund.

As at September 1973 for instance, membership of the Fund had swollen to 117. The Fund possessed at that time a pool of gold and foreign exchange amounting to $28,900m, paid in by the 117 member countries. The Fund's membership as at 24 March 1977 was 130.[11] As membership of the Fund and the pool of funds available to it grows, the financial assistance available to the members of the Fund and the Fund's area of control also increase. International co-operation (between the members) is also enhanced as more nations join the Fund. According to D.P. Whiting:[12]

There is little doubt that the very high degree of international co-operation in international monetary affairs which has existed in recent years can be attributed to the existence of the International Monetary Fund.

Tables 21.1-4 show that Nigeria's position in the Fund has continued to improve, as also has the Fund's impact and contribution to Nigeria's growth. This mutually beneficial co-existence will certainly continue to grow to the best interest of both sides.

Notes

1. Joanne Salop, 'Dollar Intervention Within the Snake', *IMF Staff Papers*, vol. XXIV, no. 1 (March 1977), p. 64.
2. J.L. Hanson, *Monetary Theory and Practice*, 5th edn. (English Language Book Society and Macdonald & Evans, London, 1974), p. 158.
3. L.V. Chandler, *The Economics of Money and Banking*, 6th edn, (Harper & Row, New York, 1973), pp. 419 and 420.
4. Hanson, *Monetary Theory and Practice*, p. 313.
5. IMF, *Surveys of African Economies*, (Washington DC, 1975), vol. 6, p. 283.
6. Central Bank of Nigeria, *Economic and Financial Review*, vol. 14, no. 1 (March 1976), p. 59.
7. Ibid.
8. Central Bank of Nigeria, 'International Economic and Financial Institutions' (mimeograph) 1977, p. 3.
9. Ibid., p. 3.
10. Ibid., p. 4.
11. IMF, 'Fund Activity', in *Finance and Development*, vol. 14, no. 2 (June 1977), p. 2.
12. D.P. Whiting, *Op. cit.*, p. 203.

NOTES ON CONTRIBUTORS

Dr W. OKEFIE UZOAGA is the Dean of the Faculty of Business Administration of the University of Nigeria, Enugu Campus and the Head of the Department of Finance for many years. Dr Uzoaga is a Reader in the Department of Finance; a former member of the Board of Directors of the Central Bank of Nigeria and the first Chairman of the Nigerian Agricultural Bank. He is the author of many learned papers published in Nigerian and foreign journals.

Dr J.K. ONOH (editor) is a Senior Lecturer in Economics, Monetary and Fiscal Policies of the Department of Finance. He is the author of the book *Strategic Approaches to Crucial Policies in Economic Development*, Rotterdam University Press, 1972. He has contributed many articles to journals and is preparing a new book on *Nigerian Central Bank: Monetary Policies and the Economy*. He is the Co-ordinator of MBA Programme of the Faculty of Business Administration, University of Nigeria, Enugu Campus and the Editorial Adviser to the *Nigerian Journal of Management*.

Mr F.O. OKAFOR is a Senior Lecturer in Finance and Investment Analysis in the Department of Finance and former Associate Dean of the Faculty of Business Administration, University of Nigeria, Enugu Campus. He is now the Acting Head of the Department of Finance and the author of many papers in the area of finance.

Dr OBI MORDI is a Senior Lecturer in Economics and Business Statistics in the Department of Management of the University of Nigeria, Enugu Campus and the Chairman of the Federal Government's NEM Insurance Company Limited. He is a keen researcher and his numerous articles in the areas of finance, management and economics have been published in journals. He is currently engaged in an extensive study of the 'Economic Structure of Nigeria and the Insurance Industry'.

Dr IBI AJAYI is a Senior Lecturer in the Department of Economics of the University of Ibadan, Ibadan. He has written a number of papers published in Nigerian and foreign journals and has conducted a number of empirical investigations of the Nigerian economy. He is the author of the book *Money in a Developing Economy (A Portfolio Approach to*

Money Supply Determination in Nigeria), published by the University of Ibadan Press, Ibadan, Nigeria.

Dr E.J. NWOSU is a Senior Research Fellow and Acting Director of the Economic Development Institute of the University of Nigeria, Enugu Campus. He is the author of a monograph *The Politics of Development Administration*, Institute for World Economics of the Hungarian Academy of Sciences, Budapest, 1974, and of the on-coming books on *Strategies in Economic Development* and *Prospects for Small Enterprise Development in Nigeria*, to be published by NOK Publishers, New York.

Dr Nwosu has also contributed numerous articles in academic journals in Nigeria and overseas and is a member of several Federal and State government agencies.

Mr P.N.O EJIOFOR is a Senior Lecturer in the Department of Management, University of Nigeria, Enugu Campus and the former Head of the Department of Business Administration, Ahmadu Bello University, Zaria. He is the co-author of the book *Nigerian Cases in Business Management* published by Cassell. He has contributed a number of articles in the areas of finance and management.

Mr A.C. EZEJELUE is a Senior Lecturer in Accounting and the Acting Head of the Department of Accountancy of the Faculty of Business Administration. He has contributed articles in the accounting field and advised the Anambra State Government on taxation affairs. He is a member of the Board of Internal Revenue, Anambra State, Nigeria.

Other contributors are Messrs C.S. Inyang, C.A. Okeke, A.N. Okoli, L.O. Mbata, S.C. Okafor, O. Unegbu, A.U. Chijindu, N.O. Odoh, F.C. Anisiuba, N. Diala-Ukah, C.C. Nweze, T.O. Ugha, M.I. Chidozie and O.A. Onwuteaka who are holders of the Bsc (Hons) degree in finance and are engaged in research or are business executives.

INDEX

315